GM 6L80 TRANSMISSIONS

HOW TO REBUILD & MODIFY

Steve Garrett

CarTech®

CarTech®

CarTech®, Inc.
6118 Main St.
North Branch, MN 55056
Phone: 651-277-1200 or 800-551-4754
Fax: 651-277-1203
www.cartechbooks.com

Edit by Wes Eisenschenk
Layout by Monica Seiberlich

ISBN 978-1-61325-730-2
Item No. SA523

Library of Congress Cataloging-in-Publication Data Available

Written, edited, and designed in the U.S.A.
Printed in the U.S.A.
10 9 8 7 6 5 4 3 2 1

CarTech books may be purchased at a discounted rate in bulk for resale, events, corporate gifts, or educational purposes. Special editions may also be created to specification. For details, contact Special Sales at 6118 Main Street, North Branch, MN 55056 or by email at sales@cartechbooks.com.

Appendix Images Courtesy Sonnax.

DISTRIBUTION BY:

Europe
PGUK
63 Hatton Garden
London EC1N 8LE, England
Phone: 020 7061 1980 • Fax: 020 7242 3725
www.pguk.co.uk

Australia
Renniks Publications Ltd.
3/37-39 Green Street
Banksmeadow, NSW 2109, Australia
Phone: 2 9695 7055 • Fax: 2 9695 7355
www.renniks.com

Canada
Login Canada
300 Saulteaux Crescent
Winnipeg, MB, R3J 3T2 Canada
Phone: 800 665 1148 • Fax: 800 665 0103
www.lb.ca

CONTENTS

Chapter 1: GM 6L80 Transmissions 4
- TEHCM 4
- Gearsets 4
- Transmission Identification 4
- RPO Identification 6
- Transmission Tag Information 7
- Inspection and Service 9
- Tools 12
- Power and Ground Testing 16
- Electrical Current Flow 17
- Adhesives, Sealers, and Lubricants 22
- Cooler Flushing 23

Chapter 2: Mechanical Electronic Components 24
- Range Reference Chart and Power Flow 24
- 6L80 Electronic Components 25
- TEHCM Shared Data and Additional Inputs 31
- Scan Tool Diagnosis, Data Parameters, DTCs, and Programming 31
- Adaptive Learning 36
- On-Vehicle Repairs and Adjustments 37
- TEHCM, TFP, TFT, Speed Sensor, and IMS Replacement 38
- Pressure Testing and Road Testing 43
- Cleaning and Inspection 45

Chapter 3: Component Service Disassembly and Assembly 51
- Torque Converter 51
- Holding Fixture 51
- Extension Housing 52
- Oil Pan Filter 52
- Pass-Through Connector 52
- TEHCM/Valve Body 53
- Pump Service 53
- 1-2-3-4/3-5-R and 4-5-6 Clutch Removal and Disassembly 63
- 1-2-3-4/3-5-R Clutch Assembly 67
- 4-5-6 Clutch Assembly 80
- 2-6 Center Support, Low/Reverse Clutch, and Low Sprag Removal 84
- 2-6 Clutch Assembly 93
- Component Service Assembly 100

Chapter 4: TEHCM Inspection and Testing 110
- GM Factory Method 110
- Aftermarket Method 111
- Valve Function 118
- Valve Body Assembly and TEHCM Installation 120
- Valve Body, Pump Valve Repair Kits, and Additional Components 124
- Oil Filter and Oil Pan Installation 125
- Fluid, Capacity, Checks, and Operation 126
- On-Vehicle Repairs and Adjustments 129
- Adaptive Learning 129
- Using a 6L80 in a Non-GM Application or GM Application Not Originally Equipped 132
- Other Aftermarket Products and Non-Internal Components 132
- Diagnostic Pointers 133

Appendix 135

GM 6L80 Transmissions

The 6L family of transmissions was introduced by General Motors in multiple applications starting with the 6L80 for the 2006 model year. As with many other GM transmission applications, the 6L units are also sold to other manufacturers for use in their vehicles.

The 6L transmissions are fully automatic 6-speed applications. The 6L applications utilize five multiple-disc clutch packs, one sprag-type one-way clutch, three planetary gearsets, one vane-style oil pump, one EC3-design torque converter, and multiple shafts.

A transmission electrical hydraulic control module (TEHCM) along with a Lepelletier and dual-pinion planetary gearsets make the 6L series unique.

TEHCM

The internal transmission control module (TCM) is more commonly known as a transmission electrical hydraulic control module (TEHCM). The TEHCM incorporates the hydraulic solenoids, temperature sensor, pressure switches, and the transmission computer (TCM) into one assembly. The TEHCM is mounted inside the transmission pan area and is attached directly to the transmission valve body. This means that all of the decisions and the control of the transmission are accomplished internally within the transmission.

The TEHCM communicates with the vehicle sensors and other control modules over a series of controller area network (CAN) data network circuits. Information is transmitted to and from the TEHCM and the other modules via CAN data, which means you need a scan tool that is capable of interpreting CAN data to communicate with the transmission. The TEHCM is programmable. Many 6L issues are not related to internal issues with the transmission; in many cases, they can be repaired by installing updated GM software.

Gearsets

The 6L units use two types of gearsets: Lepelletier and dual pinion designs. This allows the transmission to provide the available ratios without needing additional planetary gearsets.

The transmissions were developed as replacements for their 4- and 5-speed cousins to help meet ever-changing fuel-economy and emissions standards. Four different 6L configurations were released: the 6L45, 6L50, 6L80, and 6L90. The primary difference among the configurations is the physical size of the components. This makes most of the parts noninterchangeable among the different model configurations.

In addition, there are multiple part differences even within a specific transmission configuration, so it is imperative that you are sure the parts you are installing are the correct part numbers, as many updates have been implemented on all applications.

Transmission Identification

When compared with today's units, GM's numbering system for transmissions was significantly different in the past.

On the THM 400, THM 200, THM 200C, THM 350, THM 350C, THM 325, THM 125, THM 125C, and THM 425 applications, the "THM" stood for Turbo Hydra-matic, whereas the "400," "200," "350," etc. indicated the torque rating. Those with a "C" designation utilized a torque converter clutch system to provide a direct connection between the transmission and the engine during operation. Hydra-matic and Allison were the GM divisions that provided the transmission engineering and manufacturing for GM.

1980s

In the early 1980s, the numbering system changed to make it more of a worldwide approach because GM was one of the world's most dominant manufacturers and was selling engines and transmissions to various other automotive manufacturers.

Transmissions such as the THM 700-R4, 200-4R, 440-T4, and 325-4L were introduced. The "700" and "200" referenced the torque rating in Newton meters (Nm), while the "R" indicated that it was a rear-wheel-drive application. The "4" designation indicated the number of forward speeds that are available.

Changes

In the late 1980s and early 1990s, the designations began to change again. The THM 700-R4 became the 4L60, the THM 400 became the 3L80, and the 440-T4 became the 4T60. In this case, the "4" indicated that it was a 4-speed unit. The "L" indicated that it was a longitudinally mounted application (rear-wheel drive); a "T" would indicate it was a transverse-mounted application (front-wheel drive). The "60" or "80" designations indicated the unit's relative torque capacity. This may seem confusing, but it simply means that a transmission with an "80" has a higher torque capacity when compared to a "60" application within the same vehicle type. Since the number is relative, you cannot compare capacities from one unit to another, such as a 4T60 to a 4L60, because they are not the same torque rating; one is a front-wheel-drive, while the other is a rear-wheel-drive application. The updated designations were an attempt to provide a consistent numbering system across the world for all manufacturers using Hydra-matic units.

1991

In 1991, the numbering system evolved again with the addition of fully electronic control systems for many transmission applications. Prior to this point, the only electronics used on the transmission were used to control the torque converter clutch (TCC).

In 1991, the THM 400/3L80 received a complete redesign as a 4-speed unit known as the 4L80E, and in 1993, the 4L60 became the 4L60E. In addition, new front-wheel-drive applications were also introduced and updated, including the 4T60 transitioned to the 4T60E in 1991 and the 425/325-4L was replaced with the 4T80E in 1993.

The "E" designation was introduced because GM still had mechanically controlled units in production, and it wanted to eliminate the confusion between a mechanically controlled unit and an electronically controlled unit. All "E" applications utilized fully computer-controlled shifts, and most were equipped with electronically controlled line pressure. In addition, adaptive-shift software was also introduced on some models. Adaptive strategies allow the TCM to control shift feel and to adjust for clutch and seal wear within the transmission.

2006 and Later

Models from 2006 and later years have seen major introductions of GM 6-, 8-, 9-, and 10-speed applications for both rear-wheel-drive and front-wheel-drive vehicles. Again, the designations changed. The "E" designation is no longer used by GM, as all of the 6-, 8-, 9-, or 10-speed

GM 6L45/6L50/6L80/6L90 North American Usage

- Silverado, Sierra, Tahoe, Suburban, Yukon, Yukon XL, Escalade, (C/K trucks (C = 2WD, K = 4WD)
- Camaro (F-car)
- Corvette, XLR (Y-car)
- Express, Savana (G/H vans, G = 2WD, H = AWD)
- SRX (E-car)
- STS (D-car)
- CTS (D-car)
- 3500/4500 Medium-Duty Truck
- Colorado, Canyon (S/T Trucks S = 2WD, T = 4WD)

Car/truck model/body designations refer to the fourth or fifth digit of the VIN code. The fourth digit is used on cars and the fifth digit is used on trucks for the body type designation.

Not all years for the vehicles listed utilize only the 6L series transmissions, as other transmission models may also be used.

applications utilize fully integrated electronic control systems. The updated transmission designs are now utilized by GM and are sold to other manufacturers as well.

Current GM, non-hybrid transmission applications include the 6L45, 6L50, 6L80, 6L90, 6T30, 6T35, 6T40, 6T45, 6T50, 6T70, 6T75, 6T80, 8L45, 8L90, 9T45, 9T50, 9T60, 9T65, 10L60, 10L80, 10L90, and 10L1000.

As with all GM transmissions, the identification numbers/letters associated with the 6L80 have specific meanings regarding the transmission construction.

For example, for the 6L80:

Number	Meaning
6	Six forward speeds
L	Longitudinal mount (rear-wheel-drive)
80	Relative torque capacity

RPO Identification

GM has always used a process known as regular production option (RPO) codes to identify the component content for its vehicles. When a dealer orders a vehicle, every option on that vehicle, including the engine, transmission, axle ratio, radio, braking system, suspension system, A/C system, etc., is given a three-digit alpha-numeric designation. Those three-digit designations (RPOs) are used by the assembly plant to ensure the vehicle is built with the options that the dealer ordered.

For example, take a Chevrolet or GMC truck with a "Z71" decal on the truck bed. The RPO code for an off-road suspension package is Z71.

All RPO codes are three digits. Engine RPOs typically begin with the letter "L" (LT1, LT4, L88).

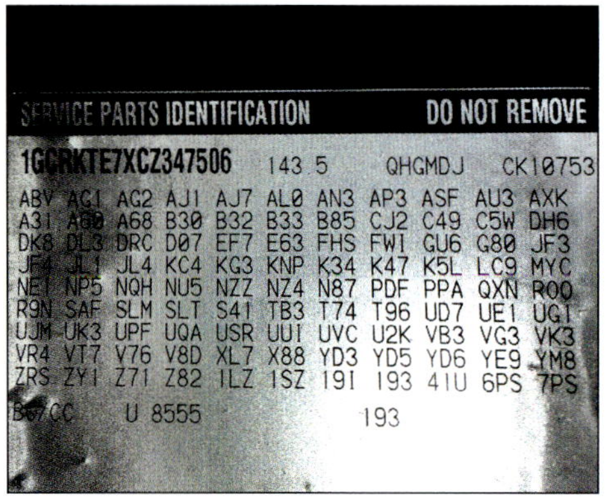

The RPO codes are listed on the RPO tag that is typically located in the glove box, center console, spare tire cover, or trunk lid for 2018-and-earlier applications. The RPO code is a three-digit designation that represents the equipment content on vehicle. Transmission RPOs start with the letter "M," engine RPOs start with the letter "L," and rear-wheel-drive final-drive information starts with the letter "G." The RPO is often required for parts ordering and to access the correct service information.

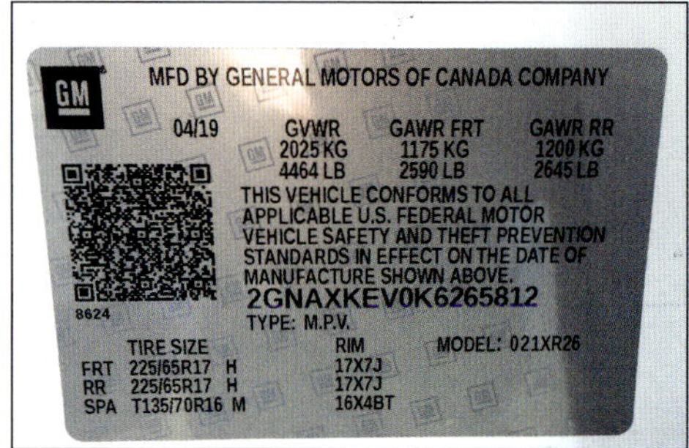

The RPO tag location and design began to change beginning in the 2018 model year. The new design tag requires a smartphone and a QR reader application to access the vehicle's RPO information. With the smartphone application open, scan the QR label. The application will then display the RPO content on your phone.

Rear-wheel-drive axle options typically begin with the letter "G" (GT4, G80). Transmission RPO codes begin with the letter "M" (MT1, M30). The RPO codes are contained on a label known as a service parts identification (SPID) label. The codes are positioned in alpha-numeric order on the label. The SPID label is typically located in one of four locations depending on the year and vehicle model: the glove box, center console, rear decklid (trunk), or on the spare tire cover.

2018 and later

Until the 2018 model year, the RPO/SPID label was located in a position that was mentioned. However, beginning with the 2018 model year, GM began to transition the label information to a different location and format. As new bodystyles and vehicle redesigns were introduced, the location of the RPO information changed. The new label requires a smartphone with a quick response (QR) reader application to access the three-digit codes. The label is now located on the driver-side B-pillar. Open your driver-side door and look at the area below the body striker. Most smartphone applications are available for free and work very well. Available applications include Data Matrix, I-Nigma, QR Scanner, QR Droid, Bar Code, and NeoReader.

To read the new design label, open the smartphone application and position the sight box for the application over the QR label area. The application will read the label and display the RPO codes as well as the vehicle identification number (VIN) and other pertinent information.

Know the RPO

As you may be wondering, why is it important to know the RPO code for the component/system you are attempting to repair? Many components share similarities, but there can

GM Transmission RPO Codes

The following chart lists all of the RPO codes for the various GM Hydra-matic/Allison 4-, 5-, 6-, 8-, 9-, and 10-speed applications for light-duty GM vehicles.

Transmission	RPO	Transmission	RPO	Transmission	RPO
4T40E	MN4	4L85E	MN8	8L90	M5U, M5X, MQE
4T45E	MN5	4L30E	ML4	9T45	M3U
4T60	ME9	4L40E	M90	9T50	M3D, M3E
4T60E	M13	5L40E	MX5	9T60	M3T
4T65E	MN3	6L45	MYA	9T65	M3V
4T65E HD	MN7	6L50	MYB	10L60	MI1
4T65E AWD	M76	6L80	MYC	10L80	MF6, MQB, MI2
4T65E Advanced	M15	6L90	MYD	10L90	MGL, MI4
4T65E	MD7	6T30	MH9	Allison 5/6-Speed LCT 1000	MW7, M74
4T80E	MH1	6T35	MNU	Allison 10-Speed 10L1000	MGM, MGU
4L60	MD8	6T40	MH8, MHB, MHH, MNH, MNK	VT20	M83
4L60E	M30	6T45	MH7, MHC, MNP, MHG	VT25	M75, M16
4L65E	M32	6T50	MHJ, MHK, M2D, MNM	VT40	MRG, MRD
4L60E Hybrid	M33	6T70	MH2, MH7, M7W, MH4	CVT7	MR8
4L70E	M70	6T75	M7V, M7X, MY9, MH6	5ET50 Electric Drive	MKE, MKV
2ML70 Electric Drive	M99	6T80	MNM	1ET25 Electric Drive	MMF
4L80E	MT1	8L45	M5T, M5N	1ET35 Electric Drive	MME

be some differences. This means that the part you are replacing could be different even though it may look identical. In many instances, the parts counterperson will ask for the option content or the vehicle's VIN so that he or she can determine the option content and make sure that you receive the correct parts for your application. In addition, component repair processes and system wiring vary, so you may need RPO information to select the correct wiring schematics or repair information.

Transmissions, as with other components, use their own unique RPOs. The 6L45 utilizes the RPO MYA, 6L50 MYB, 6L80 MYC, and 6L90 MYD for the 6-speed rear-wheel-drive applications.

Transmission Tag Information

All Hydra-matic transmissions include a tag that helps to identify the transmission. The 6L family of transmissions use a laminated tag that is mounted to a "flat" on the transmission case. The tag is typically located on the passenger's side of the case in the rear corner.

As with the RPO tag, the transmission tag contains a tremendous amount of information about the transmission, including the model code and the build/Julian date. Many transmission updates are attached to a specific Julian date, so when ordering parts, you may be required to provide the tag information to the parts person to get the correct parts for your application.

Potential Tag Issue

Take care when cleaning the tag because it is easily damaged. One suggestion is to take a picture of the tag so that you will have the information available for the parts counterperson if needed. ■

The 6L80 tag includes the following information: the model year, model code, transmission family, transmission assembly part number, Julian date, sequential serial number, plant code, broadcast code, bar code, and transmission identification.

Some of the information on the tag is very important when it comes to ordering parts and determining if your transmission was equipped with certain updates. The following information may be required by your parts counterperson.

Model Year

The model year may not be the same as the year of the vehicle on which you are working depending on the vehicle's production date.

Model Code

The model code varies depending on the vehicle platform and the type of vehicle into which the transmission is going.

Julian Date

The Julian date represents the numbered day of the year. January

6L80 Unit Specifications

The unit specifications for the 6L80 transmission are below:

- RPO: MYC
- Input torque capacity: 430 ft-lbs (583 Nm)
- Output torque capacity: 664 ft-lbs (900 Nm)
- Gear ratios: first, 4.02:1; second, 2.36:1; third, 1.53:1; fourth, 1.15:1; fifth, 0.85:1; sixth, 0.67:1; reverse, 3.06:1
- Maximum shift speed: 6,500 rpm
- Maximum GVW: 8,600 pounds
- Maximum GCVW: 14,000 pounds
- PRNDL positions: P, R, N, D, and S or M
- Two shift solenoids used (on/off design), SS1, SS2
- Six pulse width modulated (PWM) controlled pressure control solenoids (PCS): PCS, PCS2, PCS3, PCS4, PCS5, and TCC
- Bosch 32-bit TEHCM mounted internally to the transmission on the valve body (referred to as the control solenoid valve assembly in the parts information). The TEHCM incorporates the solenoids, oil pressure switches, fluid temperature sensor (TFT), and is bolted to the valve body using six bolts.
- EC3 Torque Converter 300-, 245-, 265-, or 258-mm twin plate designs. EC3 stands for "controlled capacity converter clutch," which means that the torque converter clutch will not always be fully locked. This means that the converter is designed to slip under certain driving conditions to improve drivability.
- Fluid required: Dexron VI
- Fluid capacity: 9.5L (10 qts), 9.7L (10.2 qts),11.9 L (12.6 qts) depending on model
- Clutch-to-clutch shifts: five clutches (two holding, three driving), one sprag, one-way clutch
- Planetary front (Lepelletier) output (dual pinion design)
- Vane-style oil pump
- Internally mounted TISS (transmission input speed sensor) and TOSS (transmission output speed sensor) are Hall-effect design speed sensors
- Internal mode switch (IMS) range sensor equipped
- Performance algorithm shifting (PAS) programming (downshift program)
- Performance algorithm lift foot (PAL) programming (upshift program)
- Sport mode and tap-shift equipped (tap shift allows you to manually shift the unit paddles or buttons)
- Adaptive strategies with fast-learn capabilities
- Multiple transmission only diagnostic trouble codes (DTCs)

1 is Julian date 001, while December 31 is Julian date 365. Update changes are tied to the Julian date rather than solely the model year, so when it comes to ordering parts, it may be very important.

Broadcast Code

The broadcast code is used to identify the type of transmission.

Inspection and Service

Basic inspection and service of the 6L80 begins and ends with the fluid and fluid service. For the transmission to operate correctly, maintaining the correct fluid level and fluid condition are critical. Burnt fluid or a unit that was operating low on fluid may indicate a reason for a transmission failure.

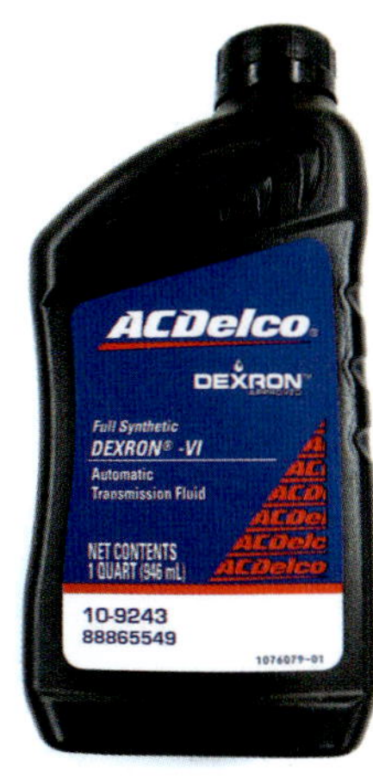

Dexron VI is the only approved fluid for 6L applications. Do not use Dexron III or other fluids in this application. Dexron VI made major improvements in oxidation resistance, lubrication capabilities, and temperature ranges when compared to Dexron III. Dexron VI is licensed by several manufacturers.

Capacities		
Capacity will vary based on your application (2008 Suburban shown)	**Specification**	
	Metric	**English**
Pan Removal and Filter Replacement (approximate capacity)	5.7 liters	6.0 quarts
Rebuild (approximate capacity)	9.9 liters	10.5 quarts
Complete Transmission System (approximate capacity)	11.5 liters	12.2 quarts
Complete Transmission System (heavy-duty cooling; approximate capacity)	11.7 liters	12.4 quarts

Fluid

The 6L80 uses Dexron VI fluid. Dexron VI is far superior to Dexron III, which it replaced. Major improvements in wear control, film strength, friction durability, and oxidation stability were achieved. Clutch-to-clutch shift transmissions, such as the 6L/6T series, require a much more robust fluid as compared to previous automatic transmission designs. Companies currently licensed to produce Dexron VI include Mobil, Chevron, Shell, SK Lubricants, and Valvoline.

Fluid Capacity

The 6L80 has five different oil pans available depending on the application. It is imperative that you have the correct oil pan. Either overfilling or underfilling the transmission can result in transmission clutch failure. Two different pan designs are used: those that are equipped with a standpipe (various standpipe heights are used) and those that are equipped with a dipstick (no standpipe is used).

Fluid capacity is strictly dependent on the vehicle application in which the transmission is used, as the pan part number is dependent on the body type. So, when it comes to fluid capacity, it is best if you reference the owner's manual for the capacity for your application.

Fluid Level

How the fluid level is checked varies depending on whether the pan is equipped with a standpipe or it uses a dipstick.

Dipstick Applications

On units equipped with a dipstick, before checking the fluid level, perform the following:

1. Start the engine and park the vehicle on a level surface. Chock the wheels.
2. Apply the parking brake and vehicle brake, and place the shift lever in Park. Move the shifter to each forward gear range as well as Reverse, pausing for 3 seconds in each range. Place the vehicle in Park.
3. Allow the engine to idle for a few minutes.
4. Observe the transmission fluid temperature (TFT) using the Driver Information Center (DIC), a scan tool, or a temperature gun to measure the oil pan temperature.

Cold Fluid Check Procedure

Use the cold-check procedure to check the fluid level when the transmission fluid temperature is between 80 and 90°F (27 and 32°C). Note that it is not as accurate as the hot-check procedure.

1. Locate the dipstick, flip the handle, pull out the dipstick, and wipe it with a clean rag.
2. Install the dipstick, pushing it back in all the way. Wait a few seconds and then pull it back out again.
3. Check both sides of the dipstick and use the lower level.
4. Inspect the color of the fluid and its condition.
5. If the fluid level is below the Cold mark (lower), add only enough fluid through the dipstick tube as needed to bring the level up to the mark.
6. If the fluid level is correct, push the dipstick back in all the way. Then, flip the handle down to lock the dipstick into place.
7. Perform a hot check after the transmission has reached operating temperature.

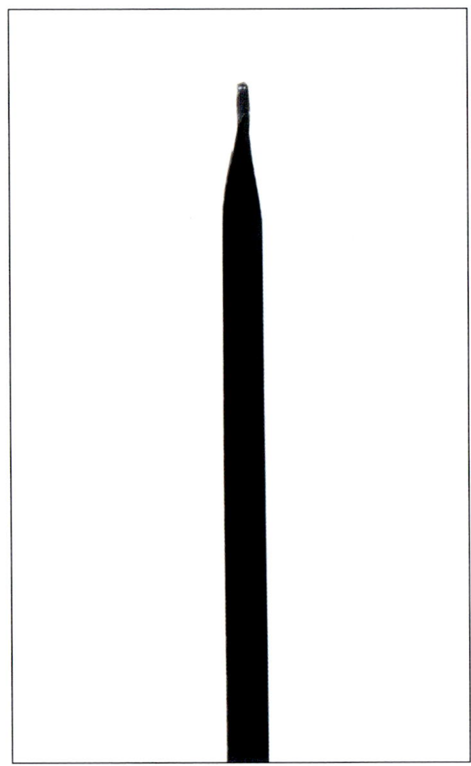

Some 6L applications use a dipstick to check the transmission fluid level. The dipstick includes hot and cold levels.

Some 6L applications are equipped with standpipes rather than a dipstick to check the fluid level. Fluid temperature is critical when checking fluid level via a standpipe. A 6L transmission must be between 86 and 122°F (50 and 80°C) to check the fluid level or you can underfill or overfill the transmission, as the level will not be accurate.

Hot Fluid Check Procedure

Use this procedure to check the transmission fluid level when the transmission fluid temperature is between 160 and 200°F (71 and 93°C):

1. Locate the dipstick, flip the handle, pull out the dipstick, and wipe it with a clean rag.
2. Install the dipstick by pushing it back in all the way. Wait a few seconds, and then pull it back out again.
3. Check both sides of the dipstick and use the lower level.
4. Inspect the color of the fluid and its condition.
5. If the fluid level is below the Hot mark (upper), add only enough fluid through the dipstick tube as needed to bring the level up to the mark.
6. If the fluid level is correct, push the dipstick back in all the way. Then, flip the handle down to lock the dipstick in place.

Standpipe Applications

Use this procedure to check the transmission fluid level when the transmission fluid temperature is between 86 and 122°F (50 and 80°C).

1. Start the engine, park the vehicle on a level surface, and chock the wheels.
2. Apply the vehicle brake and park brake. Place the shift lever in Park. Move the shifter to each forward gear range as well as Reverse, pausing for 3 seconds in each range. Place the vehicle in Park.
3. Allow the engine to idle for a few minutes.
4. Observe the transmission fluid temperature (TFT) using the Driver Information Center (DIC), a scan tool, or a temperature gun to measure the oil pan temperature.
5. With the engine running, remove the standpipe plug located in the transmission oil pan.
6. If oil runs out of the standpipe, allow it to drain until it is only dripping. Install the plug and torque it to 18 ft-lbs (25 Nm).
7. If oil fails to drip or run out, add

Split or Broken Filter

If you remove the oil pan and discover that the filter is split or broken, the cause is usually not a poorly constructed or faulty fluid filter. Instead, this issue is typically related to internal issues within the pump and/or its valving. To split the filter, high pressure must enter the suction side of the pump, which is typically due to a worn pressure regulator valve or to internal pump leakage across the pump channeling. ■

fluid through the standpipe hole or the fill port on the passenger's side of the transmission.

Filter and Fluid Service

Changing the fluid and filter on this application is a simple process. The factory pan gasket is reusable on the 6L applications. Make sure the filter is designed for your specific application and that it is a high-quality filter.

The fluid seal should be replaced anytime the filter is replaced. Use a pair of snap-ring pliers, a screwdriver, or seal puller to remove the seal. Install the new seal with a seal driver or an appropriately sized socket. Lubricate the seal before installing the filter. Wiggle the filter as you apply pressure to the filter to engage the filter seal.

1. Remove the pan bolts and drain the fluid from the pan.
2. Remove the filter and seal. Snap-ring pliers or a screwdriver work well.
3. Clean the pan, gasket, and case mating surface. Inspect the surfaces.
4. Install the filter seal using DT 47848 (or an equivalent tool) to drive in the seal.
5. Lubricate the filter seal and filter neck with transmission fluid.
6. Install the filter.
7. Install the gasket/pan and tighten the bolts to 80 in-lbs (9 Nm) using a crossing pattern. The OEM gasket is reusable if it is not damaged.
8. Fill with Dexron VI fluid.
9. Follow the fluid-level checking procedures.
10. Check for leaks.
11. Test drive the vehicle to make sure that no issues are present.

After changing the fluid and filter, if you have problems (a whine noise or no movement) getting the pump to prime, proceed as follows:

- Set the parking brake and make sure that the transmission has been filled with at least 5 quarts of fluid.

Bolt/Fastener Torque Specifications

Location	Quantity	Size	Specifications	
			Metric	English
Case Extension Housing	6	M10x1.5x40	55 Nm	41 ft-lbs
Control Solenoid Valve Assembly (TEHCM) Lower Body to Upper Body	16	M5x0.8x55; M5x0.8x45	8 Nm	71 in-lbs
Control Solenoid Valve Assembly (TEHCM) Heat Sink to Valve Body	2	M5x0.8x53	8 Nm	71 in-lbs
Upper Body to Lower Body	12	M5x0.8x36	8 Nm	71 in-lbs
Control (with Body and Valve) Valve Assembly to Case Assembly	6	M5x0.8x73	8 Nm	71 in-lbs
Oil Pan to Case	18	M6x1.0x20	9 Nm	80 in-lbs
Oil Pump to Case	13	M6x1.0x40	11 Nm	97 in-lbs
Input and Output Speed Sensor to Valve Body	2	M6x1.0x20	12 Nm	106 in-lbs
Line Pressure Case Plug	1	1/8-27 NPTF	11 Nm	97 in-lbs
Manual Shaft Detent Assembly	1	M6x1.0x14.5	12 Nm	106 in-lbs
Torque Converter Housing to Case	9	M10x1.5x50	72 Nm	53 ft-lbs

- Start the engine, move the shifter into Neutral, check the fluid level, make sure that it is full, and add fluid as required.
- Let the unit warm up until it reaches at least 155°F.
- Reset the transmission's adaptive learning with a scan tool.
- Move the shifter to Reverse with the brake depressed and count to 10.
- Move the shifter to Drive with the brake depressed and count to 10.
- Repeat the procedure.
- Check the fluid level and adjust it as necessary.

Tools

The tools needed to rebuild a 6L80 include both hand tools as well as some special tools. Hand tools, such as sockets, snap-ring pliers, hammers, pliers, and wrenches, will be needed to disassemble and assemble the transmission. Regarding some of the special tools, you may be able to improvise by using tools that you have available.

Hand Tools

Hand tools are required to remove, disassemble, repair, and install the transmission. Basic tools, such as sockets, hammers, pliers, picks, screwdrivers, and wrenches,

A full set of metric end wrenches is very helpful for 6L80 repairs.

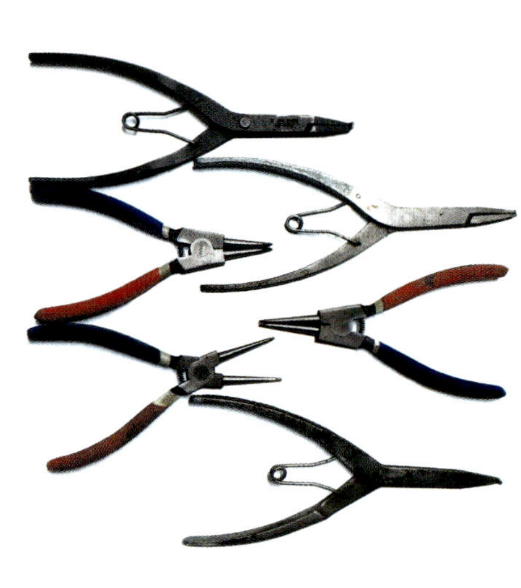

Snap-ring pliers are a necessity because the 6L80 uses multiple different snap rings.

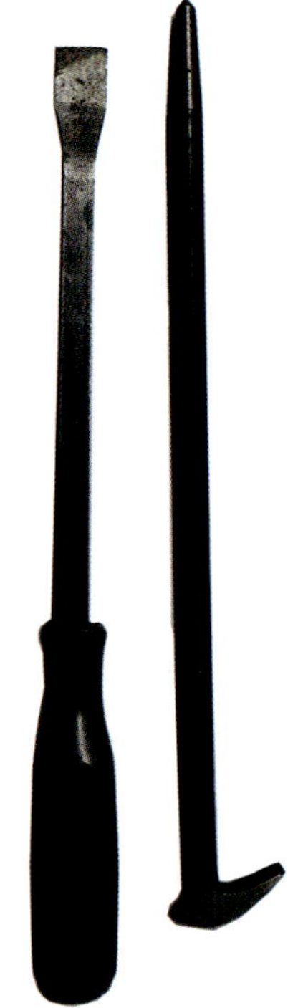

As with screwdrivers, pry bars may be helpful.

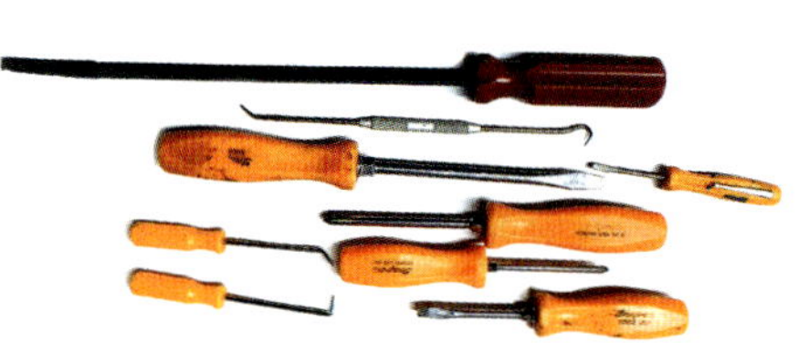

Screwdrivers and picks are used primarily to aid snap ring and valve body valve removal and installation.

Metric and Torx socket sets are required for assembly and disassembly.

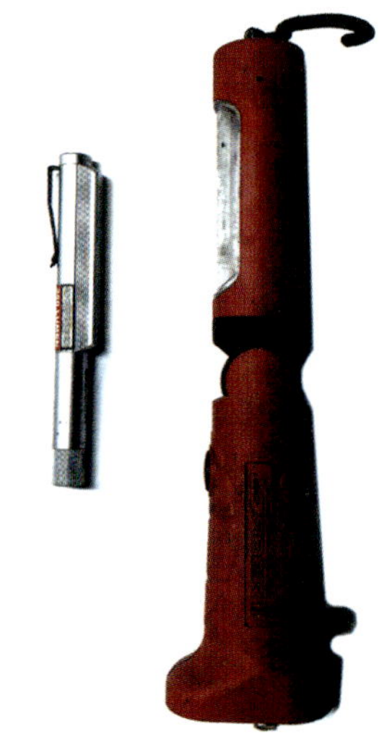

Even in well-lit work areas, handheld lights are very helpful.

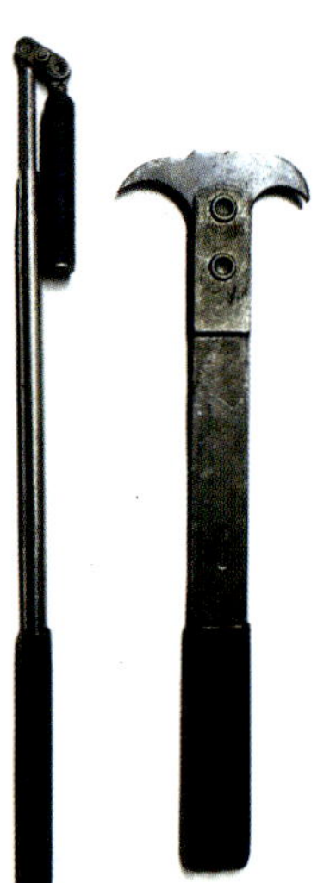

A seal remover works well for the input and output seals. A magnet is usually needed to remove small parts or parts that may have fallen into spaces that are difficult to access.

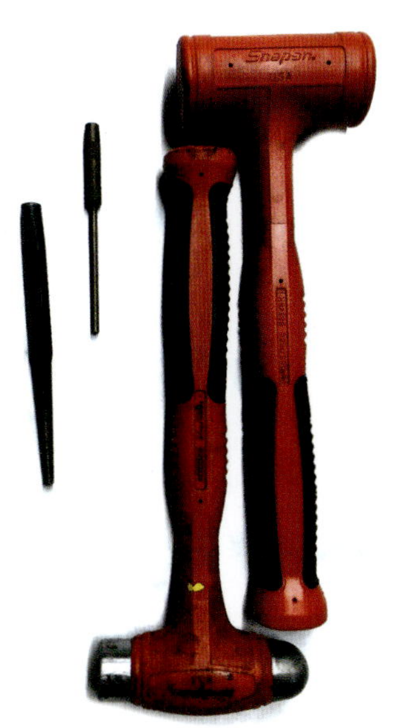

Hammers and pin punches are needed to remove many of the roll pins used in the 6L80.

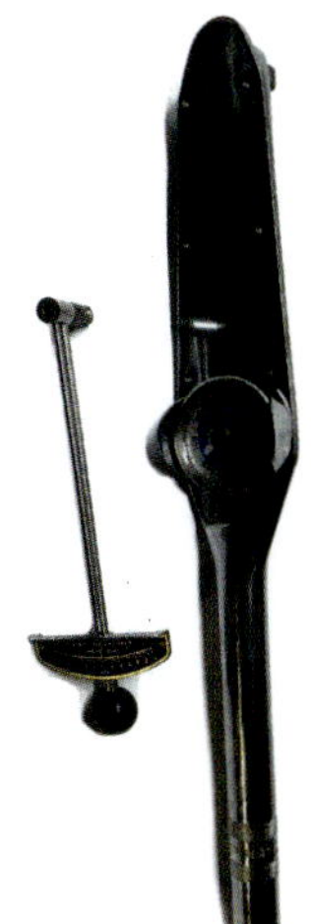

Torque wrenches are used to provide even torque at the correct value to the bolts. This is essential on components such as the pump, valve body, and bell-housing-to-case attachment bolts.

A digital volt ohmmeter is critical when testing the vehicle electrical system as well as some transmission electronic components.

Basic pliers, such as needle-nose pliers, diagonal cutters, and Vice-Grips, are needed to remove and install numerous components.

Air or an electric impact wrench makes the job much easier, especially for disassembly. Take great care if you are using one for assembly purposes because you can easily damage threads and bolts.

Clutch compressor tools are required for disassembly as well as assembly of the transmission clutch packs. If you do not have a clutch compressor, you can sometimes improvise by using pipe or another substitute from around your shop.

Various bushing drivers are required to replace transmission bushings.

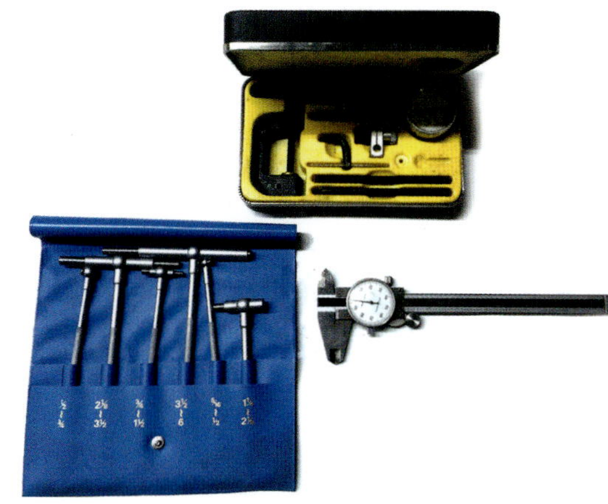

Tools such as a dial indicator, feeler gauges, and a vernier caliper are used during transmission assembly.

Adjustable clutch compressors are very handy because they will fit more than one return spring assembly diameter.

Some form of clutch compressor is required to compress the clutch piston return springs so that the piston snap ring can be removed. A compressor, hand press, arbor press, or even a drill press can be used to perform this function.

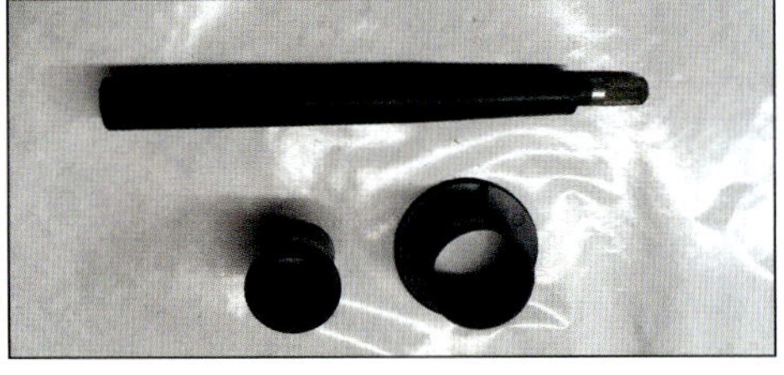

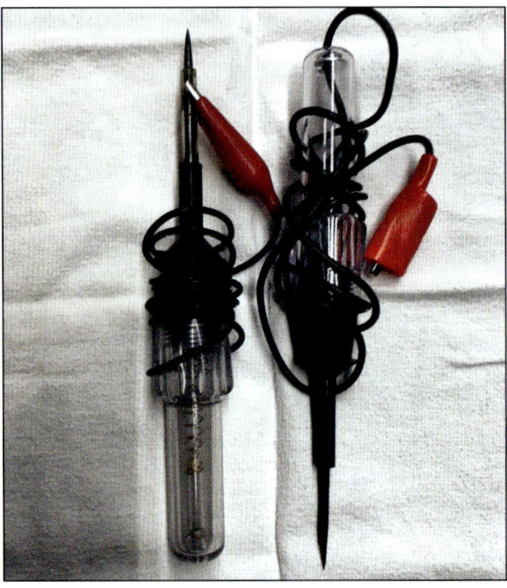

Three types of test lights are available: self-powered, low-current flow, and high-current flow. Generally, high-current flow test lights are used to check transmission powers and grounds.

Professional transmission shops use an industrial washing machine to clean transmission parts.

Some shaft seals are solid-design seals. This means that the seals must be cut with a knife to remove them. The new seal is installed using a seal protector and then sized to the correct diameter with a sizing tool.

A solvent tank is a good cleaning solution for a small shop or hobby shop. While it is more labor intensive compared to industrial washers, you can still do a good job using Stoddard solvent.

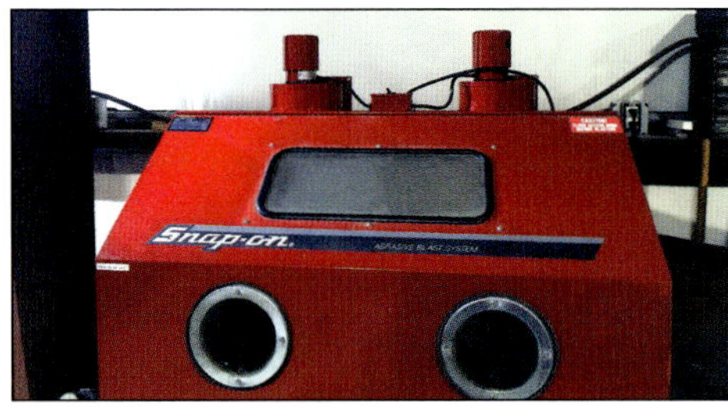

Glass-bead machines work well for external components and surfaces, but do not use them on any internal transmission surface or components.

are some of the necessary tools for tackling 6L80 repairs.

Specialty Tools

Specialty tools are those that you may or may not have access to. A torque wrench, dial indicator/dial caliper, pump puller, and clutch compressor are tools that you should rent or borrow if you do not own them because they are critical for proper service. To compress the clutches, you can use a clutch compressor fixture/foot press, an arbor press, or (if needed) a drill press with a little ingenuity to compress the springs. Access to a commercial parts washer will save you a lot of time and effort. If you do not have access to one, a solvent tank and a pressure washer

An arbor press is a great addition to any shop and can be used for many functions, such as installing bushings and bearings. In addition, an arbor press works well for compressing the clutch return springs in a transmission.

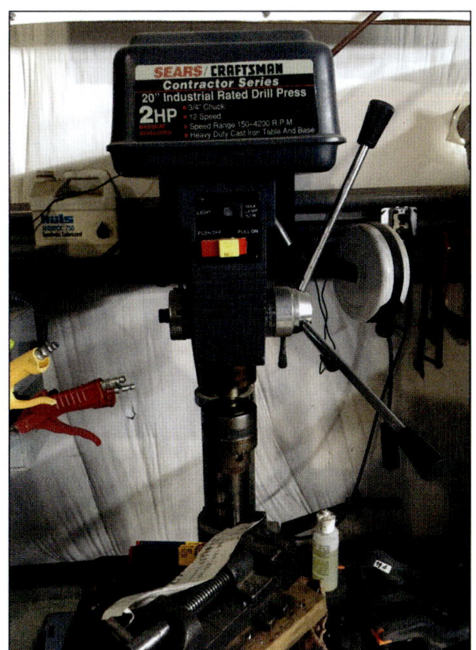

If you do not have a tool that can be used to compress a clutch return spring, consider using your drill press. With a little ingenuity, it will do the job for you.

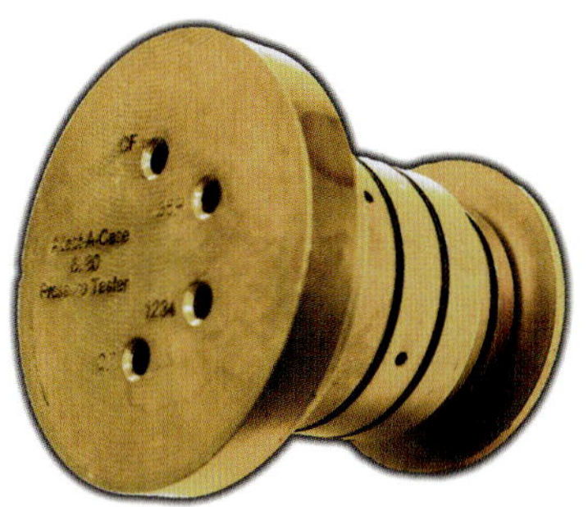

This is a pressure test tool for the 3-5-R/1-2-3-4 clutch. Part number T-135prbrac 6l80 from Adapt-A-Case can be used to bench test some clutch components.

This is a 3-5-R drum installer for the 6L80. Part number T-47781 from Adapt-A-Case helps you to remove and install the 3-5-R clutch drum.

Pump bushing and seal driver T-imnpoac 6L80 from Adapt-A-Case is used to remove and install the pump bushing and seal assembly.

Part number T-47768sac from Adapt-A-Case is used to install and properly size the turbine shaft seals.

The 6L80 giant snap-ring pliers (part number T-6800AC) from Adapt-A-Case are used to remove the center support snap ring. This snap ring is very large and strong and requires some form of giant snap-ring pliers to remove and install it from/ into the groove in the case.

This 6L80 Lifting tool T-47786AC from Adapt-A-Case allows you to lift the planetary gears in and out of the transmission case as an assembly.

may be used. A glass-bead machine works well for cleaning parts after they have been cleaned with solvent or other cleaning processes. Keep this in mind: do not glass bead any internal components or internal areas.

Some specialty tools are specific to the 6L transmissions. GM has all of the tools available through Kent-Moore Tools. The largest and most diverse aftermarket specialty tools are available through Adapt-A-Case. A special thanks to Adapt-A-Case for providing the artwork for their tools.

Adapt-A-Case's 3-5-R 6L80 t-135BRGAC can be used to install the 3-5-R drum bearing if you need to replace the bearing.

Adapt-A-Case's 6L80 T-46664AC is used to align the pump halves prior to torquing the pump bolts. Proper pump alignment is critical to prevent pump damage during operation.

Power and Ground Testing

The 6L80 is an electrically operated component just like your radio, climate control, engine, and most other systems on today's vehicles. Issues with the transmission and/or engine electrical systems can (and do) lead to transmission failure as well as repeat issues that many people misdiagnose as an internal transmission-related issue. This means that the transmission internal failure that has led you to rebuild your 6L80 may be caused by an electrical component and/or electrical circuit issue. If those issues are not found and repaired prior to you performing the rebuild, the transmission may fail again.

Power and ground supply are critical to proper 6L80 transmission operation. Many automatic transmission related issues can be addressed by checking for proper power and ground supply prior to condemning the transmission or its components as being faulty. Starting with a check of the power and ground supply is where diagnosis begins for any automatic transmission.

Battery

The battery is central to proper TEHCM and transmission operation. Everything starts and ends at the battery. The battery should be tested, preferably with a conductance-type battery tester. If you do not have access to one, most parts stores and all dealerships have conductance battery testing equipment.

In addition, the battery posts and cables should be cleaned and inspected. Keep in mind that corrosion will wick up the battery cables, creating a condition known as voltage drop, which can lead to operational issues.

It cannot be over-emphasized how important the battery and its connections are regarding proper 6L80 operation. False diagnostic

Poor connections are the biggest enemy of a properly operating 6L80. Always check the battery, its connections, as well as the transmission power and ground circuits for proper operation prior to condemning the transmission.

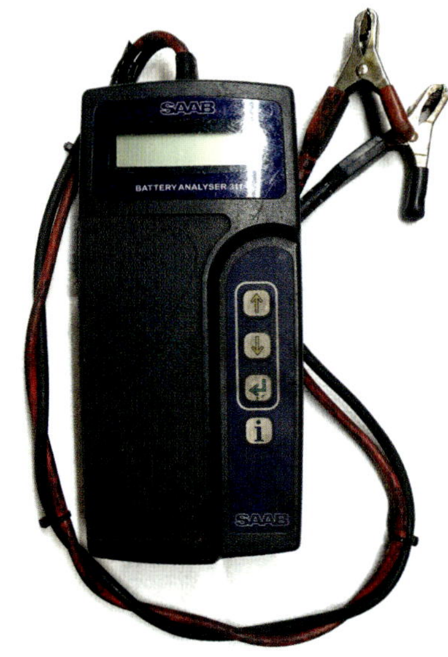

A conductance battery tester is the fastest and most reliable type of tool for testing a battery. All dealerships and most parts stores and independent repair shops can test the battery for you if you do not have access to a tester.

trouble codes (DTCs), shift concerns, as well as the transmission defaulting to limp in mode can occur if any electrical issues are present.

Circuit

When discussing an electrical system, the term "circuit" will be mentioned. A circuit is used to describe a system that starts and ends at the battery for a particular component. A circuit consists of the following:

- A power source (typically the battery)
- A ground (typically the main ground is the negative terminal of the battery). To connect the battery ground to the rest of the circuits, manufacturers use the frame, engine block, and transmission case to transmit the current flow to the ground wiring connections at the battery.
- Conductors (typically the wiring, connectors, and terminals)
- A load, lights, electrical motors, relays, or solenoids are typical components in a vehicle electrical circuit
- Circuit control (a switch or computer are typically used to control the load).
- Circuit protection (typically a fuse, fusible link, or circuit breaker are used for protection from excessive current flow)

Electrical Current Flow

Three terms are used when describing electrical operation in a circuit: amperage, voltage and resistance.

Amperage (current) is a measure of electron volume through a circuit. Amperage is the workhorse for the components. In other words, amperage is what illuminates the lights and operates the solenoids, relays, and electrical motors.

Voltage is the electrical pressure, or force, that pushes the amperage through the circuit and its components.

Resistance is the opposition to current flow (amperage) in the circuit. The higher a circuit's resistance, the lower the current flow (amperage) through the circuit, so the dimmer the light will be or the slower an electric motor will turn.

The key to understanding electrical circuits is to understand the relationship among voltage, amperage, and resistance.

Amperage

Amperage is not consumed by the electrical circuit or its components. Amperage is used to make the components operate, but it is not consumed by the component or the circuit. This means that if you were to measure the amperage flowing into a light and the amperage flowing out of the light while in operation, the amperage measurements would be the same. Factors that change the current flow through a circuit/component are the circuit voltage and resistance. The higher the voltage and/or the lower the resistance, the higher the current flow and, thus, the brighter the light. The lower the circuit voltage and/or the higher the resistance in the circuit, the lower the current flow and, thus, the dimmer the light.

Voltage

Voltage is the consumable in an electrical circuit. The key is that the component should be consuming the voltage and not the wiring or connections. In other words, first measure the voltage being delivered to the component. For the sake of argument, let's say it measures 12.5 volts. If you then measured the voltage on the ground side of the component, it should measure near 0 volts (typically, it will be less than 0.5 volts) when the circuit is in operation. The component should use almost all of the circuit voltage.

For example, if you placed your positive voltmeter lead on the power-side terminal leading to the light and your negative voltmeter lead on the ground-side terminal of the light and then energize the light, you would see the voltage that is being consumed across the light. This process is known as measuring voltage drop.

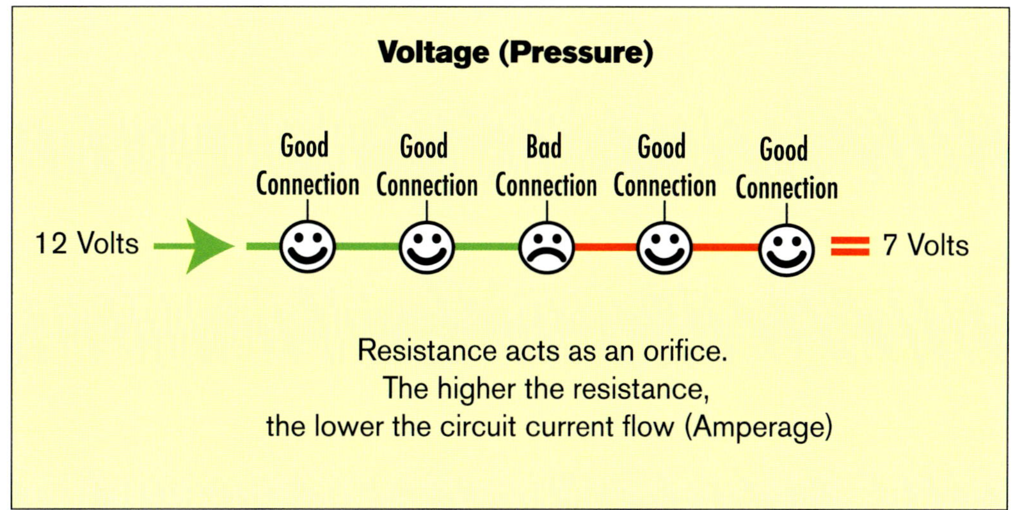

A properly charged battery should display at least 12.6 volts. Voltage supply is critical to proper transmission operation.

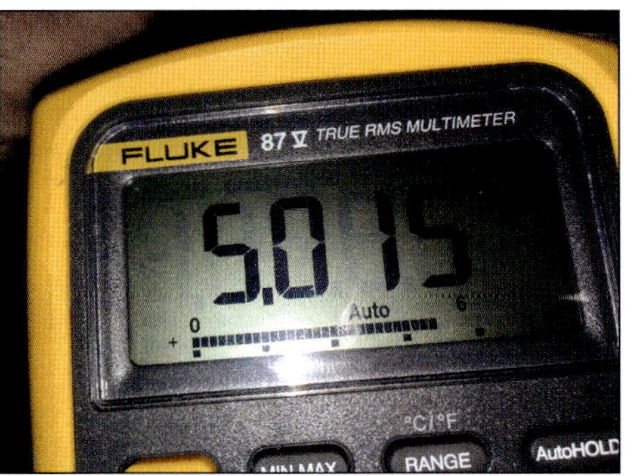

The voltage in a circuit must be consumed by the component and not the wiring or connections. Excessive voltage drop will create current flow issues in the circuit and can result in DTCs and components that operate improperly or not at all. The rule for voltage drop is 0.1 to 0.2 volt per connection with the circuit in operation. Measuring voltage drop is one of the fastest and most accurate ways of testing dynamic resistance in a circuit. A 5-volt drop, as shown, indicates a very excessive resistance issue. Resistance issues will create major transmission problems and must be addressed prior to attempting to repair issues that may appear to be transmission related.

In other words, you would see close to 12.5 volts on your meter display, indicating that the light is consuming almost all of the circuit voltage.

The key is to understand that the component is the only thing in the circuit that should be consuming circuit voltage. For example, let's say you had a bad connection in the circuit and that connection was consuming 5 volts. You would have 12 volts being applied to the connection, but only 7 volts would be available to feed the component downstream of the bad connection. Lower voltage at the component means that you are now lacking the proper electrical pressure to push the amperage through the component, and the component may not operate correctly or operate at all.

Resistance

As was described above, there is a major relationship between the resistance in a circuit and the current flow through that circuit. Resistance is typically caused by bad connections. Connection issues typically are due to the following:

- Corrosion (caused by road salt, dirt, moisture, or damaged/missing terminal seals)
- Terminal fretting (microscopic corrosion and metal transfer due to terminal vibration). Fretting is a very common cause of intermittent electrical issues.
- Loose female terminals and poor pin tension (male to female)
- Loose cable attaching bolts
- Loose connections
- Damaged wiring (broken wire strands)

Resistance can be measured in two ways: with an ohmmeter or with a voltmeter.

Ohmmeter

This is a direct static measurement of resistance, but it has many limitations. When your meter is placed in the "OHM" position, it sends a tiny amount of voltage and amperage out of the positive lead and then measures how much voltage is present on the negative lead. It then calculates the voltage drop and displays the reading as ohms on your meter. The higher the reading is, the higher the resistance is of the component/wiring.

The circuit must be deenergized; otherwise, the meter reading will not be accurate. Since the circuit is deenergized, it may test "good," but it may fail to operate correctly when it is energized.

The ohmmeter only applies a tiny voltage and amperage to the circuit so that it is not simulating the circuit in operation. For example, let's say you were measuring the resistance of a wire, and that wire had all of the strands broken except for one. When you connect the ohmmeter leads to each end of the wire, the meter will measure 0 ohms, indicating a perfect connection and no issues with the wire. If you took that same wire and connected it into a lighting circuit, you may find the light was dim or it may not light at all. You may be wondering why. The ohmmeter does not load the circuit, as it is only applying a small amount of voltage and amperage to the wire you are testing. Since you are applying such little voltage and amperage, the excessive circuit resistance due to the severed wires will not show up.

So, what does this mean? Ohmmeters are great for static checks of components, such as relay and solenoid windings if the circuit is shorted or open all the time, but they will not find issues where the solenoid or relay only develops resistance or a shorted winding condition when it is energized. Ohmmeters should not be used to test battery cable and/or connections simply because of the low-current flow characteristic of the meter, as it can easily fool you. Ohmmeters work well for sensor grounds, as they are very low-current flow circuits and the wires are typically very small with few strands.

The other issue is that manufacturers do not provide a lot of ohm-related resistance specifications, so you may be wondering if the reading you are seeing is good or bad.

Voltmeter

A voltmeter can provide an indirect measurement of circuit resistance. The advantage is that the circuit is active when you are using a voltmeter. As was discussed earlier, the circuit voltage must be consumed across the component and not across the wiring or its connections. You can measure the voltage consumed across the connections with your meter by measuring the voltage drop. Excessive voltage drop across a connection or wiring indicates excessive resistance in the circuit. A general rule when measuring voltage drop is that it should not exceed 0.1 to 0.2 volt per connection. Voltage drop techniques can be used to diagnose power- and ground-side resistance-related issues.

The 0.006-inch (0.152-mm) voltage drop shown across this circuit indicates a very good circuit connection. The voltage drop being measured in this picture is across the B+ cable and its connections, as indicated between the meter lead connections.

Power-Side Testing the 6L80

Testing the power supplied to the transmission is important. The harness connected to the transmission contains both power and a ground for the TEHCM. You can use either a voltmeter or a test light to test the power feed. An old-fashioned bulb-style test light is preferable. If you don't have a test light, you can build your own with a bulb socket and an 1157 or other light, such as a 9004 headlight. Simply attach wire ends to the socket, and you now have a high-quality test light to use that will provide sufficient load on the circuit for testing purposes.

Test lights are available as high-current flow or low-current flow versions. For testing powers and grounds, the higher current flow design should be used. A headlight works as well as a test light. A 9004 will flow 4 or 5 amps of current depending on which filament you are using. An 1157 lamp flows about 2.5 amps of current, so it makes a great test lamp for checking power and ground circuits.

Using a digital voltmeter or an LED-type test light can lead you to believe that the transmission has power even when it does not. The voltmeter (DVOM) and LED-type test lights require very little current to operate. Just like the issue with an ohmmeter (as discussed previously), if the wire is physically damaged or if you have a bad connection, the meter or LED test lamp may show that you have battery voltage available to the transmission but the circuit may not be capable of carrying enough current for the TEHCM to operate correctly.

Connect one end of your test light to a good ground. Disconnect the transmission pass-through connector (X1). Touch the other lead or the test light probe to the power supply pins in the vehicle harness connector (vehicle side) with the ignition switch in the run position. Connector X1 (vehicle harness connector connecting to the transmission), Pin 12 (pink wire), and Pin 4 (red/white) are the power feeds that need to be tested. If the light brightly illuminates, the power supplies are good.

TECH TIP

Common Connection Issues

Before testing a 6L vehicle harness for power, make sure that none of the terminals have backed out of the harness-side connector. Commonly, the terminal lock releases, and a terminal starts to back out, creating a connection issue, which can cause DTCs to set as well as communication- and transmission-related issues. ■

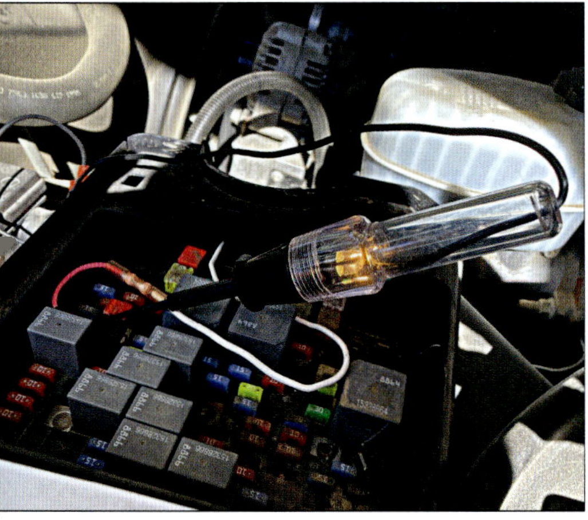

Generally high-current flow test lights are used to check transmission powers and grounds. A typical automotive test light will flow between 0.2 and 0.4 amp. LED-type test lights should not be used to test power and ground circuits because they are low-current flow devices and may indicate that the circuit/connection is good when in fact it may have resistance issues.

An 1157 light bulb works well, as it flows in the 2.5-amp range.

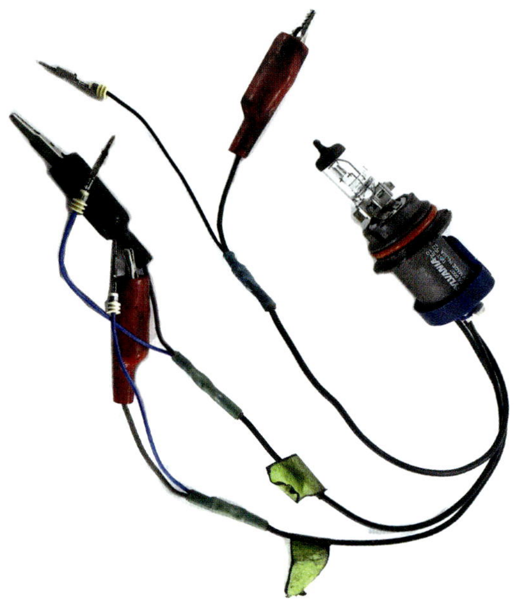

A 9004 headlight works well as a high-current flow test light. One filament flows approximately 2.2 amps, while the other filament flows around 4.5 amps.

Ground-Side Testing the 6L80

The ground can be tested using a few different methods: voltage drop with a voltmeter or with a low impendence high-current flow bulb type of test light.

The principle of measuring voltage drop is quite simple and can be used to indirectly measure resistance in a power-side or a ground-side circuit. Let's look at making a simple ground voltage drop measurement on a battery ground to highlight the principle. To check a battery ground, do the following:

- Place the voltmeter in the DC volt position.
- Connect one of the meter leads to the battery negative cable.
- Connect the other meter lead to the point on the vehicle where the ground is connected (typically the body, frame or engine).
- Turn the ignition to the ON position.
- Turn on all electrical loads: heater fan, head lights, radio, and all other components you can find to turn on.
- Read the value displayed on the meter. Typically, it should read less than 0.1 to 0.2 volt per connection. A high reading indicates circuit resistance, which must be addressed.

The same principle can be applied to the transmission ground circuit. With the connector still attached to the transmission, back probe terminal 5 of the connector. If you do not have back probing tools, a paper clip will work. Slide your probing tool parallel to the wire until you make contact with the terminal. Attach one of the meter leads to the probing tool, and attach the other lead to the battery negative terminal. Turn the ignition key to the ON position, turn all accessories/loads on, and read the meter.

Keep in mind when measuring voltage drop that you are measuring dynamic resistance of everything between the two voltmeter leads. If the reading is excessive (above 0.1 to 0.2 volt per connection), you have a ground issue. At that point, trace the wiring circuit because you have a problem somewhere between the battery negative terminal and the transmission pass-through connector. Break the circuit into sections based on the connectors and connections. Perform a voltage drop measurement between each connection and the battery negative to isolate the resistance.

Another approach is to use your test light. You may want to test the power supply and the ground for the transmission at the same time. If you already tested the power-side integrity with your test light, the ground can now be checked as well. Proceed as follows:

- With the transmission pass-through connector disconnected, locate terminal 5 (black/white wire) in the harness-side connector X1.
- With the ignition in the ON position, touch one of the test light leads (probe) to terminal 5. Touch the other lead to either power feed in the connector (Pin 12 or 4) in the harness-side connector.
- The light should be fully illuminated if the ground is good.
- If the light is dim or not lit at all, the ground is faulty.
- If the ground is faulty, you can use voltage drop to isolate the issue. Otherwise, the problem can be isolated using your test light.

6L80 Wiring at the 16-Pin Transmission Pass-Through Connector X1 (Harness Side)

Pin	Wire Color	Circuit Number/Component
1	–	–
2	–	–
3	Orange/Black	1786/ IMS to ECM Park/Neutral
4	Red/White	1840/Power
5	Black/White	451/Ground
6	–	–
7	–	–
8	–	–
9	Dark/Blue	5985/Power, IPC, DIC, Accessory Wake-Up
10	Tan/Black	2500/Data, IPC, DIC, High-Speed CAN/LAN Data, High Positive
11	Tan	2501/Data, IPC, DIC High-Speed CAN/LAN data, Low Negative
12	Pink	2139/Power
13	Tan	2501/Data, IPC, DIC High-Speed CAN/LAN data, Low Negative
14	Tan/Black	2500/Data, IPC, DIC, High-speed CAN/LAN Data, High Positive
15	–	–
16	Orange/Black	6399/ Replicated MPH/KPH to ECM without RPO NQH

Examine Connectors

When disconnecting the transmission pass-through connector, examine the connectors for evidence of transmission fluid that was trapped in the connector. The connectors should not be filled with fluid. ■

This is a good circuit voltage drop measurement. Voltage drop measurements are an easy and accurate way of testing for resistance issues when the circuit is in operation.

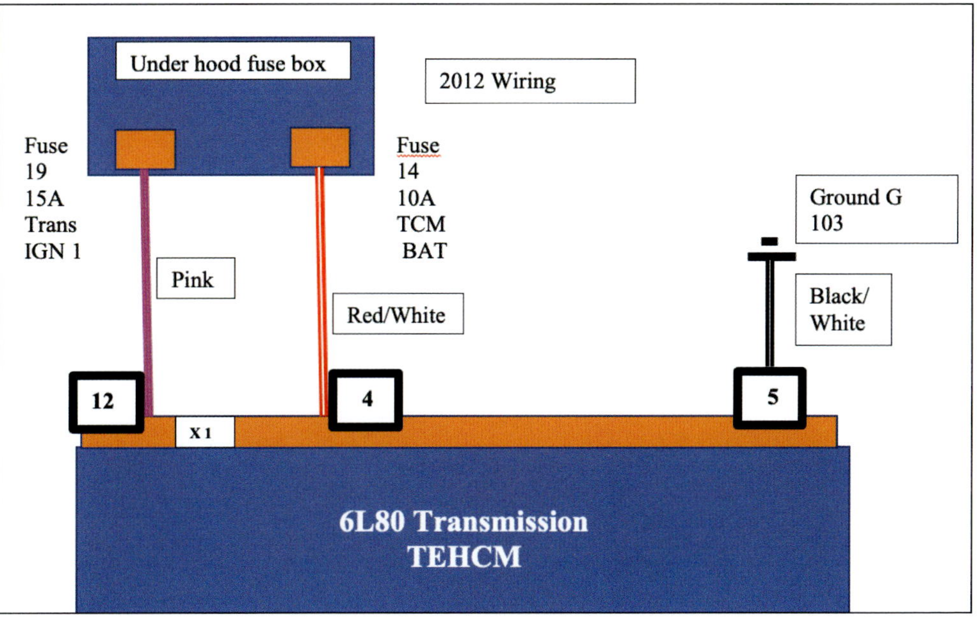

Test the power and ground of a 6L80 at the transmission prior to condemning the transmission or TEHCM. Pins 4 and 12 are power; Pin 5 is ground.

To isolate the faulty ground with your test light, attach the test light lead to the battery positive terminal. Trace the wiring to locate the circuit and its connectors. Back probe each terminal/connection with a probing tool and your test light. When the light fully illuminates, you have found the issue. The problem is located somewhere between the point where the light fully illuminated and the last point where the light was dim.

If fluid is present in the pass-through connector, any of the following symptoms may occur:

- False DTCs
- No engine crank when key is in the start position
- Start and stall
- No scan tool communication with various computers
- Transmission defaults may be present
- The driver information PRNDL indicator may be blank and not show the gear position

Adhesives, Sealers, and Lubricants

None of the gaskets or seals used in the 6L80 require any type of

Power, ground, CAN data, and park and neutral input is fed to the vehicle controls through the X1 connector, which is plugged into the transmission.

sealer. Rubber seals should be lubricated with Dexron VI or an approved transmission assembly lube, such as Transjel.

When installing the torque converter bolts, use Loctite Blue 242 thread locker on the threads.

Seal and Gasket Service Kits

Seals and gaskets need to be replaced any time that a transmission is rebuilt. A quality kit is a necessity. Some kits include gaskets and seals only; others include clutch plates. Some kits also include the filter and the molded clutch pistons. Most companies have kits available in multiple content configurations. Several companies sell kits for the 6L transmission. Precision International, TransTec, and Seal Aftermarket are some of the larger suppliers. Precision International is the OEM supplier for GM.

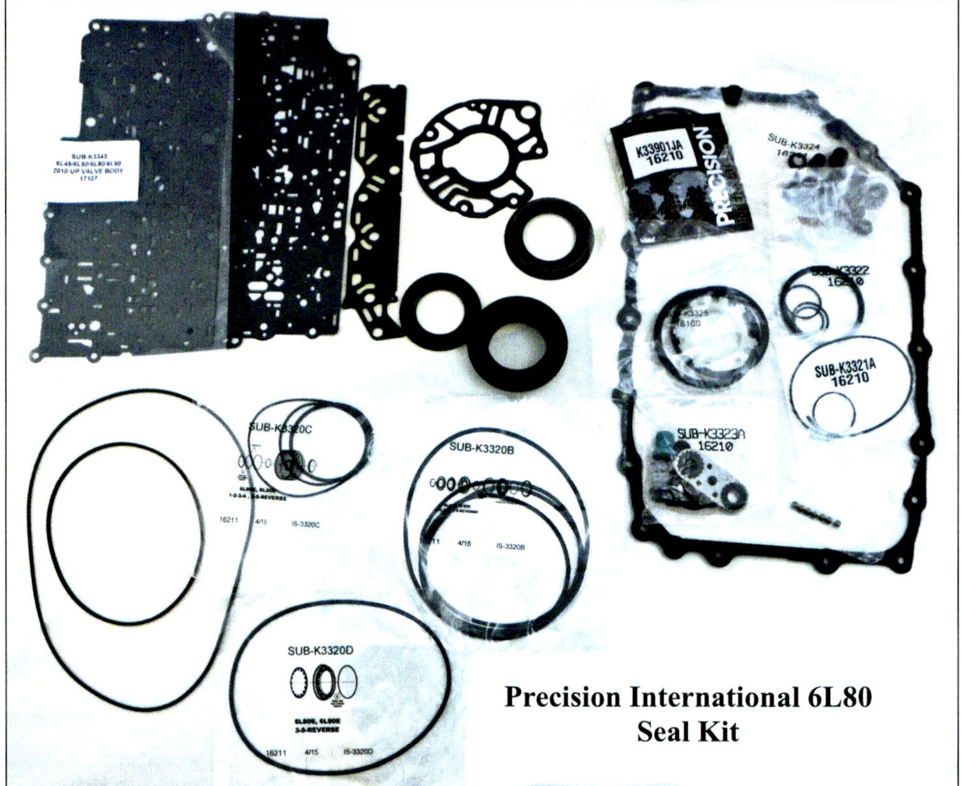

Transmission kits are available in several configurations, such as seals and gaskets; seals, gaskets, and clutches; seals, gaskets, clutches, and filters; and seals, gaskets, clutches, filters, bearings, and bushings. Some kits are available prepackaged with all of the seals labeled for which component they fit; others are delivered in bulk bags.

> **TECH TIP**
> ### Automotive Grease
> Under no circumstance should you ever use any automotive-type grease, such as chassis or wheel-bearing grease, in an automatic transmission. Automotive greases do not break down completely and can lead to plugged filters and ultimately pump and transmission failure. ■

Cooler flushing or replacement is critical to transmission life. Cooler return flow is fed to the transmission lubrication circuit so that a restricted cooler will not lead to transmission failure.

Assembly Lubricants

Transmission components, seals, bearings, and bushings need to be lubricated prior to assembling the transmission. The type of lubricant depends on the component that is being assembled.

Several types of lubricants are used including:

- Automatic transmission fluid
- Transmission assembly specialized lubricants, such as Transjel, Trans Assembly Goo, synthetic transmission assembly lube, or Vaseline

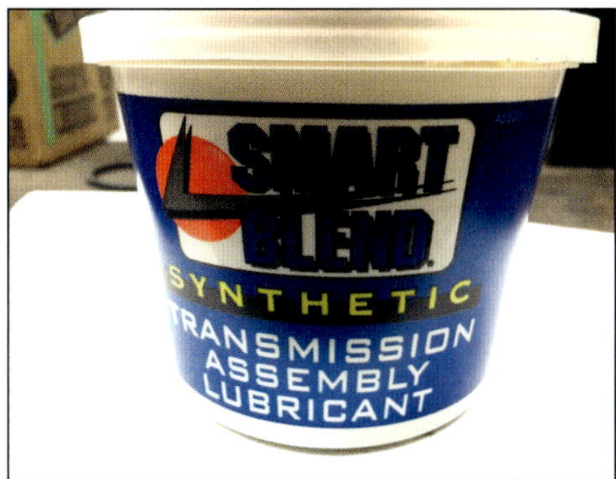

Assembly lubes, such as Transjel, Assemblee Goo, and synthetic assembly lube are available to help with component assembly and lubrication. Do not use automotive greases, such as chassis or wheel bearing greases, as they can lead to filter restrictions and transmission failure.

Seals, Clutch Piston Seals, and Sealing Rings

The type of lubricant used varies based on the preference of the assembly technician. Most rebuilders use a specialized lubricate such as Transjel. Some old timers use a home hardware product known as "door ease," which is then over-coated with automatic transmission fluid. Others simply coat the seals with automatic transmission fluid.

Components and Bearings

Most components, such as the gears and all the bearings, should be lubricated with automatic transmission fluid.

Bushings and Thrust Washers

These components are typically coated with a specialized lubricant, such as Transjel, or automatic transmission fluid.

Cooler-flushing solvent is available in cans from many parts stores.

Valve Body, Valves, and Bores

All transmission valves and valve bores should be coated with automatic transmission fluid.

Oil Pump

Most rebuilders coat the pump gears, vanes, rotors, and slides with a specialized lubricant, such as Transjel, or automatic transmission fluid. Most rebuilders pack the pump with lubricant to ensure that the pump will properly prime immediately on the first start.

Cooler Flushing

Any time that the transmission is rebuilt or a new transmission has been installed, the transmission cooler must be cleaned. Contamination and metal particulates tend to pack into the cooler, which restricts the cooler flow. The oil returning from the transmission is used for transmission lubrication, so a restriction in the cooler flow can result in total transmission failure. A few methods are used: a professional cooler-flushing machine with an aerosol cooler-flushing solvent or replacement of the cooler or the radiator, which typically houses the cooler.

MECHANICAL ELECTRONIC COMPONENTS

The 6L80 uses five multiple-disc clutch packs and one sprag one-way clutch to provide six forward speeds and one reverse range. The clutch packs, when hydraulically applied, drive or hold different planetary gearset members to provide the various gear ratios as well as vehicle direction. Some of the clutches are combined in one housing.

Starting in the front of the unit is the oil pump assembly. Behind the oil pump is the 1-2-3-4/3-5-reverse clutch drum, the Lepelletier gearset, and the 4-5-6 clutch with the turbine shaft attached to the clutch housing. The 4-5-6 clutch damper and intermediate shaft follow. The 1-2-3-4 clutch hub and 2-6/3-5-R clutch hub is next in line. Following the two clutch hubs is the 2-6/low/reverse clutch drum (center support), followed by the dual-pinion planetary gearset and finally the output ring gear with the output shaft attached.

All of those components are positioned in the transmission case. The components are fed hydraulic pressure (clutch apply and lube pressure) via passages in the pump, case, and transmission shafts.

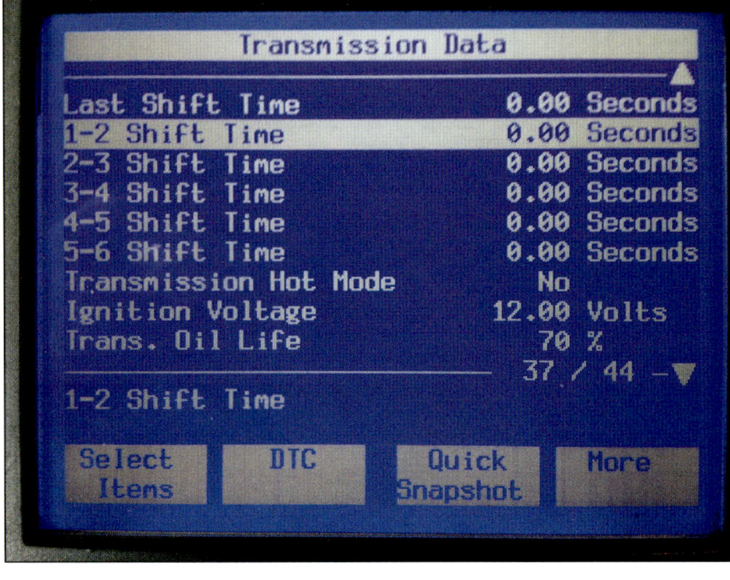

The 6L80 uses five multiple-disc clutches, one sprag one-way clutch, three planetary gearsets, five shafts, and one vane-style oil pump.

Range Reference Chart and Power Flow

All of the clutch components used in the 6L series units are named after the gears in which they are used. For example, a 2-6 clutch is used for second gear as well as sixth gear, and a 4-5-6 clutch is used in fourth, fifth, and sixth gears.

The 6L80 requires a combination of two clutches to provide a forward or reverse gear ratio. If only one clutch applies, the transmission will be missing the two gears that the clutch activates. If the clutch in question is starting to fail, the slip becomes apparent in the highest gear in which the clutch is used prior to it slipping in both gears for which the clutch is used. This is due to the load on the clutch; the higher the gear (lower the gear ratio), the higher the torque load is on the clutch.

If more than two clutches are applied at one time, the vehicle will tend to tie up on that shift. Tie-up issues are typically related to internal seal leakage or cracks/warpage in the pump or valve body.

Monitoring the gear ratio with a scan tool is a great way to determine if a clutch is slipping. Each gear

Range Reference Power Flow									
Range	**Park Neutral**	**Rev**	**1st Braking**	**1st**	**2nd**	**3rd**	**4th**	**5th**	**6th**
1-2-3-4 Clutch	–	–	On	On	On	On	On	–	–
3-5-R Clutch	–	On	–	–	–	On	–	On	–
4-5-6 Clutch	–	–	–	–	–	–	On	On	On
2-6 Clutch	–	–	–	–	On	–	–	–	On
Low/Reverse Clutch	On**	On	On	On*	–	–	–	–	–
Low Sprag	–	–	–	On	–	–	–	–	–
Gear Ratios	–	3.06-1	4.02-1	4.02-1	2.36-1	1.53-1	1.15-1	.85.1	0.67-1

*With some 6L80 applications, the low/reverse clutch is applied during launch in D-range first gear. As soon as the vehicle reaches 2 to 3 mph, the clutch is released. This feature provides additional torque capacity as the vehicle attempts to move forward. The application of the low/reverse clutch during launch can complicate diagnosis if you are not aware of how it is programmed. A faulty low sprag can fool you, as one would expect that the transmission would not move forward. This is not the case if the vehicle is equipped with the programming described above. In this instance, the transmission will start to move; then, it will appear that the transmission has dropped into Neutral, as the vehicle reaches 2 mph and the low/reverse clutch releases.

** The low/reverse clutch is applied in Park and Neutral ranges. This feature is used on multiple GM transmission families. This feature is used to reduce "garage shift" engagement times, as the low/reverse clutch is required for both first- and reverse-gear operation.

Planetary Power Flow							
Planetary and Gear	**Rev**	**1st**	**2nd**	**3rd**	**4th**	**5th**	**6th**
Lepelletier Front (Input)	x	x	x	x	x	x	–
Dual Pinion (Output) Front set	x	–	x	x	–	x	x
Dual Pinion (Output) Rear set	–	x	x	x	x	x	x

Note that "x" indicates that the planetary is in use.

provides a specific ratio. The TEHCM calculates the ratio based on input and output speed sensor signal frequency. The TEHCM then provides the information to the other vehicle modules via the CAN data bus. The scan tool receives the speed information via its CAN-bus connection.

Planetary noise diagnosis is based on when the planetary is in use. Typically, the planetary will make a whining noise that may include a vibration that can vary in intensity based on the speed and torque being applied to the planetary. Use the Planetary Power Flow chart to identify which planetary may be causing your concern.

6L80 Electronic Components

The 6L80 utilizes multiple electronic components to control the operation of the transmission. Electrical inputs (sensors/switches) provide information to the TEHCM/TCM regarding the operation of the transmission while output devices (solenoids) are used by the TEHCM/TCM to control the operation of the transmission.

TEHCM

The 6L80 uses an integrated solenoid body and TCM. The assembly is typically referred to as a transmission electrical hydraulic control module (TEHCM), or if you are referencing GM parts information, it is called a control solenoid with body assembly. The TEHCM is mounted internally of the transmission and bolted to the transmission valve body.

The TEHCM assembly houses the following components:

- 6 PWM high-side driven-pressure control solenoids: PCS line, PCS2, PCS3, PCS4, PCS5, and TCC
- 2 shift solenoids (ON/OFF design): SS1,SS2
- Bosch 32-bit TCM
- 1 transmission fluid temperature (TFT) sensor
- 2 thermal couples for computer circuit board overtemperature protection
- 4 transmission fluid pressure (TFP) switches. TFP 1 indicates the position of the 3-5-R clutch regulator control valve. TFP 3 indicates the position of the 2-6 clutch regulator control valve. TFP 4 indicates the position of the 1-2-3-4 clutch regulator control valve. TFP 5 indicates the position of the low/reverse clutch regulator control valve.

The 6L80 is equipped with an electrohydraulic device known as a transmission electrical hydraulic control module (TEHCM). The TEHCM houses the transmission computer (TCM), six pulse width modulated pressure control solenoids, two on/off solenoids, four clutch pressure switches, and the temperature sensors. If it is faulty, the TEHCM is designed to be replaced as an assembly. The TEHCM requires programing if it is replaced.

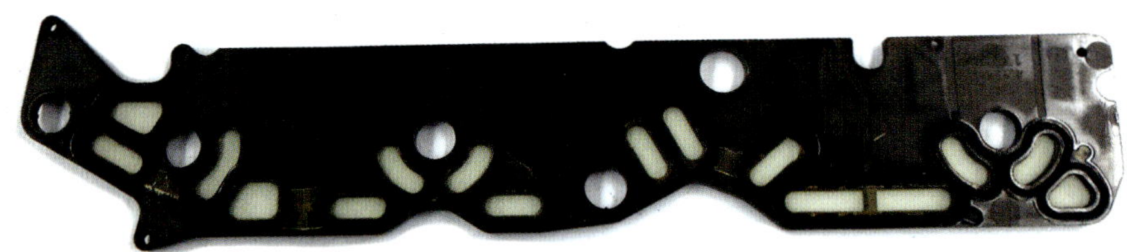

The filter plate is located between the valve body and the TEHCM. It filters the fluid traveling into the TEHCM solenoids and is designed to be replaced anytime the TEHCM and valve body are separated.

Since the TEHCM is an integrated device, if a TEHCM component fails, the complete TEHCM assembly will require replacement. The exception is the pressure switches. If a pressure-switch membrane fails, aftermarket kits (Sonnax, TransGo) are available to allow you to service the membranes rather than replacing the assembly. If a pressure switch electrically fails, the TEHCM will require replacement.

Replacing the TEHCM also requires that you replace the filter plate that fits between the valve body and the TEHCM. GM requires the filter plate be replaced any time the TEHCM is unbolted from the valve body. GM engineering studies have shown leakage issues when the filter plate is reused.

Multiple TEHCM part numbers are available, so make sure that you are installing the correct one. If the TEHCM is being replaced, it will require programming before it will operate correctly. Failing to program the TEHCM can cause transmission failure or the TEHCM to command the transmission into a default gear.

Global A/Global B

Many late-model GM 6-, 8-, 9-, and 10-speed vehicles use a communication data bus structure known as global A or global B. This was an update that integrated the theft-deterrent system into most of the vehicle control modules. When the ignition key is rotated to the ON position, the master module — typically the body control module (BCM)—will poll all of the modules on the CAN data bus. If a module fails to send the BCM back the correct coded sequence, the BCM will send a lockout signal to the PCM/ECM to inhibit vehicle operation. If the PCM is inhibiting engine start, the symptom will typically result in a start/stall. The engine will run for 2 seconds and then stall. The theft light may or may not be illuminated.

In addition, the BCM will send a coded message to the module in question, locking out that module permanently. In simple terms, this means that modules, including late-model TEHCMs, can no longer be swapped from vehicle to vehicle on many late-model applications.

PCS Solenoids

The TEHCM houses six PWM pressure control solenoids and two on/off solenoids. The PWM pressure control solenoids (PCS 2, 3, 4, and 5) are used to control clutch regulator valves within the valve body. The clutch regulator valves are used to control the apply-and-release pressure for each of the clutches. As the solenoid duty cycle command changes, the pressure to the clutch it is controlling also changes. The solenoid commands can be monitored with a scan tool.

Each clutch has its own clutch regulator valve and solenoid to control its pressure: PCS2, PCS3, PCS4, and PCS5. PCS2 controls the 3-5-R clutch regulator valve, which controls the 3-5-R clutch. PCS3 controls the 1-R/4-5-6 clutch regulator valve, which controls the low/reverse and 4-5-6 clutches. PCS4 controls the 2-6 clutch regulator valve, which controls the 2-6 clutch. PCS5 controls the 1-2-3-4 clutch regulator valve, which controls the 1-2-3-4 clutch.

In addition, a PWM solenoid (PCS line) is used to control the transmission main system oil pressure known as line pressure. The line pressure PCS is used to control the oil pump pressure regulator valve, which controls oil pump output pressure.

The torque converter clutch is controlled by the TCC PCS. The TCC system used with the 6L80 is a EC3 design. The EC3 TCC systems allow slippage during many different driving conditions, so do not be alarmed if you see TCC slip rates on your scan tool ranging between 0 and 100 rpm during moderate steady throttle. The TCC PCS controls the TCC regulator valve, which is used to regulate the pressure feeding the torque converter clutch pressure plate. TCC is available in first through sixth gear, but it typically applies in fourth, fifth, and sixth gear depending on the TCM software as well as engine load and other factors.

The PCS solenoids are of two different designs: normally low (NL) and normally high (NH). This is a Bosch designation, which refers to the output pressure from the solenoid when it is turned off electrically. A normally low solenoid has no output pressure when it is off electrically. A normally high solenoid has output pressure when the solenoid is in the off position electrically. PCS 2 and PCS 3 TCCs are normally high design solenoids while PCS 4, PCS 5, and PCS lines are normally low design solenoids.

Solenoid Application Chart

Gear	Shift Solenoid 1 Forward Control	Shift Solenoid 2 Reverse Control	3-5 REV Clutch PCS 2 NH	LOW REV 4-5-6 Clutch PCS 3 NH	2-6 Clutch PCS 4 NL	1-2-3-4 Clutch PCS 5 NL	Gear Ratio
Park	On	On	Off	On	Off	Off	–
Reverse	On	Off	On	On	Off	Off	3.064
Neutral	On	On	Off	On	Off	Off	–
1st Braking	On	On	Off	On	Off	On	4.027
1st	Off	On	Off	Off	Off	On	4.027
2nd	Off	On	Off	Off	On	On	2.364
3rd	Off	On	On	Off	Off	On	1.532
4th	Off	On	Off	On	Off	On	1.152
5th	Off	On	On	On	Off	Off	0.852
6th	Off	On	Off	On	On	Off	0.667

The solenoid on/off that is referenced in the solenoid application chart is referring to the hydraulic position of the solenoids. "On" means that it is hydraulically applying pressure to the valving and clutches, while "Off" means that the solenoid is not applying pressure to the valving and clutches. The command position shown on your scan tool may indicate the hydraulic commanded position as indicated in the chart, or it may indicate the electrical commanded position of the solenoid, which may be opposite from the chart depending on the brand of your scan tool and its software.

PCS 2, PCS 3, PCS 4, and PCS 5 control the shifts by controlling which clutch applies. In addition, they work to control shift aggressiveness by controlling the rate of the clutch apply through the regulator valves that they control. Shift feel is also controlled by the clutch compensator circuits.

The TEHCM TCM controls both the power and the ground for the PCS solenoids. If a short occurs, current flow is limited by the TCM to approximately 0.9 amp.

On/Off Shift Solenoids

The TEHCM houses two on/off design solenoids: Shift solenoid 1 and Shift solenoid 2. Both are normally closed (NC) designs, which means that when the solenoid is turned off electrically, the solenoid has 0 output pressure. Shift solenoids 1 and 2 are used to control the direction the vehicle moves (forward or backward). Primarily, shift solenoid 1 controls when the transmission is capable of moving forward as well as engine braking in M1 range. Shift solenoid 2 controls reverse engagement. Shift solenoids 1 and 2 are used to control the clutch select valves within the valve body, which control the vehicle's direction of travel. As with the PCS solenoids, the shift solenoid status can be monitored with a scan tool.

Transmission Fluid Temperature Sensor

The transmission fluid temperature (TFT) sensor is mounted externally on the TEHCM. The sensor is used by the TCM as one of the inputs to control shift points, TCC, and shift feel (line pressure). The temperature sensor is an NTC (negative temperature coefficient) sensor. NTC-design thermistors change resistance based on a change in temperature. The resistance change is the inverse of the temperature change. In other words, as the temperature decreases, the sensor resistance increases; an increase in temperature results in the sensor resistance decreasing.

The TCM sends 5 volts to the sensor and then monitors the voltage drop across the sensor. The TCM-measured voltage drop is then used by the TCM to determine the transmission fluid temperature.

The TCM software has a mode known as "hot mode" to help prevent damage to the transmission. On the 6L80, hot mode occurs at 270°F (132°C). Hot mode may change the TCC PCS solenoid line pressure commands for the transmission in an attempt to lower excessive transmission fluid temperature. If the overheat condition persists, the TCM will signal the BCM, which will signal the IPC (instrument panel cluster) driver information center. The driver may receive a message regarding the transmission overheating condition that may instruct the driver to pull over and stop until the transmission is no longer overheating. TFT can be monitored with a scan tool.

TCM Thermal Couples

Mounted to the TCM substrate (circuit board) are a pair of overtemperature sensors, which are used by the TCM to monitor the temperature of the TCM circuit board. If the circuit board temperature exceeds 287°F (142°C), the TCM will shut down and the transmission will enter a default mode that only allows reverse, third, and/or fifth gears. TCM temperature can also be used to calculate if the TFT sensor has failed by comparing the temperature measured by the TFT versus the TCM circuit board temperature. A DTC P0711 will set if that condition is present. TCM internal temperature may be one of the parameters available on your scan tool depending on the scan tool brand and its software.

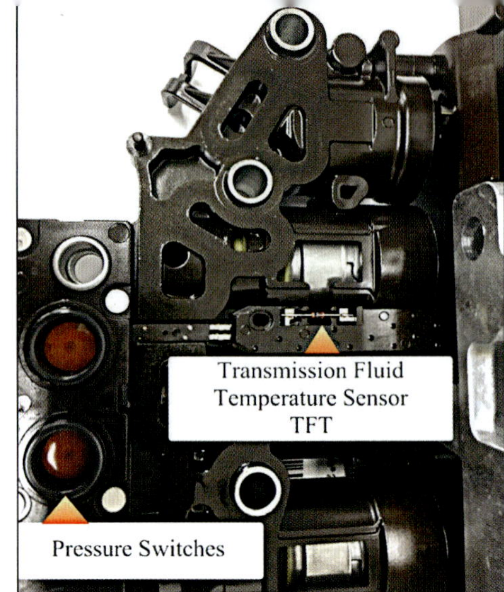

Transmission fluid pressure (TFP) switches are used to monitor the operation of the transmission clutch hydraulic circuits. TFP-related DTCs are very common on the 6L80. The fluid temperature sensor monitors the temperature of the fluid in the transmission pan. Default actions can occur if the fluid temperature is too high.

Transmission Fluid Pressure Switches

The TEHCM houses four hydraulically controlled transmission fluid pressure (TFP) switches. The TCM monitors the position of the switches to determine if the clutch regulator valves are supplying pressure to the clutches. Four pressure switches are used—one for each clutch control solenoid. The clutch pressure switches are designed to change position as the clutch is turned on or off. The pressure switches monitor the position of the clutch regulator valves, which are controlled by the solenoids. The TCM uses the switch position to determine solenoid and clutch regulator issues. When the TCM turns a PCS on or off, it expects to see a corresponding change in the

6L80 Transmission Fluid Pressure Switch Scan Tool Values				
Range/Gear	**TFP Switch States**			
	TFP Switch 1	**TFP Switch 3**	**TFP Switch 4**	**TFP Switch 5**
Park/Neutral	High 12 volts	Low 0 volts	Low 0 volts	Low 0 volts
Reverse	Low 0 volts	Low 0 volts	Low 0 volts	Low 0 volts
1st, Engine Braking	High 12 volts	High 12 volts	Low 0 volts	Low 0 volts
1st	High 12 volts	High 12 volts	Low 0 volts	High 12 volts
2nd	High 12 volts	Low 0 volts	Low 0 volts	High 12 volts
3rd	Low 0 volts	High 12 volts	Low 0 volts	High 12 volts
4th	High 12 volts	High 12 volts	Low 0 volts	Low 0 volts
5th	Low 0 volts	High 12 volts	High 12 volts	Low 0 volts
6th	High 12 volts	High 12 volts	High 12 volts	Low 0 volts
6th (Possible additional gear state depending on the TCM software)	High 12 volts	Low 0 volts	High 12 volts	Low 0 volts

pressure switch state. If the pressure switch state does not change, a DTC for that solenoid/clutch regulator valve will set, leading the TCM to command default actions.

Pressure switch issues are quite common on 6L applications, as fluid debris tends to cause issues. Service kits are available from aftermarket suppliers, such as TransGo and Sonnax, to address contamination issues.

The pressure switches are an NC design, meaning that when no pressure is applied to the switch membrane, the switch will be closed, connecting the circuit to ground. As pressure is applied to the switch, it will open, which will remove the ground path for that switch. The TCM provides a bias voltage to each switch; when it is open, the TCM will see the bias voltage it was supplying to the switch. When the switch is closed, the TCM will see near 0 volts as the circuit is grounded through the switch. Pressure switch operation can be monitored with a scan tool.

TFP 1 indicates the position of the 3-5-R solenoid/clutch regulator control valve. TFP 3 indicates the position of the 2-6 solenoid/clutch regulator control valve. TFP 4 indicates the position of the 1-2-3-4 solenoid/clutch regulator control valve. TFP 5 indicates the position of the low/reverse solenoid/clutch regulator control valve.

Note: On 6L80 applications, TFP 2 is not used; this is not the case with some other GM transmission families.

Internal Mode Switch

The internal mode switch (IMS) is bolted to the transmission valve body, and its plunger is connected to the valve body manual valve. The IMS is connected electrically to the TEHCM/TCM and ECM. The IMS changes position based on the transmission shift linkage, which is controlled by the driver and shift

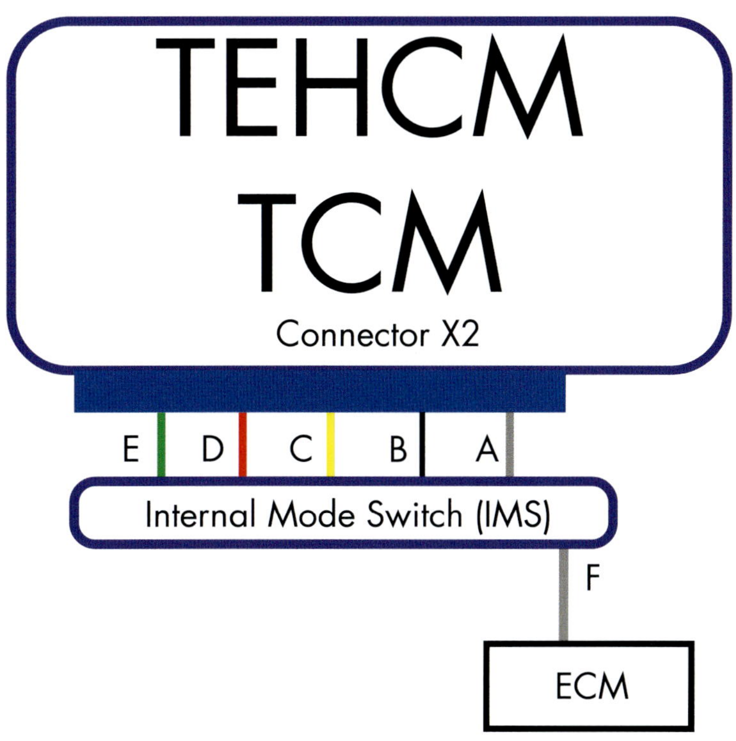

lever. The IMS acts as the shifter lever/range position sensor or manual valve position sensor so that the TEHCM knows the shifter position. This information is used by the TEHCM to determine the number of shifts and to command manual downshifts (or manual range) when the driver manually downshifts the transmission.

In addition, a dedicated circuit connects the Park/Neutral input from the switch directly to the engine control module (ECM) for engine start. IMS values can be monitored with a scan tool and should match the chart if it is functioning correctly.

The internal mode switch (IMS) acts as a shift lever position sensor for the TCM. As you change range, the IMS will signal the TCM regarding the range you have selected. The IMS can be tested and replaced separately.

Input and Output Speed Sensors

The 6L80 uses a pair of two-wire, Hall-effect, magneto-resistive type of speed sensors to feed component rotational speed information to the TEHCM. The sensors are fed an 8.3- to 9.3-volt supply voltage from the TEHCM TCM. The sensors produce a square-wave output, which is fed directly to the TEHCM via the sensor wiring. The frequency of the square wave varies based on the component rotational speed.

The input and output sensors are combined into one assembly so that if one sensor fails, the new part will include both sensors. The input speed sensor (ISS) monitors the speed of the 1-2-3-4/3-5-R clutch drum. The output speed sensor (OSS), which is also known as the vehicle speed

IMS Scan Tool Values Based on Shift Lever Position

IMS Scan Tools Values Gear Selector Position	Scan Tool Signal A IMS Pin E	Scan Tool Signal B IMS Pin D	Scan Tool Signal C IMS Pin C	Scan Tool Signal P IMS Pin B
Park	Low	Hi	Hi	Low
P to R	Low	Low	Hi	Low
Reverse	Low	Low	Hi	Hi
R to N	Hi	Low	Hi	Hi
Neutral	Hi	Low	Hi	Low
N to D	Hi	Low	Low	Low
Drive 6	Hi	Low	Low	Hi
Drive 6 to Drive 4	Low	Low	Low	Hi
Drive 4	Low	Low	Low	Low
Drive 4 to Drive 3	Low	Hi	Low	Low
Drive 3	Low	Hi	Low	Hi
Drive 3 to Drive 2	Hi	Hi	Low	Hi
Drive 2	Hi	Hi	Low	Low
Open	Hi	Hi	Hi	Hi
Invalid (DTC Sets)	Hi	Hi	Hi	Low
Invalid (DTC Sets)	Low	Hi	Hi	Hi
Not all ranges may be available on all applications. The transition from one range to another is also shown. Low = 0 volts, continuity to ground, Hi = 12 volts, open circuit.				

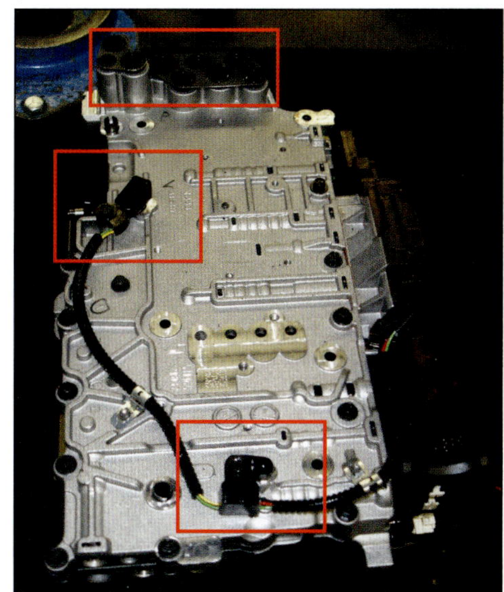

The input speed sensor (ISS) and output speed sensor (OSS) are housed as a single assembly. The sensors produce a square wave output that is fed to the TCM. If the sensor requires replacement, it is important to make sure that you are replacing it with the correct one. Two design output planetaries are used in the 6L80: unigear and non-unigear. The sensors are different based on the design. Installing the incorrect sensor can lead to sensor failure and DTCs. The TEHCM/valve body assembly must be removed to replace the sensors because they are mounted to the underside of the valve body.

sensor (VSS) monitors the speed of the output speed sensor tone wheel mounted on the output planetary.

The ISS is primarily used for gear ratio and TCC slip calculations. The OSS is used to calculate gear ratio, control upshifts and downshifts, line pressure, and TCC.

TEHCM Shared Data and Additional Inputs

While the TEHCM receives information from sensors/switches that are mounted internally of the transmission, most of the information the TCM requires to control shifting and pressures comes from information that is supplied by other modules, such as the engine control module (ECM), body control module (BCM), chassis control module (CCM), and electronic brake control module (EBCM).

The throttle position sensor (TPS), accelerator pedal position (APP) sensor, brake pedal position (BPP) sensor, engine speed, engine coolant temperature (ECT) sensor, manifold absolute pressure (MAP) sensor, mass airflow (MAF) sensor, intake air temperature (IAT) sensor, TAP switches, and pitch/yaw sensor are examples of externally mounted sensors that are used by the TEHCM TCM to control transmission operation. Sensor information is transmitted to the TEHCM TCM from the other modules via the CAN communication bus.

Proper transmission operation is dependent on accurate information from the sensors that act as inputs to the TCM. With that in mind, any time you have a transmission concern, make certain that the issue is not related to something other than an internal transmission related issue prior to condemning the transmission.

Scan Tool Diagnosis, Data Parameters, DTCs, and Programming

A quality scan tool is critical to assist with the diagnosis of 6L80-related issues. The scan tool should allow you to check for DTCs that are stored, freeze frame and failure record information related to the DTCs, provide sensor data, and allow output override capabilities to control the transmission.

Data Parameters

Dozens of parameters are available on 6L80 applications. Parameters are related to sensor input values, TCM calculations (ratio and torque), and output commands (the solenoids

Key-on, engine-off data is shown. Engine torque can be used to diagnose if the engine software has been modified, which can lead to transmission damage. Engine RPM is supplied to the TCM from the ECM and is used to help diagnose slip-related concerns. "Calc. Throttle Position" indicates the position in which the ECM believes the throttle plates are located. This information is supplied by the ECM. Input and output speed sensor data can be used to help diagnose issues with the speed sensors. "ISS/OSS Supply Voltage Data" represents the 9-volt bias signal provided to the sensors from the TCM.

and pressure control). Data parameters are provided by the various control modules to aid in diagnosis.

DTCs

DTCs are a form of contact tracing for your vehicle. A DTC indicates the area of the vehicle system that has an issue. It does not necessarily mean the component is faulty; however, it does indicate that something is likely wrong that relates to that component/circuit/system.

For example, let's say that you had a DTC related to the IMS. Several possibilities exist, including an issue with the wiring, a problem with the IMS connection to the manual valve, a faulty TEHCM, or a faulty IMS.

It is imperative that you scan all vehicle modules because, in simple terms, today's transmission is no longer a transmission. It is part of a complete powertrain system. This means that issues in other systems can/will cause issues with transmission operation. A good example that is quite common is how clutch dam-

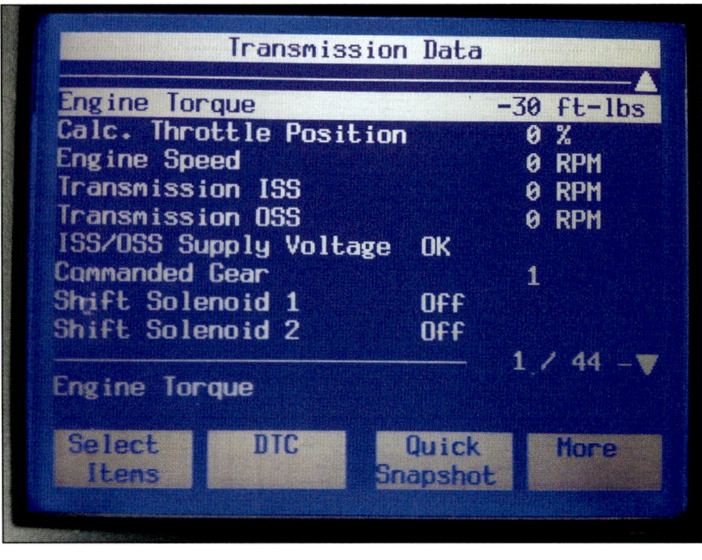

Key-on, engine-off data is shown. "Commanded Gear" represents the TCM commanded gear position. "Shift Solenoid 1" and "Shift Solenoid 2" data represents the commanded position for the on/off solenoids hydraulically.

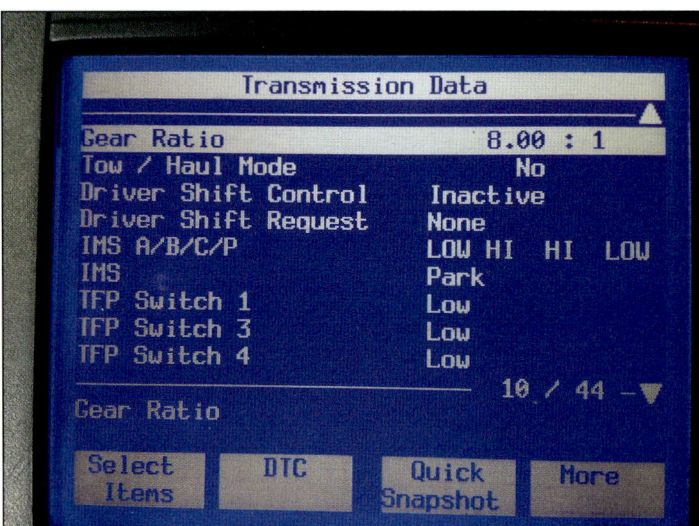

Key-on, engine-off data is shown. "Gear Ratio" represents the calculated transmission gear ratio, which can be used for shift and slip diagnosis. "Tow/Haul Mode" represents the actions of the driver to engage or disengage the tow haul switch on the shift lever, while "Driver Shift Control" data represents the commands from the driver to shift the transmission using the tap shift feature. The IMS data indicates the position of the IMS switches based on the position of the shift lever. The TFP data represents the position of the TEHCM pressure switches.

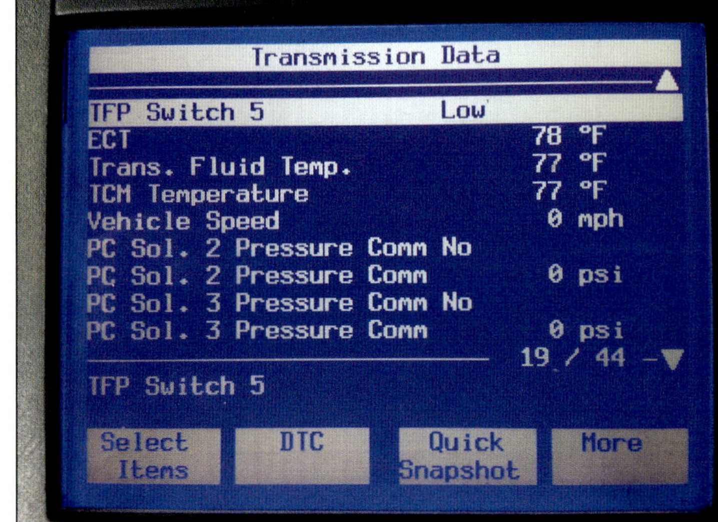

Key-on, engine-off data is shown. "ECT" represents the engine coolant temperature value provided by the ECM, while "Trans. Fluid Temp" represents the transmission fluid temperature measured by the TCM. TCM temperature is provided by a temperature sensor mounted on the TCM circuit board and is used to diagnose TCM overtemperature issues. "Vehicle Speed" represents the calculated mph/kph based on the output speed sensor rotational speed value. The "PC Sol" commanded position represents the calculated pressure commands for the various pressure control solenoids. These values represent the commanded pressure that is applied to the various clutches.

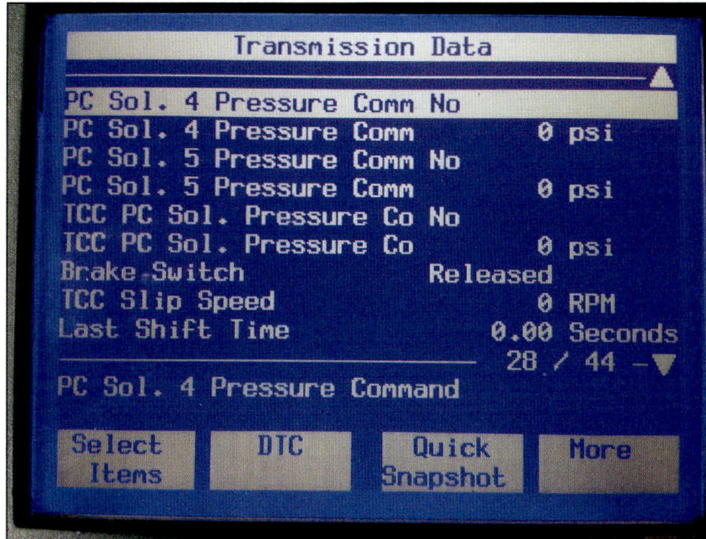

Key-on, engine-off data is shown. The "PC Sol" commanded positions represent the calculated pressure commands for the various pressure control solenoids. These values represent the commanded pressure that is applied to the various clutches. Brake switch position indicates the position of the vehicle brake pedal and is used to disengage the TCC. TCC slip indicates the calculated slip in RPM of the torque converter clutch. Last shift time data represents the calculated shift time for the last shift performed in seconds. This data is used to diagnose shift flare as well as aggressive shift concerns.

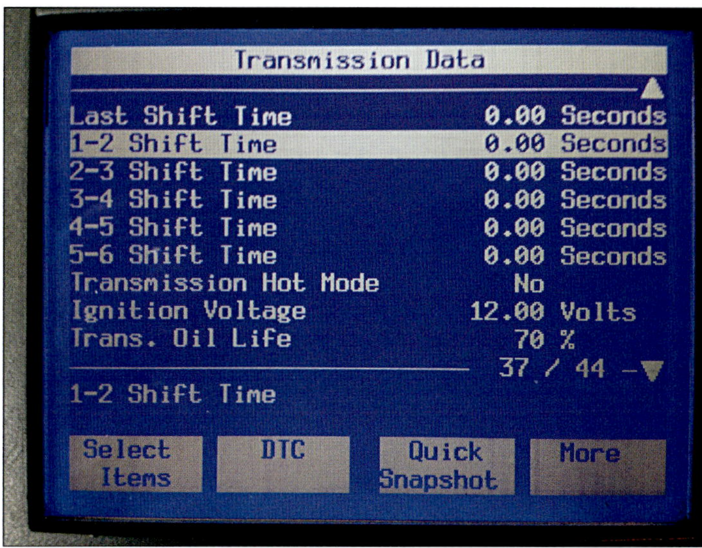

Key-on, engine-off data is shown. Shift times are available for each shift. This represents the calculated shift time for the last shift that occurred. This data is only valuable if the shift was an adaptable shift. Shift times are used to help isolate issues with clutch apply, such as flares, bumps, and hard shift concerns. "Hot Mode" indicates if the transmission has been forced into a default state by a fluid overtemperature condition. "Ignition Voltage" represents the battery voltage supply that is available to the TCM. "Transmission Oil Life" indicates the available fluid life before the transmission fluid should be changed.

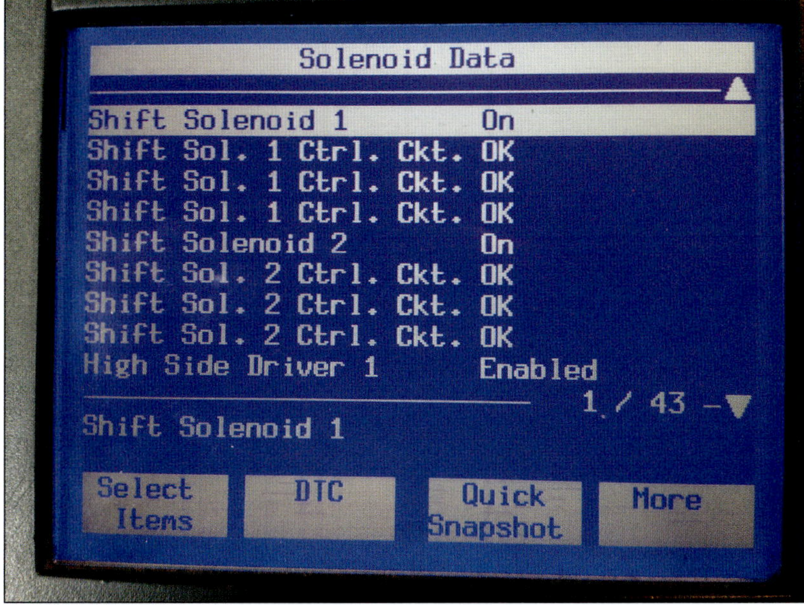

Key-on, engine-off data is shown. Solenoid control circuit feedback values are displayed for each solenoid. "Ok" indicates that the solenoids/circuits do not have electrical-related issues, while a fault indication represents an electrical issue with the solenoid/circuit. The solenoids are fed voltage via a high-side driver, which is represented with the data. When the high-side driver indicates "Enabled," the solenoids are being fed voltage by the TCM.

age may be caused by a driver using an oil-coated type of aftermarket air filter. The oil from the filter element coats the factory MAF sensor element, which skews the MAF sensor airflow value that is being sent to the ECM. The ECM then communicates the incorrect engine load value to the TCM. The TCM then calculates the wrong line pressure solenoid command value, leading to low clutch pressure and ultimately transmission clutch failure. GM has issued bulletins regarding this issue.

All 6L80 DTCs are OBD II–compliant five- or seven-digit (enhanced) codes. The five-digit codes are the standard OBD II–compliant DTCs, while the sixth and seventh digits on a seven-digit enhanced DTC are symptom indicators. This enhanced

Character	Representation
P	Powertrain
0	This is a generic DTC, so the meaning is the same for any manufacturer.
1 or 2	Manufacturer-specific DTC.
7, 8, or 9	Transmission-related concern.
11	This character provides information about the component or concern that is causing the DTC. In this instance, the concern indicates an issue related to the fluid temperature sensor or circuit.

DTC design will help to separate things such as a short-to-ground condition from a short-to-voltage condition. The additional sixth and seventh digits of an enhanced DTC cannot be read with some brands of scan tools.

Here is an OBD II–compliant five-digit DTC example: P0711.

You may not be able clear the DTC and/or its default actions on late-model vehicles, even though the scanner indicates the DTC is cleared. For example, you may have a service engine soon (SES) lamp illuminated and you clear the DTC, but the lamp may not turn off even though the DTC is supposed to be cleared. So, how do you get the SES lamp off after you clear the DTC with your scan tool? Review the parameters that the controller uses to set the DTC. Operate the vehicle, making sure to match the DTC parameters used for setting the code. Typically, this will take more than one drive cycle. The controller will test for the fault, and if all is well, it will turn off the lamp and fully clear the DTC. This process was implemented because people were trying to cheat to get their vehicles through the local emissions certification for vehicle licensing.

If you have a DTC set, be sure to access the appropriate shop manual information.

Programming

The TEHCM TCM requires programming to function correctly if it was replaced. Programming the TEHCM TCM requires the use of a J2534 programming interface, a quality scan tool, and a subscription to the GM SPS programming service via AC Delco. If you do not have access to the programming equipment, have a dealer or qualified independent shop do the programming for you. If you are reusing the TEHCM, check its software level to see if it is equipped with the latest software load. Check your software level for free by accessing the GM TIS2 website: tis2web.service.gm.com/tis2web.

Once you have accessed the website, load your VIN into the "VIN" box on the screen and press the "Get CAL ID" icon. The next screen to load will display the calibration

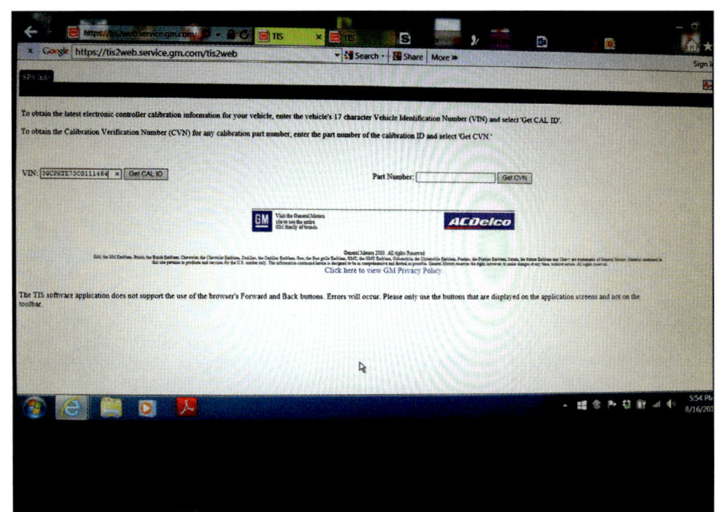

GM has a calibration identification website available so that you can check your TCM software level. More transmission issues are repaired today with software than by any other means. The website address is tis2web.service.gm.com/tis2web and is available free of charge.

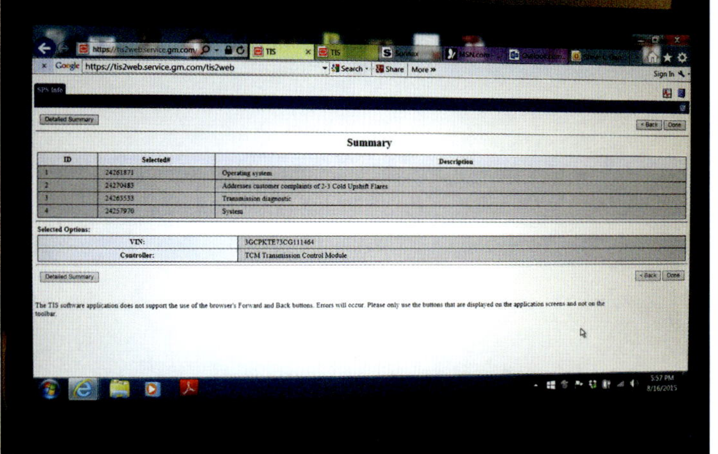

With the click of a mouse, you can access all of the calibration information for your vehicle, including the TCM. The site is VIN-code specific so the calibration information that is displayed is for your vehicle only. A history of the calibration, including the CAL ID number and the reason for the calibration update, is typically displayed.

tables for your VIN. You can choose various controllers for access to the calibration numbers available. If you choose the TCM/transmission icon, the next screen will display the calibration numbers available for your TCM application. The display will show the various calibrations that are available for your application and

Common 6L80 DTCs

DTC	Description
P0218	Fluid overtemp
P0562	System high voltage
P0563	System low voltage
P0601	TCM ROM
P0602	TCM not programmed
P0603	TCM long-term memory reset
P0604	TCM RAM
P0634	TCM overtemp
P0658	Solenoid high-side driver low volt
P0659	Solenoid high-side driver high volt
P0667	TCM thermal couple performance
P0668	TCM thermal couple low voltage
P0669	TCM thermal couple high voltage
P0711	TFT sensor performance
P0712	TFT low voltage
P0713	TFT high voltage
P0716	ISS performance
P0717	ISS circuit low voltage
P0722	OSS circuit low voltage
P0723	OSS signal intermittent
P0741	TCC stuck off
P0742	TCC stuck on
P0751	Shift solenoid 1 stuck off
P0752	Shift solenoid 1 performance
P0756	Shift solenoid 2 performance
P0776	PCS 2 stuck off
P0777	PCS 2 stuck on
P0796	PCS 3 stuck off
P0797	PCS 3 stuck on
P0815	Upshift switch circuit (TAP)
P0816	Downshift switch circuit (TAP)
P0826	Upshift/downshift switch circuit
P0842	TFP switch 1 low voltage
P0843	TFP switch 1 high voltage
P0851	P/N input low voltage
P0852	P/N input high voltage
P0872	TFP switch 3 low voltage
P0873	TFP switch 3 high voltage
P0877	TFP switch 4 low voltage
P0878	TFP switch 4 high voltage
P0961	Line pressure PCS performance
P0962	Line pressure PCS low voltage
P0963	Line pressure PCS high voltage
P0965	PCS 2 performance
P0966	PCS 2 low voltage
P0967	PCS 2 high voltage
P0969	PCS 3 performance
P0970	PCS 3 low voltage
P0971	PCS 3 high voltage
P0973	Shift solenoid 1 low voltage
P0974	Shift solenoid 1 high voltage
P0973	Shift solenoid 2 low voltage
P0974	Shift solenoid 2 high voltage
P0989	TFP switch 5 low voltage
P0990	TFP switch 5 high voltage
P1621	TCM long term memory performance
P1684	TCM power up temp performance
P1685	TCM power-up temp low voltage
P1686	TCM power-up temp high voltage
P1751	Shift valve 1 performance
P1825	IMS invalid range position
P1876	Upshift/downshift switch low voltage
P1831	TCC PCS solenoid low voltage
P1832	TCC PCS solenoid high voltage
P1915	IMS wrong range
P2534	Ignition switch voltage low
P2714	PCS 4 stuck off
P2715	PCS 4 stuck on
P2719	PCS 4 performance
P2720	PCS 4 low voltage
P2721	PCS 4 high voltage
P2723	PCS 5 stuck off
P2724	PCS 5 stuck on
P2728	PCS 5 performance
P2729	PCS 5 low voltage
P2730	PCS 5 high voltage
P2762	TCC PCS performance
P2763	TCC PCS low voltage
P2764	TCC PCS high voltage
P2771	4x4 circuit low
P062F	TCM long term memory performance
P06AC	TCM power-up temp performance
P06AD	TCM power-up temp low voltage
P06AE	TCM power-up temp high voltage
P30BD	Engine stall prevention
P0182E	IMS invalid

typically the reason for the update.

Compare the numbers displayed on the GM TIS2WEB SPS system to the value you see listed as "CAL ID" in your scan tool data parameters. If the values displayed on your scan tool are the same as the latest one displayed on the GM website, the calibration is up to date. Keep in mind that this website format changes often, so the screens may not look exactly as the picture portrays.

Adaptive Learning

The 6L80 software is equipped with a feature known as adaptive learning. The adaptive learning feature is designed to ensure that the transmission shifts and operates the same at 100,000 miles as it did at 100 miles. Multiple types of adaptive learning are used, but the most common type is the upshift/downshift adapts.

When repairs are performed that can affect shift quality, the stored adaptive values must be cleared and new adaptive values must be relearned for the transmission to operate correctly. A quality scan tool is required to complete this process.

The 6L80 TCM has the ability to learn the shift times of all the transmission upshifts and downshifts; this is known as "shift adapts." The TCM measures the clutch apply/release rates to determine the shift time. This is accomplished by the TCM monitoring the shift command plus the input and output speed sensors frequencies during the shift. The TCM commands a shift and then monitors for a change in the input speed sensor frequency. By measuring the time between when the solenoid was commanded to make a shift and the time when it sees an input speed sensor change showing the shift is complete, the TCM can determine the shift time.

The measured shift time is then compared to the desired shift time by the TCM for that vehicle load and shift. If the shift time was too short, the TCM will command less pressure the next time that particular shift is commanded again. If the shift time was too long, the TCM will increase the pressure when that particular shift happens again. The corrected shift pressure offset values are stored in the TCM memory to be used on the next shifts. While the system is very sophisticated, keep in mind that the TCM is monitoring the shift times for all the up/downshifts at various various throttle openings and storing that information in the TCM memory for use on the next shift that meets that criteria.

The shift adapt pressure offset values are learned and stored in the TCM memory for each shift. If repairs are performed on the transmission that can affect shift times, it is important that the shift adapt stored values be reset and relearned.

Clearing Adapts and Relearning Adapts

The shift adapts should be cleared and relearned if any of the following occur:

- The transmission was replaced
- The transmission was rebuilt
- The valve body was replaced or repaired
- Any repair that could impact shift times was performed, including replacing or reprograming the TEHCM TCM

Clearing the adaptive memory is accomplished with a quality scan tool. The reason that the adapts must be cleared is that you were likely repairing the transmission because of an issue with the transmission. The TCM will have learned and attempted to correct for the issues present within the transmission.

For example, if the seal for the 2-6 clutch was worn, the 1-2 and/or 5-6 shifts may flare. The TCM will learn the shift time and provide a positive pressure offset in an attempt to correct for the worn seal on the next shift. Then, you install new seals, the leakage is no longer present, and the transmission has been repaired. However, the TCM does not know that you have repaired the transmission, of course. The TCM then shifts the transmission using the pressure offsets that were stored for the worn transmission. This can cause transmission damage as well as and upset the driver, as it takes a lot of shifts at various different throttle openings and temperatures to get the values relearned for the new transmission.

Clearing the adapts clears all the adaptive memories. Clear all DTCs prior to clearing the adapts. Follow the instructions on your scan tool to clear the adapts. Once the adapts are cleared, new transmission adapts need to be relearned. Some scan tools have the ability to perform a "fast learn," which shortens the length of time it takes to relearn the adapts. Once the fast learn has been performed, a road test should be performed, up/downshifting the transmission through all gears at various different throttle openings. If your scan tool does not have the ability to perform a fast learn, you should perform an extensive road test, operating the vehicle through all of the up/downshifts at various throttle openings and temperatures. On late-model

Resetting 6L80 Transmission Shift Adaptive Values with a Scan Tool

applications, a scan tool parameter is available, indicating when the adapt updates are complete.

Keep in mind that fast learn capabilities are not available on some models and model-year applications. The 1-2 and 3-2 shifts are the most difficult to learn for the 6L80 application, so it is likely that it will take some extended driving while cycling through those shifts to attain an acceptable shift feel for the driver.

On-Vehicle Repairs and Adjustments

Addressing issues with the 6L80 many times includes making adjustments and the replacement of faulty components. As with other fully electronic transmissions, the 6L80 uses numerous electronic components that can and do fail, creating transmission operational issues as well as DTCs, which may be set in the TCM or ECM memory. Replacement of the electronic components in most cases is very straightforward and simply requires the component be removed from the transmission and replaced with a new component. The exception is the TEHCM, which requires reprogramming and must have an adaptive relearn process be performed prior to returning the vehicle to the owner.

Shifter Cable

Two shifter cable designs are used on the 6L80: one-piece and two-piece. The biggest difference you need to be aware of is that the socket on the two-piece design must be unbolted from the transmission shift linkage because it will be damaged if you try to pry it off the attaching ball. Follow these steps for adjustment:

1. Place the steering column shift lever in the Park position and chock the wheels.
2. Move the transmission manual shaft lever into the Park position.
3. Open the cable white cover and unlock the cable locking teeth using a screwdriver. Grasp the shift cable shifter end in your left hand and the shift cable transmission end in your

The shift cable will require adjustment. The white tab locks the cable in position.

One Assembly

Keep in mind that the TCM, solenoids, TFT, and pressure switch components are part of the TEHCM assembly and are not serviced separately. ■

TEHCM Reprogramming

If a new TEHCM was installed, it will require reprogramming. Once it is programmed, the adapts need to be relearned. ■

right hand. Align the two ends and slide them together. Once you slide the two-piece cable together, it will no longer come apart, as it locks permanently into position.

4. Release the transmission end; this will allow the spring to apply tension to the cable.
5. Open the white cover on the shifter end of the cable. Push down the natural-colored lock button. This will engage the locking teeth on the transmission end of the cable.

Transmission Mounts

The transmission mounts should be inspected for wear and damage. A collapsed mount can cause vibrations to be transmitted into the vehicle body, leading to driver-related complaints. Inspect the mount for cracks and the rubber for being separated from the metal.

TEHCM, TFP, TFT, Speed Sensor, and IMS Replacement

The IMS and/or the speed sensors can be replaced separately from the TEHCM. It is important to remember that the various part number speed sensor designs are available based on the transmission planetary design, so always double-check your replacement sensor part number. If the TFP or TFT sensors are faulty, the TEHCM will require replacement, as they are not sold separately.

TEHCM, TFP, and TFT Replacement

Drain the fluid from the transmission, and remove the pan and filter. Disconnect the IMS connector and the TEHCM pass-through connector by popping up the connector lock on the TEHCM.

Lay out the valve body/TEHCM bolts as you remove them on a clean workbench. Note the position of the different bolt lengths. Installing the bolts in incorrect locations can result in major issues. Bolts used are two M5x53 to attach the TEHCM to the valve body heat sink on the side, four M5x55, and five M5x45.

The TEHCM is bolted to the valve body. It is easiest to remove the TEHCM if you remove the valve body with the TEHCM attached as an assembly from the transmission. The TEHCM can then be separated from the valve body. The valve body/TEHCM is attached to the transmission using six bolts. Depending on the year, the bolts may be conventional hex-head designs or E12 Torx Plus designs.

Disconnect the speed sensor and IMS connectors from the TEHCM. Once the valve body and TECHM assembly have been removed from the transmission, the nine bolts attaching the TEHCM and filter plate to the valve body can be removed. Two of the bolts are located on the side of the TEHCM near the TCM. At this point, the TEHCM and valve body may be separated from each other.

The bolts are three different lengths, so it is critical that they be reinstalled into the correct holes.

Install a new filter plate and the new TEHCM onto the valve body. Align the components and install the 9 bolts used to attach the TEHCM and new filter plate to the valve body. Be sure to install the 2 M5x53-mm bolts located on the side of the TEHCM. Finger-tighten all the bolts. It is critical that the bolts be installed in their correct locations. Connect the speed sensor and the IMS electrical connectors to the TEHCM. Tighten all 11 bolts to 71 in-lbs (8 Nm) using the proper torque sequence, starting in the center and moving outward in a crossing pattern. The 2 bolts on the side of the TEHCM holding the TCM to the heat sink should be torqued last.

Install new pump and center support seals into the case and onto the valve body.

Install the valve body/TEHCM assembly into the case aligning the connector with the pass-through connector. Install the pass-through connector and push it into place. Lock the pass-through connector latch but do not force the locking tab into position, as damage can occur. Install the 6 remaining bolts attaching the assembly to the case. Torque

Replacing the TEHCM, TFP, and TFT

1 *The six valve body numbered bolts require removal for the TEHCM/valve body assembly to be removed. The other circled bolts will be removed once the TEHCM/valve body are on the workbench and you want to separate the valve body and TEHCM. Do not remove any bolts other than the six numbered bolts until the TEHCM/valve body are on the bench. In addition, two heat sink bolts located on the side of the TEHCM must be removed to separate the TEHCM from the valve body. Make sure to set the bolts out on your workbench so you can install the bolts back into their correct positions as three different lengths are used. Bolts used for TEHCM/valve body mounting are two M5x53 (used to attach the TEHCM to the valve body heat sink on the side), four M5x55 and five M5x45.*

2 *The input and output speed sensors are mounted to the top of the valve body. This means the TEHCM/valve body assembly must be removed to replace the sensor. The ISS/OSS sensors are one assembly and are connected electrically to the TEHCM.*

3 *The IMS is bolted to the bottom of the valve body assembly and connected electrically to the TEHCM. To replace the IMS, disconnect the switch assembly and unbolt it from the valve body. To install it, bolt the IMS into position and torque the bolts to 71 in-lbs (8 Nm); then, reattach the electrical connector.*

4 *When you are ready to install the TEHCM/valve body assembly into the case, a set of seals connecting the valve body to the center support need to be installed prior to installing the valve body.*

5 *When attaching the valve body to the TEHCM, do not forget the heat sink bolts located on the side of the TEHCM. These bolts are 53 mm long, and it is critical that you do not install the wrong bolts in these holes, as damage to the valve body will occur. These bolts are the last to be torqued when following the torque sequence.*

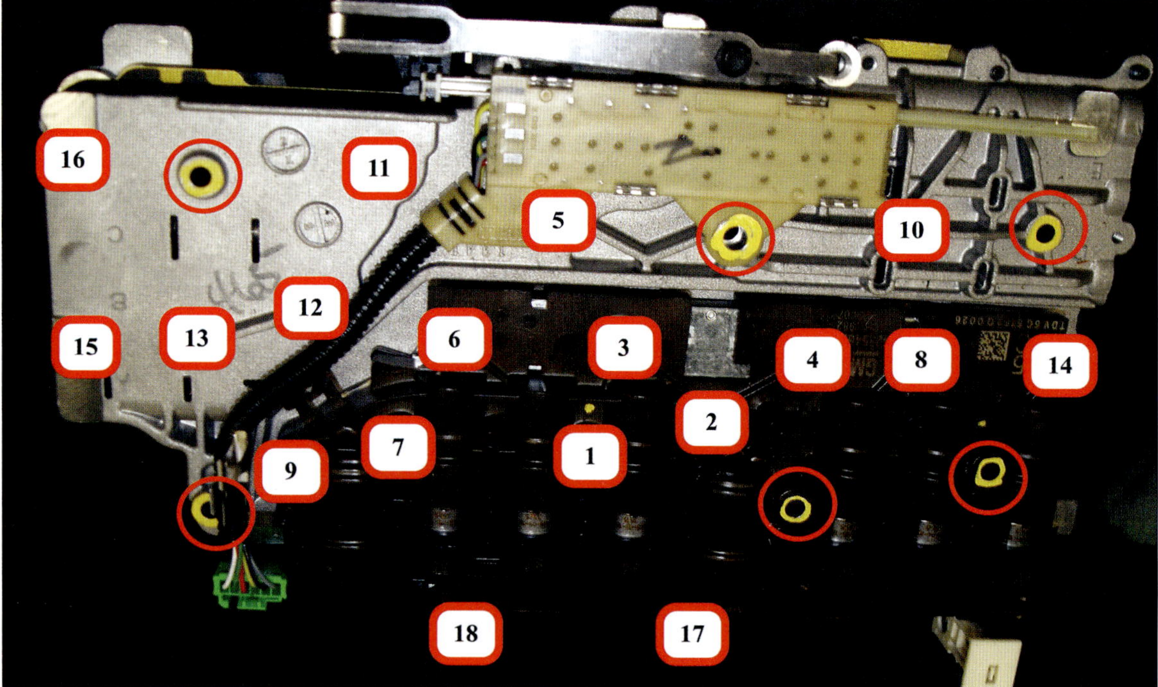

6 *When attaching the valve body to the TEHCM, a torque sequence must be followed. Torque the bolts in the sequence shown to 71 in-lbs (8 Nm).*

all the bolts, including the 6 attaching bolts to specification of 71 in-lbs (8 Nm) using the proper torquing sequence.

Install a new filter, install the pan, gasket, and Dexron VI fluid. Adjust the fluid level.

Speed Sensor Replacement

Two speed sensor assembly designs are available that fit the 6L80 applications. The sensor design that is used is based on the output shaft tone ring and planetary design (unigear or non-unigear). The sensors

Late-model applications use a unigear output planetary gearset. The unigear output gearset can be identified by the one-piece ring gear/output shaft that houses two ring gears and the output shaft in the one assembly. The unigear design uses a different part number speed sensor assembly compared to the non-unigear design speed sensor assembly. The speed sensor designs cannot be interchanged; if they are, failure can occur.

The non-unigear gearset is used on earlier applications. It can be identified by looking at the ring gear. The two ring gears are held into the housing with snap rings. A spacer separates the two ring gears. The non-unigear design uses a different part number speed sensor assembly compared to the unigear design speed sensor assembly. The speed sensor designs cannot be interchanged; otherwise, failure can occur.

The speed sensors are mounted to the top of the valve body assembly. To service the speed sensors, the TEHCM/valve body must be removed from the transmission. Both the input and the output speed sensors are contained as one assembly. The sensors are fed 8.3 to 9.3 volts from the TEHCM/TCM with the sensors outputting a signal back to the TCM as a square wave that varies frequency based on the sensor tone wheel rotational speed. Different sensor part numbers are available based on the type of output planetary gearset design (unigear versus non-unigear).

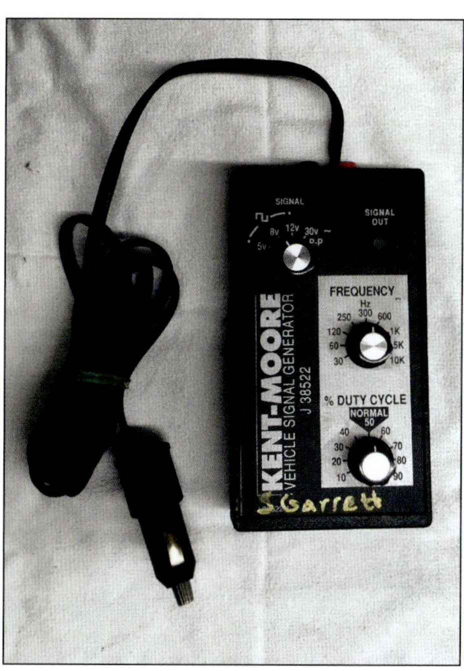

A signal generator can be used to isolate a speed sensor issue from a TEHCM/TCM issue. Connect the signal generator to the sensor TCM terminals, set the generator to provide an 8-volt square wave, and monitor the speed signals with your scan tool. If the scanner indicates a speed sensor signal for each of the sensor inputs, the sensor is faulty. If the scan tool indicates 0 mph, the TEHCM is faulty.

designs are not interchangeable, and failure will occur if you install the incorrect design assembly. Compare your new/old parts before installing the sensor assembly.

Speed sensors can be tested by using a signal generator, which is connected to the speed sensor connector at the TEHCM to provide a speed signal to the TCM. The signal generator is set to provide an 8-volt square wave to the TCM as a substitute for the speed sensor signals.

GM has an umbilical cord special tool (DT 47825-10) that attaches to the TEHCM/valve body with the assembly removed from the transmission. The cord is attached to the TEHCM/valve body assembly and the vehicle harness side connector. A scan tool is then attached to the vehicle so that speed inputs can be monitored.

With input from the signal generator, you should see a speed signal on your scan tool. If the signal is present on your scan tool, the sensor assembly will require replacement. If the scan tool registers 0 rpm, the TEHCM is faulty and will require replacement.

To test or replace the speed sensors, the TEHCM/valve body assembly must be removed from the transmission as outlined in TEHCM replacement section above. This requires that it be unbolted (six bolts) from the case. With the assembly on the bench, flip it over to expose the speed sensors. Install the new sensors and connector and reinstall the assembly. Torque the six attaching bolts to the specification of 106 in-lbs (12 Nm).

Install a new filter, install the pan, gasket, and Dexron VI fluid. Adjust the fluid level.

IMS Replacement

Diagnosis of the internal mode switch (IMS) can be accomplished with your scan tool prior to transmission disassembly by monitoring the IMS values outlined earlier

IMS Bench Testing				
Range Selected	**IMS Pin E**	**IMS Pin D**	**IMS Pin C**	**IMS Pin B**
Park	Continuity	OL	OL	Continuity
P to R	Continuity	Continuity	OL	Continuity
Reverse	Continuity	Continuity	OL	OL
R to N	OL	Continuity	OL	OL
Neutral	OL	Continuity	OL	Continuity
N to D	OL	Continuity	Continuity	Continuity
Drive 6	OL	Continuity	Continuity	OL
Drive 6 to Drive 4	Continuity	Continuity	Continuity	OL
Drive 4	Continuity	Continuity	Continuity	Continuity
Drive 4 to Drive 3	Continuity	OL	Continuity	Continuity
Drive 3	Continuity	OL	Continuity	OL
Drive 3 to Drive 2	OL	OL	Continuity	OL
Drive 2	OL	OL	Continuity	Continuity

in this chapter. If the values do not match the chart, either the IMS or the TEHCM are likely defective.

The IMS can be bench tested using an ohmmeter. It is easiest if the IMS is tested prior to removing the valve body from the transmission. Disconnect the sensor connector from the TEHCM. Using a terminal probing tool or a paper clip, attach your ohmmeter to the appropriate leads at the connector that you just disconnected. Move the shift lever located on the driver's side of the transmission through the ranges. As the shifter is moved, the meter should display a resistance reading of less than 10 ohms or OL (open circuit) depending on which range you have selected.

As you move it through the ranges, the reading will show some ranges with continuity while other ranges will indicate an OL. All you are looking for is that the switch is capable of closing and opening. If the meter stays locked on OL or if it shows continuity in every range (stays locked in one position), the IMS is faulty. If the first circuit tests good, move to the other circuits and repeat the process.

- Connect one meter lead to pin A (Gray) and the other to pin B (Black) on the IMS.
- Connect one meter lead to pin A (Gray) and the other to pin C (Yellow) on the IMS.
- Connect one meter lead to pin A (Gray) and the other to pin D (Red) on the IMS.
- Connect one meter lead to pin A (Gray) and the other to pin E (Green) on the IMS.
- Connect one meter lead to pin A (Gray) and the other to pin F (White) on the IMS.

To replace the IMS, drain the fluid and remove the pan and filter. Remove the connector attaching the IMS to the TEHCM TCM. Remove the bolts attaching the IMS to the valve body and remove the IMS.

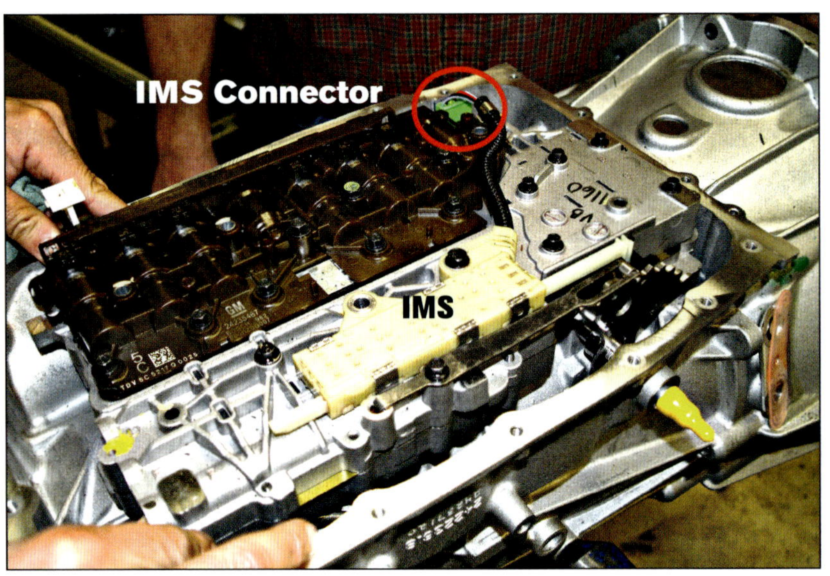

The internal mode switch (IMS) is an input to the TEHCM TCM. The IMS provides a high- or low-voltage signal on multiple circuits to the TCM based on the position of the shifter/manual valve. As you move the shifter, the voltage sequence changes to indicate the range you have selected. The IMS is bolted to the valve body and connected to the TEHCM TCM via a harness and connector. Replacing the IMS is as simple as unbolting the IMS, disconnecting the connector, and installing a new IMS. The IMS slide will need to be aligned with the manual valve when it is being reinstalled. The IMS can be checked with your scan tool prior to disassembly or with an ohmmeter when disconnected.

The IMS can be bench tested by using an ohmmeter. Connect one meter lead to pin A; then, connect the other lead to pin B. Repeat this process for each of the other pins: A to C, A to D, A to E, and A to F. Rotate the shifter through the ranges. Depending on the range selected, the meter will show either continuity or OL. You are not really concerned about which ranges indicate OL or continuity but rather that the signal does not stay locked in one position (OL or continuity) in all ranges. To check the sensor for each range, refer to the resistance chart in this chapter.

Install a new IMS, making sure to align the IMS slide with the manual valve. Torque the bolts to 71 in-lbs (8 Nm). Attach the IMS electrical connector.

Install a new filter, pan, and gasket. Add Dexron VI fluid, and adjust the fluid level.

Pressure Testing and Road Testing

Pressure testing is required any time the transmission fails to move (forward or backward) or if you have a transmission that exhibits hard shifts or slipping shifts and resetting and relearning the adaptive values have no impact on the shift quality.

Pressure Testing

The process will require a pressure gauge and a quality scan tool capable of controlling the transmission pressure control solenoid. Follow these steps:

1. Block the wheels, start the engine, set the parking brake, and place the transmission in Park. Use a scan tool to inspect for any current or previous DTCs. If current DTCs are set, address them first, as high line pressure is a default action for numerous DTCs.
2. Check the transmission fluid level and adjust as necessary.
3. Turn the engine off. Inspect the manual shift linkage at the transmission for proper function.
4. Remove the line pressure test port plug that is located on the passenger side of the transmission bellhousing. Install a pressure gauge into the test port.
5. Start the engine. Using your scan tool, access the Transmission Output Controls menu for

6L80 Line Pressure Values		
Scan Tool Line PCS Solenoid Commanded Position In (Kpa). Note that the scan tool value may vary from pressure gauge value due to software.	**Approximate line pressure values shown on pressure gauge, 1500 engine RPM**	
	KPa	**PSI**
No scan tool command	310 to 550	45 to 80
200 KPa commanded	655 to 900	95 to 130
400 KPa commanded	1100 to 1310	160 to 190
600 KPa commanded	1520 to 1725	220 to 250
800 KPa commanded	1860 to 2070	270 to 300

If you are faced with a slippage issue, shift feel issues, or a no-movement condition, a mainline oil pressure test must be conducted. Using the tap located on the passenger's side of the transmission case, attach a pressure gauge to the transmission. Using your scan tool, change the pressure command with the engine running. If the pressure is low or high, check for DTCs that may result in a pressure issue and address those first. If no DTCs are found, issues with the pressure regulator or line pressure solenoid may need to be addressed.

the Line PCS Solenoid. Control the Line PCS Solenoid in Park/Neutral with the engine speed at approximately 1,500 rpm and the TFT between 95 and 131°F (35 and 55°C). Use your scan tool to command line pressure to increase and decrease, allowing the pressure to stabilize between increments. Compare the pressure readings on the gauge with the line pressure table.

6. Readings that exceed the specifications by plus or minus 10 percent indicate an issue with the transmission, such as the pressure control solenoid, pressure regulator valve, filter, or fluid level. Turn off the engine and disconnect your scan tool.
7. Remove the line pressure gauge. Install the line pressure test hole plug and tighten to 97 in-lbs (11 Nm).

Road Testing

Road testing the vehicle is crucial for the proper diagnosis of transmission-related issues as well as to confirm that the transmission is operating correctly after repairs have been performed. Proper road testing requires the use of a quality scan tool so that different parameters can be monitored during transmission operation.

Scan Tool Checks

Perform this procedure first to ensure that the electronic transmission components are functioning properly. If these components are not checked, a simple electrical condition could be misdiagnosed.

1. Connect the scan tool.
2. Ensure that the gear selector is in Park and that the parking brake is set.
3. Start the engine. Scan for DTCs and address any current DTCs before moving to the next step.
4. Verify that the following scan tool data can be obtained and is functioning properly: engine speed, transmission ISS, transmission OSS, vehicle speed, IMS, commanded gear, gear ratio, line PC Sol, pressure command, brake switch, ECT, TFT, TCM temperature, calculated throttle position, actual throttle position, ignition voltage, TFP Switch 1, TFP Switch 3, TFP Switch 4, TFP Switch 5, PCS 2 Pressure Command, PCS 3 Pressure Command, PCS 4 Pressure Command, PCS 5 Pressure Command, Shift Solenoid 1, Shift Solenoid 2, TCC PCS duty cycle, and TCC slip speed.

Monitor the data values with the key on and engine off as well as with the engine running and compare the results to the service manual standards or to data from another known good vehicle.

Garage Shifts

Follow these steps:

- Set the parking brake. Start the engine and allow the transmission to warm up. With the engine running, apply the brake pedal.
- Move the gear selector through each gear range: P/R, R/P, R/N, N/R, N/D, D/N, D/M, and M/D.
- Pause 2 to 3 seconds in each gear position. Verify that the gear engagements are not delayed (they should take less than 2 seconds), and they should not be harsh. Monitor the engagement with the scan tool by observing the ISS/turbine shift speed sensor value. ISS should drop to 0, showing when the engagement is complete.

Harsh engagement may be caused by high engine idle speed, incorrect line pressure, or high line pressure resulting from a DTC being set.

Delayed engagement may be caused by low idle speed, low fluid level, incorrect line pressure, the TFT being too cold, shift selector linkage out of adjustment, or incomplete adaptive learning.

TCC and Shift Controls

The TCM calculates the upshift/downshift points based on MAP, MAF, TFT, ECT, throttle position, and vehicle speed. The TCM compares the values to values stored in a shift point table in the vehicle software. When it is appropriate for the vehicle to upshift or downshift, the TCM commands the appropriate pressure control solenoid on or off.

The key parameters to monitor for shift control operation include gear ratio; TCC slip; PCS 2, PCS 3, PCS 4, PCS 5, and TCC PCS commands and feedback values; and engine RPM to determine if a shift has occurred and if the clutch is slipping or not.

The TCC system used in 6L80 applications is an EC3 design. This design makes it difficult to feel the TCC apply, as it uses a PWM control system to control TCC apply and release. EC3 systems are also designed to slip at steady load and steady throttle openings, which should be considered normal. Normal TCC slip rates vary from 0 to 100 rpm while on flat roads with steady throttle and the TCC commanded on. Excessive slip rates indicate an issue with the system, such as a faulty torque converter, TCC apply valve or TCC regulator valve stuck or worn, TCC circuit hydraulic leakage, or a faulty TCC PCS.

Downshifts

Follow these steps:

1. Attach your scan tool and monitor the commanded gear shift time parameters. Accelerate the vehicle in drive range at light throttle (5 to 15 percent) until third gear is just achieved.
2. Quickly increase the throttle angle until the commanded gear position indicates that a downshift to second gear was commanded. Note the shift feel and shift time. Repeat this process for each shift, 4/3, 5/4, and 6/5.
3. Note any harsh, soft, or delayed shifts or any slipping conditions. Note any noise or vibration.
4. Follow the same process using manual shift control either with the shift lever or by using the driver shift controls on the steering wheel.

A commercial washer is the most efficient way to wash most transmission parts. If you do not have access to a commercial washer, a pressure washer and solvent tank can be used.

Cleaning and Inspection

Component inspection and cleaning are important steps in any quality rebuild. All of the components must be fully inspected for excessive wear and damage. Once properly inspected, the components should be cleaned so that they can be lubricated and reassembled.

Components

The most critical process when rebuilding a transmission is making certain that all components are clean when they are installed. Cleaning the case and its components can be accomplished using various processes, including the following.

- A commercial washer is used in professional transmission shops to clean the majority of the components.
- A solvent tank can be used if you do not have access to commercial washing equipment.

Brake cleaner works well for small parts including valve body components.

Any type of transmission failure will lead to contaminants collecting in the transmission cooler, which is typically part of the radiator. The contaminants must be flushed, otherwise transmission damage or failure may occur. The use of a commercial flushing machine is the best solution.

If you do not have access to a flushing machine, you may consider using aerosol cans filled with a cooler-flushing solvent. While this procedure is not as desirable as a commercial machine or cooler replacement, it works in most instances. Run multiple cans through the cooler, flushing in both directions. Make sure to blow out the cooler fully with compressed air when you are done. Also, check the cooler's flow volume when you are done.

- Spray cans of brake cleaner work well for smaller components as well as the valve body.

Cooler

The transmission oil cooler requires flushing any time you are rebuilding or installing a remanufactured unit. A clean cooler is critical for transmission operation and life. The cooler tends to trap contamination from the damaged transmission. Those contaminants will travel into your newly built transmission, causing valves to stick as well as major lubrication issues with the new transmission. This can lead to premature transmission failure. Cooler flushing can be accomplished by using a commercial transmission flushing machine, which is the preferred method, or by using multiple cans of spray cooler flush that are available from your local parts store.

Component Inspection

Planetaries, shafts, drums, clutches, bearings, snap rings, the valve body, pump, and the case must be inspected for damage and wear.

Ball Wear

Check ball wear is common on earlier 6L applications. Commonly, the balls will get caught in the spacer plate, which leads to slipping or a no-apply of the clutch that the ball is controlling. No movement forward is a common complaint when the 1-2-3-4 clutch check ball gets stuck. The check balls should always be

Worn check balls are a common 6L80 issue. Many times, the balls will stick in the spacer plate holes, resulting in clutch apply issues. The balls are supplied in most seal/gasket kits and should be replaced anytime the unit is apart.

replaced in the 6L applications and are typically included in seal/gasket kits.

Planetaries

Inspect the planetary gear teeth for cracks and excessive wear, and the pinion washers should be inspected for damage. Most transmissions have a measurement for pinion washer wear that can be accomplished with the use of a feeler gauge. The feeler gauge is placed between the pinion washer and the pinion. If wear is excessive, the planetary carrier will require replacement on most applications.

Inspect the planetary gears and thrust washers for damage and wear. If the washers or planetary show wear, make sure to fully inspect for lubrication circuit restrictions and leakage as well as the transmission fluid cooler for restrictions.

Inspect the splines where the clutch discs ride for wear. Grooves in the drum splines can lead to the discs sticking in those splines and clutch failure.

Shafts

Shafts should be inspected for spline wear and for being twisted.

Inspect all the shaft splines for wear, evidence of twisting, as well as cracks. If performance software is installed in the ECM, consider making various performance updates to the transmission, as excessive torque will damage the transmission.

On trucks that are used hard, it is common for the center support lugs to wear. This allows the support to shift position in the case, causing leakage between the support and the valve body. Leakage can cause slippage and failure of the 2-6 and/or low/reverse clutches.

Drums

Drums should be inspected for cracks, which is common on the 6L applications. If cracked, the drum must be replaced. In addition, the drum splines and bushings should be checked for wear and replaced if needed.

Center Support

The center support houses the 2-6 clutch, low/reverse clutch, and the low sprag. The support should be examined for lug wear, which will allow the support to rock back and forth in the case lugs, which may lead to clutch failure. If the lugs are damaged, the support must be replaced.

Clutches

Typically, clutches are replaced during a rebuild, so inspection is not generally required. It is suggested that

The 3-5-Reverse clutch drum has a tendency to develop cracks in the weld area of the drum. Leakage in this area will generally lead to slippage and finally clutch failure. The dot matrix–stamped drums are updated, but even those drums should be leak tested prior to assembly, as the cracks are not always visible. Keep in mind that some of the drums have an air-bleed hole, so do not confuse a leak from the air bleed and a leak in the drum weld. The drum should be replaced if it is cracked.

Cracks in the 1-2-3-4 piston are common, so closely examine the piston. An updated piston is available from GM and the aftermarket to address this issue.

Cracks and fractured housings are common, so closely examine the housing. An updated piston housing is available from GM to address the issue.

an OEM-type clutch be used, such as BorgWarner, Exedy, or Raybestos. Both the friction and the steel plates should be replaced. If you decide to reuse your clutches, the friction discs need to be inspected for flaking, discoloration, warpage, spline wear, and for being burnt. The steel plates will need to be inspected for flatness, lug wear, heat checks, and general wear.

While clutch damage can occur with any of the clutch packs, the 4-5-6 clutch pack is the most prone to damage on this application.

Spline

All shaft and gear splines should be examined for wear and damage. If excessive wear or damage are present, the component will require replacement.

Inspect the sun gear splines for damage and wear.

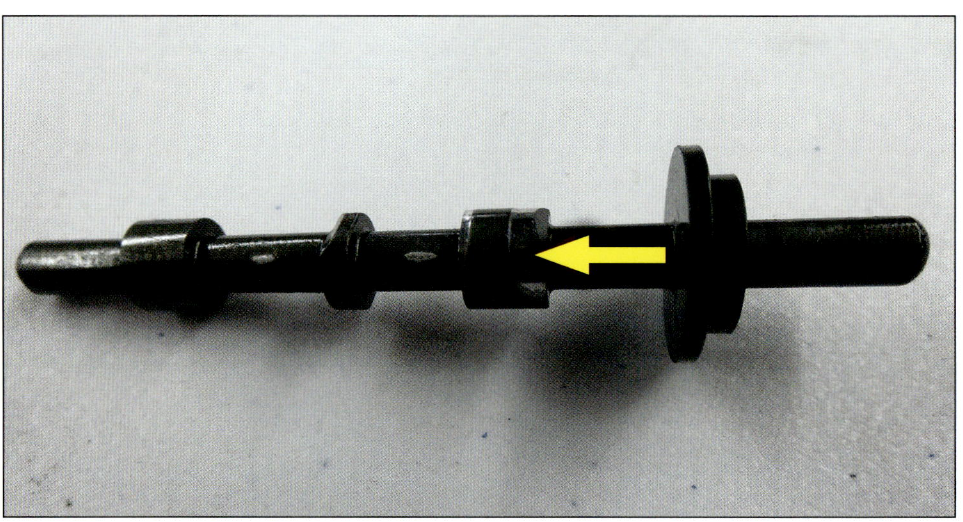

This is one of the top three issues with the 6L80: the lands on the valve tend to wear due to valve side-loading issues. Aftermarket valves are available to address the issue from TransGo, Superior, and Sonnax. A worn pressure regulator valve will affect the transmission line pressure, which will have a dramatic effect on clutch life.

Pump failure is the most common 6L failure: generally, the torque converter fails, leading to metal contamination reaching the pump and ultimately pump failure. This contamination typically restricts the oil cooler, so cooler contamination will need to be addressed. GM sells the parts as an assembly while the aftermarket will allow you to buy any part needed. Keep in mind, the rotor/slide clearance should be checked prior to installing the completed assembly in the transmission. The procedure is covered in Chapter 3.

Inspect all of the lugs in the case for excessive wear and damage.

Valves and Oil Pump

The 6L80 has many issues with valve wear, so the valves and bores located in the oil pump as well as the valve body must be inspected for wear. Updated valves and repair kits are available if excessive wear is present.

Oil Pump Damage

Oil pump damage is the most common 6L80 issue, so always inspect the pump for wear and damage. If the pump is damaged, the torque converter and pump will require replacement. Metal from the failing torque converter migrates to the oil cooler and pump, which leads to the damage. In addition, the cooler will either need to be properly flushed or replaced; otherwise, the failure may occur again.

Bearings

Clean the bearings with solvent. Most transmission bearings cannot be disassembled for inspection, so if you plan on reusing them, apply force to the bearing while rotating it. If any roughness is felt, replace the bearing. Most suppliers have bearing kits available that will provide all of the bearings for the unit under one part number.

Snap Rings

Snap rings can be damaged during disassembly. Inspect the snap ring for distortion and damage/wear to its surfaces. When in doubt, install a new snap ring.

Case

Inspect the case for cracks and wear in the lug areas.

Bushings

Inspect all bushings for wear and damage. GM does not service most of the bushings and requires the dealer to replace the component if a bushing is worn or damaged. Bushings are available through aftermarket suppliers, but be aware of some cheap bushings, as they may not maintain the correct tolerances and may perform worse than the old bushing that you removed. A quality US company producing bushings is Dura-bond, which is an OEM supplier for many engine and transmission bushings.

All of the bearings must be checked for damage. Bearings are available to replace any that are needed.

Transmission bushing are used to support and hold the components in proper alignment within the transmission. Think of them as a bridge that you use to cross a river. The bridge holds all of the cars crossing the bridge in proper position, allowing them across the river. If the bushings are worn, the shafts and housings lose alignment. This leads to clutch failure because the seal rings in the unit may no longer be properly aligned, leading to leakage. Inspect the bushings for wear and damage. If you find worn bushings, closely inspect the lubrication circuit and cooler for evidence of a flow issue.

Low Sprag

Low sprag wear is common on this application. Inspect the sprag elements as well as the inner and outer races for discoloration and wear.

Clutches are usually replaced during a typical overhaul. If you are not going to replace the clutches, inspect them for flaking, spline damage, and warpage. The steel plates should be inspected for lug wear, warpage, and excessive heat checking.

Some of the 6L80 components use a friction weld process during manufacturing. Inspect the friction weld areas for cracks and damage.

Friction Weld

Inspect the planetary gearset friction weld for evidence of cracks.

3-5-R Bearing Seal Damage

Sometimes the 3-5-R drum is in good shape, but the bearing or seal is damaged. The seal and bearing are sold separately and can be replaced without replacing the drum.

The low sprag is an uncommon failure, but it is seen from time to time. Inspect the sprag elements for wear.

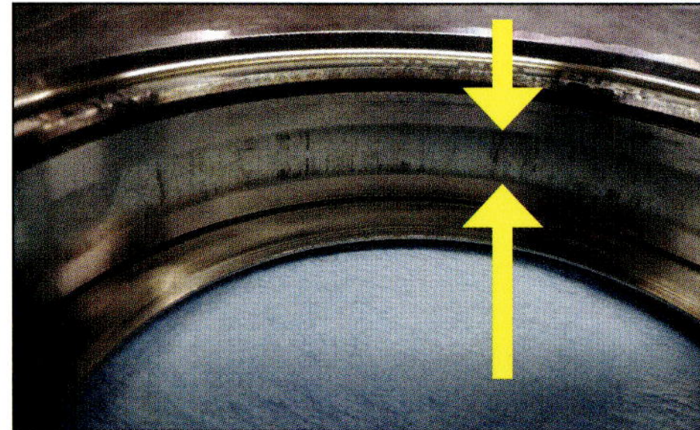

The inner and outer races for the sprag should be inspected for wear and damage. If a worn sprag is found, the complete unit is available from GM. The sprag element is available from the aftermarket. If a race is damaged, the complete sprag must be replaced.

While it is uncommon, the green-colored seal in the 3-5-R drum bearing does fail and should be inspected for damage. Some kits include this bearing/seal.

CHAPTER 3

Component Service Disassembly and Assembly

The disassembly, inspection, and service of a 6L80 transmission requires you to be organized and detail oriented. The internal service of the unit is discussed by each component within this chapter. The disassembly, inspection, and assembly of the component is addressed, and the installation of each component is covered in the transmission assembly section of the chapter.

Torque Converter

To remove the torque converter, rotate and pull the converter away from the pump assembly. Keep in mind that the torque converter is heavy. If you are planning to reuse the converter, flip it upside down in a drain pan and drain as much fluid as possible. Once drained, flip the converter with the hub side facing up and cover the hub hole.

Holding Fixture

The holding fixture (GM DT 8763-B) for the 6L applications mounts to the lugs in the case and can be mounted to a workbench. Some aftermarket fixtures can be attached to an engine stand. If you do not have access to a transmission mounting fixture, some technicians stand the transmission on its end on a pair of boards over a small bucket or use an old transmission case as a stationary stand.

GM as well as several aftermarket companies sell a holding fixture for the 6L80 that can be attached to a workbench or an engine stand to make servicing the unit easier.

If you do not have access to a holding fixture, an old transmission case that you can stand on end also will work. The old transmission case is not as nice to use as a holding fixture, but it will work to stand the transmission upright to service the internal components.

Several pan configurations are used, so if you are replacing your pan, make sure that the replacement is correct for your application. Some pans are equipped with standpipes, while others are not. The OEM gasket is designed to be reusable if it is not damaged. Holding the pan in position are 20 M6x18 bolts. When the filter is removed, break the old filter apart to inspect the contaminants, as that will give you a good idea of what to closely inspect when the unit is apart.

Extension Housing

Some applications utilize an extension housing. The housing is held in place by six bolts. Remove the bolts and remove the housing. A large square-cut seal is used on the outside diameter, while a lip seal acts as a dust seal on the rear of the housing. A bushing that is internal to the housing should be inspected for wear. A collar with a seal is slip-fit onto the output shaft and should be removed, and the seal should be replaced on some applications.

The six highlighted bolts must be removed from the valve body and the TEHCM. This will allow the valve body and the TEHCM to be removed as an assembly. Some applications use hex-head bolts, while others use Torx-plus fasteners. To remove the valve body and the TEHCM, slide the white TEHCM electrical connector up.

Oil Pan Filter

Rotate the transmission with the input shaft facing up and allow any fluid to drain. Once it is drained, rotate the transmission with the oil pan facing up and remove the 20 (M6x18) bolts. Remove the pan and gasket (the OEM gasket is reusable). Rotate and pull on the filter to remove it. Break the filter apart to inspect the type and quantity of contamination present. This will provide a good idea of what to inspect for when the transmission is fully disassembled. Use a screwdriver or snap-ring pliers to remove the filter seal.

Pass-Through Connector

The TEHCM pass-through connector located in the passenger-side rear corner of the case can be removed now or once you have the TEHCM/valve body removed. If you choose to remove it now, pull the TEHCM connector lock to release the slide connector. Slide a DT47715 (or an equivalent) connector removal tool over the pass-through connector. Push on the tool to release the connector locks and remove the connector. The connector can be removed without the tool, but the tool makes the process much easier and faster. Otherwise, you can simply wait until the TEHCM/valve body is removed to gain access to the connector, which is the typical choice if you do not have access to a connector removal tool.

TEHCM/Valve Body

The TEHCM is bolted to the valve body. To remove the TEHCM, it is easiest if you remove the valve body with the TEHCM attached. The TEHCM can then be separated from the valve body when the TEHCM/ valve body is on the bench. To remove, unlatch the white electrical connector on the rear corner of the TEHCM. The TEHCM/valve body is attached to the transmission using six bolts. Depending on the year, the bolts may be conventional hex-head designs or E12 Torx plus designs. Remove the TEHCM/valve body from the transmission.

Pump Service

The following section contains the steps to properly rebuild the 6L80 pump assembly. As with other 6L80 components, organization and a clean work area are critical to a proper pump rebuild.

Removal

The pump is bolted to the bellhousing assembly. Unlike many other rear-wheel-drive automatics, the 6L family of units does not require a pump-pulling tool to remove the assembly. The pump is removed by removing the bellhousing and pump as an assembly. Once the bellhousing/pump assembly has been removed, the pump can be separated from the bellhousing by removing the pump attaching bolts.

Position the transmission with the input (turbine) shaft facing up. To remove the bellhousing/pump assembly, remove the TCC O-ring from the input (turbine) shaft. Remove the nine M10x50 bellhousing bolts. At this point, the bellhousing/pump assembly can be separated from the transmission case by lifting it straight up.

To separate the pump from the bellhousing, rotate the bellhousing so that the pump is facing up once you have it on the bench. Remove the 13 M6x40 bolts that attach the pump to the bellhousing. Separate the pump stator support from the bellhousing by lifting it off the bellhousing.

The pump cover/stator support assembly has a gasket located between the stator support and the cover assembly. Sometimes the gasket will fail, which can lead to clutch failure as the 1-2-3-4, 4-5-6, and 3-5-Reverse clutches are fed through the support. Depending on where the gasket failure is located, one or more clutches may slip or not apply at all. In addition, tie-up issues can occur.

GM does not allow dealer technicians to service the gasket. Instead, it instructs the technician to replace the pump cover/stator support assembly if it fails an air or vacuum test. The logic used by GM engineering is that the support is assembled using automated equipment, which preloads the support and torques all of the bolts in one step. They were concerned that people would not properly preload the stator support as they torqued the bolts. As torque is applied and released on the stator support splines during transmission operation, the support could move, leading to gasket failure.

Some aftermarket shops replace the gasket as part of a rebuild. Some shops air test the gasket, and if it is not leaking, they do not service it. The gasket and O-ring seal are generally included in the overhaul gasket set. To service the gasket/seal, remove the six bolts holding the support to the cover. Remove the support from the cover using an arbor press and clean the parts with solvent. Install a new O-ring and gasket and mount the support to the cover with the bolts. Preload the support in the clockwise direction, and while holding it in that position, torque the bolts using a crossing pattern to 120 in-lbs (13 Nm).

Removing the Pump

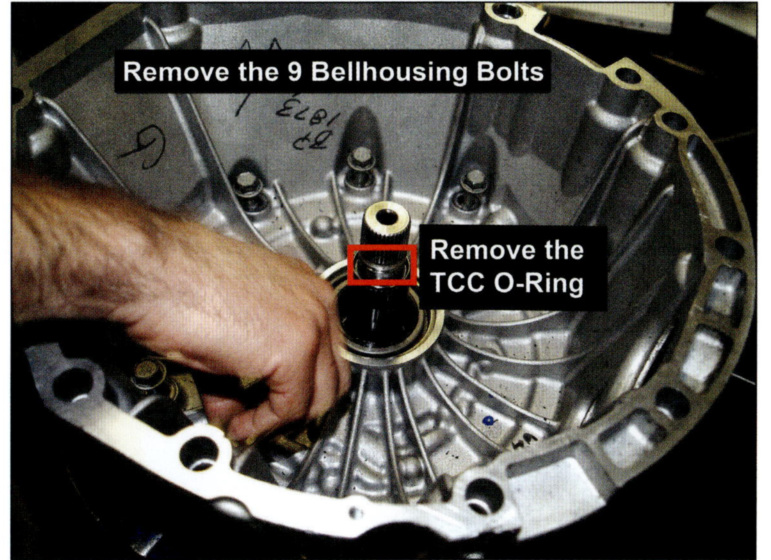

1 ***Remove the TCC O-ring from the turbine shaft. Remove the nine M10x50 bolts from the bellhousing.***

2 *Wiggle and lift the bellhousing and pump assembly to separate it from the case.*

3 *Remove the 13 M6x40 bolts attaching the stator support/ pump body to the bellhousing.*

4 *Wiggle and separate the stator support from the bellhousing side of the pump.*

5 *The stator support is retained by six bolts. Only remove the bolts if you want to replace the gasket under the support.*

6 *A gasket is used on 6L80/6L90 applications that seals the stator support to the pump body. Three clutches are fed through the support, so a leak in the gasket can result in clutch failure. GM does not service the gasket and instead instructs technicians to replace the pump body/stator support if the gasket is leaking. Many aftermarket technicians do replace the gasket, as it is included in most gasket/seal kits, while other shops only replace it if it is leaking. The gasket can be vacuum tested or air tested for leakage if desired. The stator support is a light press fit into the pump body. If you choose to replace the gasket, remove the six bolts attaching the components. Replace the O-ring and gasket and preload the support in the counterclockwise direction while torquing the bolts to 120 in-lbs (13 Nm) using a crossing pattern.*

Inspection

Pump damage is very common on 6L applications. Pump damage is typically caused by torque converter failure. Prior to disassembling the pump components, inspect the rotor for a dot that is typically located close to the converter drive lug. If no dot is found, mark the rotor with dye or a scribe so that you can easily distinguish which side of the rotor is facing up. This makes reassembly easier.

Disassemble the pump components by carefully prying out the slide spring with a screwdriver. With the spring removed, remove the rotor, vanes, slide and slide seal, spacers, and slide pivot pin. Lay the parts on a clean rag in order. Inspect the rotor and slide for damage and wear. Inspect the vanes for wear. Vane kits are available from GM as well as aftermarket suppliers. Inspect the pumping chamber and the stator support pump body for wear and damage, such as scoring, roughness, and other physical damage. Damage will require the pump be replaced, or the bellhousing pump pocket will require re-machining. Inspect the stator support side of the pump for the same issues. It can be machined if needed.

The 6L80 uses a vane-style variable-displacement pump. Note the rotor position prior to disassembly; most will have a dot that faces up. If no marks are seen, mark the rotor with a marker or scribe on the side facing up. When disassembled, inspect the components for wear and damage. Lay a straightedge across the bellhousing and check the bellhousing for warpage with a feeler gauge. Warpage in excess of 0.001 inch (0.0254 mm) will require that the bellhousing be machined or replaced. If the bellhousing or the stator support side of the pump was machined or replaced, the pump rotating component end clearance and the transmission end play must be checked.

Keep in mind that if machining is performed or components are replaced, the pump component end clearances must be checked. Clean the bellhousing surfaces, and place a straightedge across the bellhousing surface to check the pump and bellhousing machined surfaces for warpage. Attempt to place a feeler gauge between the straightedge and the bellhousing/pump surface. Warpage should not exceed 0.001 inch (0.0254 mm) Keep in mind that if the pump was replaced or machined, the rotor/slide end clearance and the unit end play must be checked. The rotor slide end clearance specification is 0.001 to 0.002 inch (0.0254 to 0.0508 mm).

GM does not use an end play specification, as it only replaces

Pump damage is the most common issue with 6L applications. If the pump is damaged, either it will require machining or it will need to be replaced. If machined or replaced with a re-machined assembly, the rotor/slide end clearances and the unit end play need to be checked and addressed.

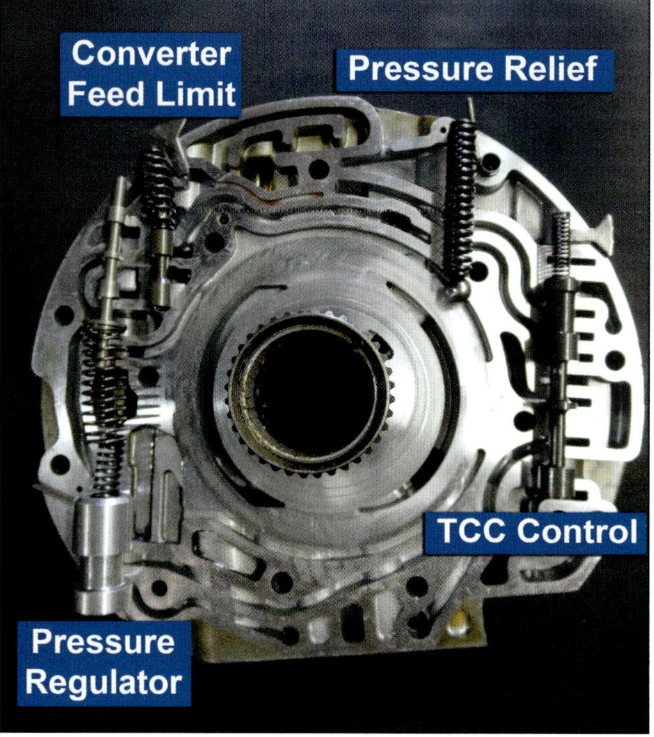

Disassemble the pump valves and inspect the valves and bores for wear and damage. If it is not damaged or worn, clean the pump components and lubricate them with transmission fluid and reassemble.

the pump/bellhousing with a new assembly. In the aftermarket, this is not generally the case. So, check the input shaft end play after the unit has been reassembled. The specification target is 0.004 to 0.006 inch (0.102 to 0.152 mm). Typical end play on a 6L80 generally runs between 0.006 and 0.035 inch (0.152 and 0.889 mm). Aftermarket shims are available from Superior Transmission products to address input end play issues.

Worn pressure regulator valves are the second most common issue on 6L applications. Service valves to address the issue are available from aftermarket suppliers, such as TransGo, Superior, and Sonnax.

Cleaning

Pump parts can be cleaned with solvent. The pump should be disassembled, and all the valves need to be taken out of the pump body and inspected. Flat-blade screwdrivers and picks work well to help remove the components. Be careful not to damage the valve or the bores. Lay the valves, springs, and retainers on a clean cloth so that they can be inspected and cleaned. The valves and their bores need to be inspected for wear and damage. The aluminum sleeves and the pump body contain orifices that need to be cleaned. Some of the orifices are contained in the cup plugs, which are driven into the pump body.

Pressure regulator valve wear is very common on 6L applications, so the valve must be closely inspected. Pressure regulator valve repair kits are available from several different companies, such as Trans Go, Superior, and Sonnax.

The stator support pump body and bellhousing pump surfaces need to be checked for flatness with a straightedge. Inspect all of the pump channeling for damage.

Rebuilding

Once the pump parts have been inspected and cleaned, the pump can be reassembled. Replacing the front seal and torque converter pump bushing located in the bellhousing are next. The front seal must be replaced. The bushing is typically replaced by transmission rebuilders, but be aware that some cheaper bushings may not maintain the proper hub-to-bushing clearance, so if the bushing is in good condition, it may be a judgement call if you choose to replace it or not.

GM does not sell the bushing and requires the dealer to replace the bellhousing assembly if the bushing is damaged. Replacing the bushing requires a properly sized bushing driver and the purchase of an aftermarket bushing. Note the exact position of the bushing before you press out the old bushing. Press in the new bushing at the same depth using the same orientation as the old bushing.

Multiple seals are located in the bellhousing assembly. Remove and replace the cooler line seals if the transmission is not equipped with a cooler thermo valve block. If the transmission is equipped with a cooler bypass valve block located on the side of the bellhousing, unbolt the block, disassemble it, and replace the seals. Reassemble the valve block and reattach it to the bellhousing.

Inspect the front pump bushing for excessive grooving and wear. If it is damaged, it will require replacement. A properly sized bushing driver is required to remove and install the bushing. Make sure that it is installed straight and to the correct depth.

The seal is a light press fit and can be pushed into place with an installer tool or just by using your fingers. Install the snap ring once the seal is fully seated in the bore.

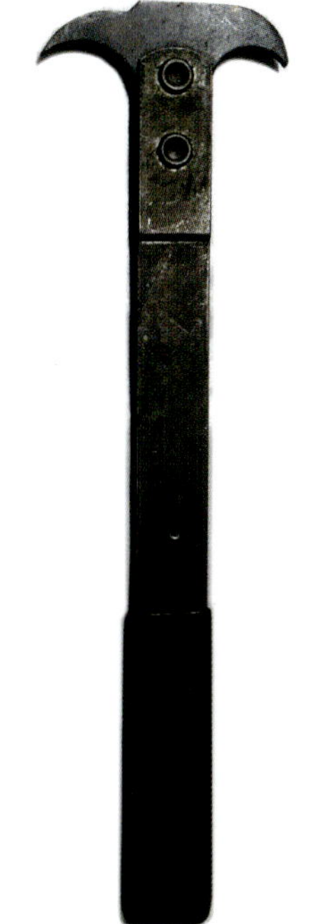

A seal remover works well to remove the front seal.

If the transmission has burnt clutches and/or fluid, one of the common causes is a faulty cooler bypass valve block. When the block malfunctions, the transmission will overheat due to the valving restricting flow to the oil cooler. If you suspect that the valve block is the cause of your concern or your transmission had been running hot, replace the assembly.

To replace the front seal, remove the snap ring and use a seal removal tool to remove the front seal. Clean the seal bore and install the new seal and snap ring. GM does not make a seal driver for this seal, but you may find a seal driver for another application that will work. The seal is not tight in the bore and can be pushed into place with light pressure on most applications. If you have some transmission components, such as a servo cover for a 4T60E or anything that will allow you to push evenly on the seal, it will make installation easier.

Selective Parts and Measurements

If the pump and its parts are in good condition, they can be reused. If any parts are damaged, they can be replaced. GM sells rotors and

Rotor Size		
GM Part Number	**Millimeter**	**Inch**
24248569	17.948 to 17.961	0.7077 to 0.7071
24248570	17.961 to 17.974	0.7071 to 0.7076
24248571	17.974 to 17.987	0.7076 to 0.7081

Slide Size		
GM Part Number	**Millimeter**	**Inch**
24222668	17.948 to 17.961	0.7077 to 0.7071
24224131	17.961 to 17.974	0.7071 to 0.7076
24224132	17.974 to 17.987	0.7076 to 0.7081

slides in selective sizes as well as vane kits for the pump. If the bellhousing bore or stator support pump body is damaged, either the pump or the components must be replaced or re-machined. If you are purchasing a new or rebuilt pump, ask your supplier if the pump was properly clearanced prior to installing it. An improperly clearanced pump can lead to pump failure or pressure-related issues.

If your pump parts were machined, check the pump clearances prior to assembly. One of two methods can be used: using Plastigauge or measuring the pump bore depth with a depth micrometer or dial caliper.

If you choose to use the measurement technique, measure the depth of the pumping chamber bore and the thickness of the rotor and the thickness of the slide. Compare the bore depth to the slide and rotor thickness measurements. The correct rotor and slide selection should provide 0.0008 to 0.002 inch (0.02032 to 0.0508 mm) of end clearance between the flat area of the bellhousing machined surface and the slide and rotor. If the measurement is not correct, choose the correct rotor or slide for from the chart for your application.

Using Plastigauge is a simpler method. The pump components need to be clean and dry. Install the rotor and slide. Place small pieces of green Plastigauge in two or three locations on the rotor and slide. Install the fluid pump cover body and torque the 13 M6x40 bolts to 97 in-lbs (11 Nm) using the proper sequence. Remove the bolts and separate the pump cover body from the bellhousing. Using the scale provided with the Plastigauge, measure the clearance. It should measure between 0.001 and 0.002 inch (0.0254 and 0.0508 mm).

If the measurement indicates an end play clearance issue, note which component (rotor or slide) is incorrect. Measure that component and compare it to the chart. Order the GM part number based on the part size that you require.

If the pump was machined, the rotor/slide end clearance must be checked. Plastigauge works well; the specification is 0.0008 to 0.0020 inch (0.020 to 0.051 mm).

- Slide to pump body end play clearance: 0.0008 to 0.0020 inch (0.020 to 0.051 mm)
- Rotor to body end play clearance: 0.0008 to 0.0020 inch (0.020 to 0.051 mm)
- Three slide and rotor sizes
- Plastigauge works well for the measurements

Assembly

Once the pump components have been inspected and any wear issues with the pump have been addressed, reassemble the pump. New seals from the rebuild kit will be used.

Install the Plastigauge across the rotor and slide in multiple locations. Bolt the pump back together and torque to the specification. Unbolt the pump halves and measure the Plastigauge with the built-in measuring tool. Selective size rotors and slides are available.

Bellhousing Side

If you are replacing pump parts, such as the rotor or slide because it was damaged but the rest of the pump is in good condition, measure the damaged part's thickness. Replace the rotor or slide with the same size as listed in the chart on page 58. If the pump components have been machined, take the measurements described previously prior to pump final assembly. This means that the pump slide and rotor need to be installed clean and dry to make the Plastigauge measurements. Once the measurements are complete, remove the slide and rotor, lube the components, and reassemble them.

When you are ready to assemble the components, lube the pump parts with transmission fluid or Transjel assembly lube. Install the slide, rings, seals, and slide pivot pin and spring. An O-ring seal is used to apply pressure to the large slide seal ring on the bottom side of the slide. A groove in the bottom of the slide houses the O-ring followed by the slide seal ring. Lube those components before installing them.

Use two slide decrease chamber seals, a round backup seal, and a rectangular Teflon seal. The backup seal is installed against the slide, and the rectangular seal fits between the backup seal and the pump wall.

Slide Spring

To install the slide spring, several methods and tools can be used, including the following:

- A pair of channel-lock pliers will work to compress the spring. A screwdriver can then be used to push the spring into position.
- An adjustable (crescent) wrench can be used to compress the spring. Place the spring between the jaws and turn the adjuster until the spring is properly compressed. Use a screwdriver to push the spring into position.
- A small engine valve-spring compressor works well. Compress the spring; then, use a large flat-blade screwdriver or other flat tool to push the spring into position.

Rotor and Vanes

Install the rotor and vanes as follows: Install one of the cast-iron vane guide rings, the plastic vane guide ring, and the rotor. Make sure to install the rotor with the dot or the dye/scribe mark that you previously made facing up. Be sure that the vane guide ring is properly aligned with the notches in the bottom of the rotor. Install the vanes with the rounded side facing the slide ID. Once the vanes have been installed, install the final vane ring.

If you are reusing the vanes, you will likely notice witness marks on one end of the vane. They are from the contact between the rotor and the vane. The vanes should be installed with the witness marks facing the rotor so that they are positioned as they were prior to disassembly. Make sure that all of the parts are approximately flush with the pump machined surface. If any of the components are higher than the machined surface, something was assembled incorrectly, and it will need to be addressed. If it has been properly assembled, lube the slide and rotor flat surfaces with Transjel.

Stator Support/Pump Body Cover Side

Lubricate all of the valves and bores and install the four valves, springs, and retainers. Make sure that the machined surfaces are clean and dry. Insert the pump cover assembly into the bellhousing and align the 13 bolt holes.

Install a pump alignment tool, such as the GM DT 46664 (or an equivalent), to align the bellhousing and stator support. Tighten the alignment tool to align the parts. Tighten the 13 attaching bolts in the proper sequence to (97 in-lbs (11 Nm). Remove the alignment tool and install the large-diameter bellhousing/pump seal onto the bellhousing/pump assembly.

Assembling Pump Components

1 ***The pump utilizes a slide, rotor, vanes, vane rings, slide pivot pin, slide ring, and various seals. The seals are serviced as part of the overhaul kit, while the other components must be purchased separately if they need to be replaced.***

2 *The slide O-ring is installed first followed by the slide seal ring. Lubricate the components.*

3 *Use two slide decrease chamber seals, a round backup seal, and a rectangular Teflon seal. The backup seal is installed against the slide, and the rectangular seal fits between the backup seal and the pump wall. Once in position, install the pivot pin and spring.*

4 *Installing the slide spring is a challenge if you have never done it before. A screwdriver, adjustable wrench, small engine valve-spring compressor, or water pump pliers work well to help get the spring into position.*

5 *Using a water pump–type pliers is another method that can be used to install the slide spring. Compress the spring with the pliers. Then, use a screwdriver to push the spring into place.*

6 *Install the rotor, vanes, guides, and vane rings into the pump, making sure to properly orient the parts. Fully lubricate the pump components.*

7 *Lubricate all of the valves and bores and install the 4 valves, springs, and retainers. Make sure that the machined surfaces are clean and dry. Insert the pump cover/stator support assembly into the bellhousing and align the 13 bolt holes. Install a pump alignment tool, such as the GM DT 46664 (or an equivalent), to align the bellhousing and stator support. Tighten the alignment tool to align the parts.*

8 *Tighten the 13 M6x40 attaching bolts in the proper sequence shown to 97 in-lbs (11 Nm). Remove the alignment tool and install the large-diameter bellhousing/pump seal onto the bellhousing/ pump assembly.*

Install the thrust washer onto the stator support assembly. Use Trans-jel to retain the washer. GM recommends that the washer be replaced as it is a wear item.

Install the three new stator support rings. These seal rings control the feed for the 3-5-R/1-2-3-4 clutch assemblies.

Pump Ring Updates and Seal Ring Installation

Two different ring designs have been used. An update was made due to delayed reverse and/or forward engagement issues at cold temperatures as well as shift flare on the 2-3 shift when cold. An updated stator support and rings were introduced to address the issue. Which ring type you select from your overhaul kit is based on the ring design with which your unit is equipped. The update was a running change during the 2009 model year. The ring designs are not interchangeable.

The early-design rings are directional. Inspect the early-design ring and you will find that one side of the ring has a groove, dot, paint mark, or arrow on it. The bottom ring closest to the stator support/pump is installed with the groove, dot, paint mark, or arrow in the ring facing up, away from the stator support. The other two rings are installed with their grooves, dot, paint mark, or arrow facing down toward the stator support/bellhousing. In addition, the ring ends are flat, and when installing them, make sure that the ends of the rings are not sticking out. Otherwise, ring damage will occur. Failing to install the rings correctly may result in clutch apply issues.

The updated ring design is held into the support by lugs that fit into

Install a new stator support thrust washer. Two design stator support seal designs have been used. The seal designs are not interchangeable. Install the rings.

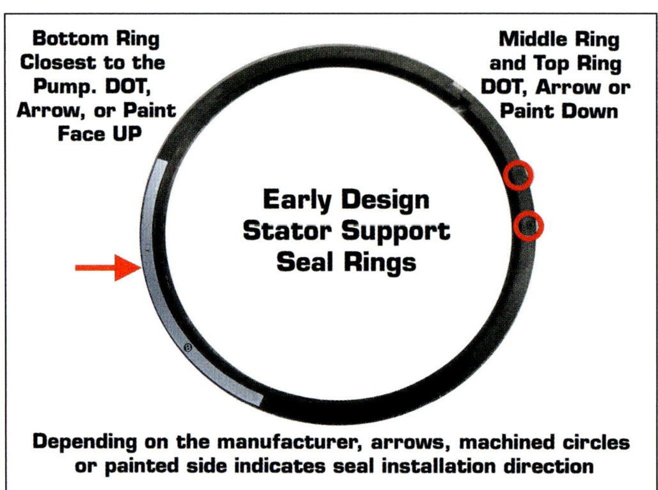

Early-design pumps use butt-cut rings. The rings are directional and must be installed correctly; otherwise, pressure-related issues may occur. The rings use a groove, dot, paint mark, or arrow to identify the direction the rings should be installed onto the stator support. The bottom ring closest to the pump/stator support is installed with the identification mark facing up. The middle and upper rings are installed with the identification marks facing down.

The updated ring design is held into the support by lugs that fit into notches machined into the support. Backup rings are positioned behind the Vespel rings to provide pressure on the rings. Install the components.

notches machined into the support. Backup rings are positioned behind the Vespel rings to provide pressure on the rings. Install the components. The pump and bellhousing assembly is almost complete.

Filter Seal Installation

The last step is to install the filter seal into the pump. Using a flat driving tool or the GM tool DT 47848, drive the seal into position in the pump.

At this point, the assembly is complete, and it should be set aside until you are ready to install it onto the case. Be aware that if the pump was machined or replaced with a rebuilt pump, you will need to check unit end play. Superior Transmission Products manufactures aftermarket shims to address end play issues.

Install the seals based on their design.

Using a flat driving tool or the GM tool DT 47848, drive the seal into position in the pump. Lubricate the seal. Set the completed pump aside on your workbench.

1-2-3-4/3-5-R and 4-5-6 Clutch Removal and Disassembly

At this point, begin to remove the clutches and planetaries from the transmission case. To remove the 6L80 internal components, grab the input (turbine) shaft and lift the components out of the case. The 1-2-3-4/3-5-R, 4-5-6 clutches and front planetary gearset will come out as a unit with the input shaft.

Separate the 1-2-3-4/3-5-R clutch drum from the 4-5-6/turbine shaft assembly. Place the 1-2-3-4/3-5-R clutch drum on your bench with the open side facing you. Remove the large snap ring holding in the clutches using a pick or small screwdriver. Remove the friction/steel clutches and wave plate. The clutch discs closest to the snap ring you removed is the 3-5-R clutch. The 3-5-R clutch wave plate sets down against the 3-5-R apply ring, which also needs to be removed. At this point, you can now remove the 1-2-3-4 clutches and wave plate.

The clutch layouts are as follows:

3-5-R Clutch	
6L45/ 6L50/ 6L80	Four internally splined plates, four externally splined plates, and one wave plate
6L90	Four or five internally splined plates, four or five externally splined plates, and one wave plate

1-2-3-4 Clutch	
6L45/ 6L50/ 6L80	Five internally splined plates, five externally splined plates, and one wave plate
6L90	Five or six internally splined plates, five or six externally splined plates, and one wave plate

A= 3-5-R/1-2-3-4 Clutch
B= Front planetary gear set
C= 4-5-6 Clutch and input Shaft
D= 2-6/3-5-R Clutch hub
E= 1-2-3-4 Clutch hub
F= 4-5-6 Clutch dampener and shaft
G= 2-6/Low Reverse clutch and center support
H= Low sprag clutch
I= Output dual pinion planetary
J= Output ring gear and output shaft

The components are housed in the case starting with the 3-5-R/1-2-3-4 drum, front planetary, input shaft 4-5-6 clutch, 2-6/3-5-R clutch hub, 1-2-3-4 clutch hub, 4-5-6 clutch damper and intermediate shaft, center support and clutches, low sprag, and planetary gearsets. Various bearings are positioned between the components.

To remove the 6L80 internal components, grab the input (turbine) shaft and lift the components out of the case. The 1-2-3-4/3-5-R, 4-5-6 clutches and front planetary gearset will come out as a unit with the input shaft. Remove the 3-5-R, and 1-2-3-4 clutch snap rings, clutches, steel plates, backing plates, and wave plates.

Piston Removal and Return Spring Compression

To remove the clutch pistons, some form of compression tool is needed along with a way to compress the return spring. Some of the clutches utilize multiple pistons, an apply piston, and a compensator or clutch dam piston. GM 6L units use a compensator hydraulic circuit to feed the compensator/clutch dam piston. The compensator circuit provides pressure to the piston, which opposes the movement of the clutch piston. This system is used to control shift feel.

To remove the pistons, place your clutch compression tool on the piston. If you do not have access to clutch compression tools, you may be able to make your own using some correctly sized pipe or heavy-wall PVC pipe, which you cut out a

Spring Interchangeability

The Belleville return springs used in the 1-2-3-4 and low/reverse clutches look very similar and are extremely close in size. However, the springs are not interchangeable, so make sure that they are not mixed up. ■

Wave Plate Identification

The wave plates for the 1-2-3-4 and 3-5-R clutches have been updated. They can be identified based on the number of external tangs. The 3-5-R wave plate was updated from 12 to 18 tangs. The 1-2-3-4 clutch wave plate was updated from 9 to 18 tangs. ■

If you do not have access to the OEM or aftermarket clutch compression tools, you can make your own.

slot on one side so you can access the snap ring.

Compress the clutch return springs with a snap press, foot press, arbor press, drill press, or even by using some ready rod, nuts, and a couple of flat plates. Compress the springs only far enough to remove the snap ring. Over-compression can damage the compensator/clutch dam pistons.

Clutch pistons are sometimes difficult to remove. Once the piston is ready to come out, it may be necessary to apply air pressure to remove the piston from the housing. Tapping the housing while upside down on your workbench may also work.

Lay out all of the parts on a clean rag in the order they were removed from the drum.

1-2-3-4 Piston and Compensator Piston Removal

GM clutch compression tool DT 37734 (or an equivalent) can be used. Compress the return spring; then, remove the snap ring with a pair of snap-ring pliers and a pick. Remove the compensator/clutch dam piston, Belleville return spring, and 1-2-3-4 piston.

Be sure to closely inspect the 1-2-3-4 piston for cracks. 1-2-3-4 piston cracks are common and will lead to clutch failure, slippage, or no-apply concerns. GM has updated the piston design. In addition, aftermarket pistons are available to address the issue. The updated GM piston design typically have part number 24238700 cast into the piston.

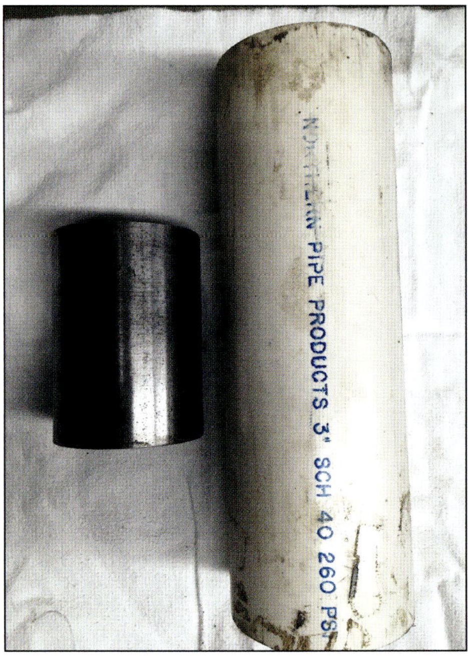

Tubing of the right diameter can be used. Cut out a slot in the side to allow access to the piston snap ring.

Removing and Inspecting the 1-2-3-4 Piston

1 ***GM clutch compression tool DT 37734 (or an equivalent) can be used. Compress the return spring. Then, remove the snap ring with a pair of snap-ring pliers and a pick.***

2 *Remove the compensator/clutch dam piston, Belleville return spring, and 1-2-3-4 piston.*

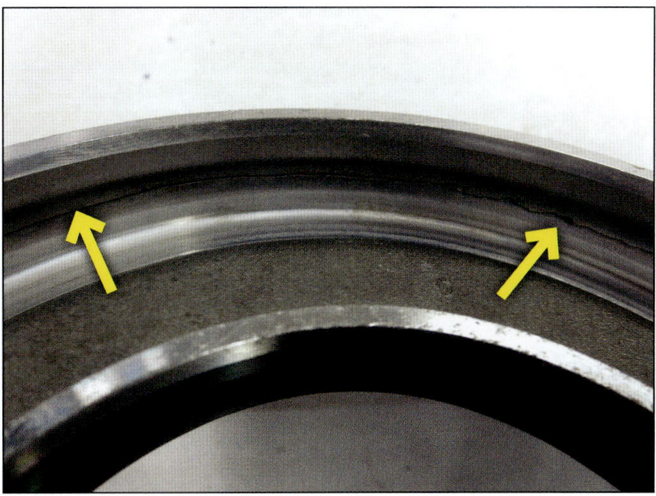

3 *Closely inspect the 1-2-3-4 piston for cracks. 1-2-3-4 piston cracks are common and will lead to clutch failure, slippage, or no-apply concerns. GM has updated the piston design. In addition, aftermarket pistons are available to address the issue.*

3-5-R Piston and 1-2-3-4 Piston Housing Removal

GM clutch compression tool DT 47867 (or an equivalent) can be used. Compress the return spring and remove the snap ring with a pair of snap-ring pliers and a pick. Remove the 1-2-3-4 piston housing, return spring, and 3-5-R piston.

As with the 1-2-3-4 piston, the 1-2-3-4 piston housing has a tendency to develop cracks. Inspect the center area of the housing for cracks or breakage. An updated piston housing design is available from GM to address this issue.

The 1-2-3-4, 3-5-R drum was updated for the cracking issue, but it does not mean that the new drum will not crack. Even the updated drum should be checked for leakage. The updated drum design can be identified by a dot matrix bar code stamping on the drum.

Drum Bearing Replacement

If you are replacing the drum, make sure that the new drum has the support bearing installed. Many replacement drums do not contain the bearing, and the bearing/seal must be installed prior to installing the drum into the transmission.

Clean and inspect all of the components. Inspect the clutch drum bearing and seal for damage. Check to make sure the bearing rotates smoothly when it is turned. Inspect the seal for tears. If the seal or bearing is damaged, the bearing/seal assembly will require replacement. Some seal/gasket kits contain the bearing/seal assembly.

A blind-hole or bridge puller can be used to remove the bearing/seal assembly. Install the new bearing/seal assembly and push it in with an arbor press (or an equivalent tool) until it is flush to 0.012 inch (0.3 mm) below the top of the drum surface.

Inspect the pistons and drum for cracks. Inspect the wave plate.

For 3-5-R/1-2-3-4 piston housing clutch snap ring removal, GM clutch compression tool DT 47867 (or an equivalent) can be used. Compress the return spring and remove the snap ring with a pair of snap-ring pliers and a pick. Remove the 1-2-3-4 piston housing, return spring, and 3-5-R piston.

TECH TIP

Clutch Drum Damage Check

The 3-5-R/1-2-3-4 early-design clutch drums tend to develop cracks in the drum weld area. The drum needs to be air tested for leaks. To test for leakage, apply soapy water to the drum weld area. Blow compressed air from the inside of the drum toward the weld area. If you see any bubbles, the drum is cracked and must be replaced. Most 6L 3-5-R/1-2-3-4 drums contain an air-bleed hole near the weld area, which will need to be plugged when air testing. When replacing the drum, be aware that the 6L80 and 6L90 drums are of different heights and contain different clutch counts. ■

As with the 1-2-3-4 piston, the 1-2-3-4 piston housing also has a tendency to develop cracks. Inspect the center area of the housing for cracks or breakage. An updated piston housing design is available from GM to address this issue.

The 3-5-R/1-2-3-4 early-design clutch drums tend to develop cracks in the drum weld area. The drum needs to be air tested for leaks. To test for leakage, apply soapy water to the drum weld area. Blow compressed air from the inside of the drum toward the weld area. If you see any bubbles the drum is cracked and must be replaced. When replacing the drum, be aware that the 6L80 and 6L90 drums are of different heights and contain different clutch counts.

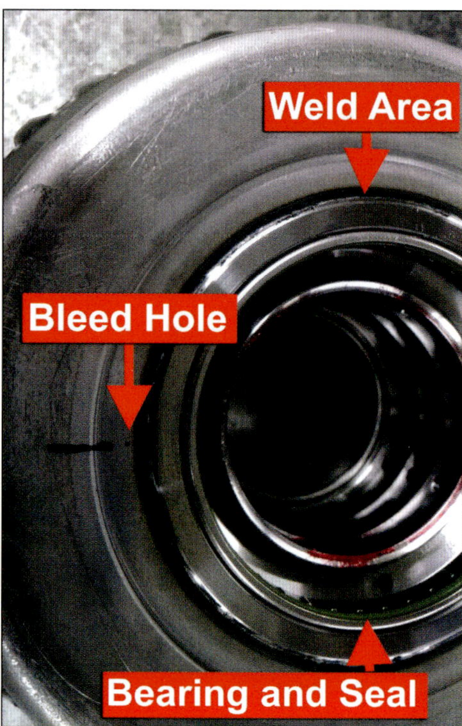

Most 6L 3-5-R/1-2-3-4 drums contain an air-bleed hole near the weld area, which will need to be plugged when air testing.

Inspect the seal and bearing for damage. If damaged, remove the old bearing. If you are replacing the drum, make sure that the new drum has the support bearing installed. Many replacement drums do not contain the bearing, and the bearing/seal must be installed prior to installing the drum into the transmission.

Make sure to press or drive the bearing straight. Install the new bearing/seal assembly and push it in with an arbor press (or an equivalent tool) until it is flush to 0.012 inch (0.3 mm) below the top of the drum surface.

Inspect and replace any damaged or worn components.

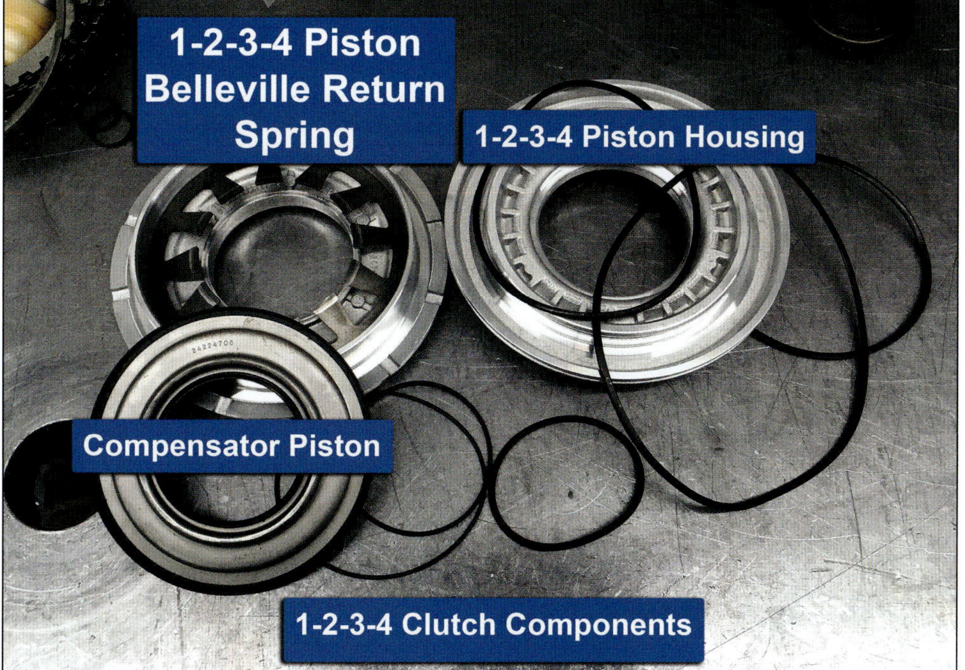

The 3-5-R/1-2-3-4 clutch housing contains the components for both clutches. The 1-2-3-4 components include the 1-2-3-4 piston, 1-2-3-4 piston housing, the piston return spring for the 1-2-3-4 clutch, and the compensator piston. In addition, various seals for the components are housed in this area. Some seals are replaced separately, while the compensator piston is a molded design component. Cracks in the 1-2-3-4 piston and housing are common, so always inspect the components.

Inspect the inside diameter of the drum where the pump seal rings ride below the drum bearing for excessive wear. Typically, seals and clutch discs are replaced. If you are going to reuse the clutches, inspect the steel plates for heat checking. Inspect the friction discs for flaking and spline issues.

1-2-3-4/3-5-R Clutch Assembly

Assembly is basically the reverse of disassembly. Lube the seals with transmission fluid, Vaseline, or Transjel. Select the correct seals for the 1-2-3-4/3-5-R clutch assemblies by comparing them to the seals you removed. Some seal service kit brands are available prepackaged with the seals in sealed packs, which identify where the seal is to be used. This type of kit will make your task much easier if you are not well versed with the transmission, as some seals are very close in size.

3-5-R Clutch Piston and 1-2-3-4 Piston Housing

Three seals (two O-rings and one D-ring) are used on the hub of the 3-5-R clutch drum. The bottom and largest in diameter is the 1-2-3-4 clutch housing seal, followed by the smaller-diameter 1-2-3-4 clutch housing seal. Finally, the 1-2-3-4 clutch inner seal, which is the smallest in diameter, is located in the upper seal groove on the hub.

Lubricate and install the two bottom clutch housing seals onto the drum hub. Do not install the top "D" seal on the hub at this point. Install the 3-5-R piston seals and lubricate the seals and drum seal surface. Carefully install the 3-5-R piston by applying pressure in various areas of

The 3-5-R/1-2-3-4 clutch housing contains the components for both clutches. The 3-5-R components include the 3-5-R piston and the piston return spring. In addition, the seal for the piston is housed in this area. Keep in mind that the return spring is directional.

the piston. Push in the piston until it is bottomed in the drum. Install the Belleville return spring with the center tangs up. Make sure that the spring is centered on the piston.

Install the seals on the 1-2-3-4 piston housing. Install the 1-2-3-4 piston housing. Using the DT 47867 compression tool (or an equivalent), lightly compress the 3-5-R Belleville return spring and install the piston snap ring. GM makes a tool to help with the snap ring installation (DT 47782-1 or DT47782-2), but it can also be done safely with a pair of snap-ring pliers and a little patience. Make sure that the snap ring is fully seated by using a screwdriver.

Install the upper D-shaped seal on the clutch drum hub. The rounded side of the seal should face toward the outside of the clutch drum. The flat side of the seal should face toward the drum hub.

Reassembling the Clutch Piston

1 Three seals (two O-rings, one D-ring) are used on the hub of the 3-5-R clutch drum. The bottom and largest in diameter is the 1-2-3-4 clutch housing seal followed by the smaller diameter 1-2-3-4 clutch housing seal. Finally, the 1-2-3-4 clutch inner seal, which is the smallest in diameter, is located in the upper seal groove on the hub. Lubricate and install the two bottom clutch housing seals onto the drum hub. Do not install the top "D" seal on the hub at this point. Install the 3-5-R piston seals and lubricate the seals and drum seal surface. Carefully install the 3-5-R piston by applying pressure in various areas of the piston. Push in the piston in until it is bottomed in the drum.

2 *Install the Belleville return spring with the center tangs facing up.*

3 *Install the seals on the 1-2-3-4 piston housing. Install the 1-2-3-4 piston housing. Using DT 47867 (or an equivalent compression tool), lightly compress the 3-5-R Belleville return spring and install the piston snap ring. GM makes a tool to help with the snap ring installation (DT 47782-1 or DT47782-2), but it can also be done safely with a pair of snap-ring pliers and a little patience.*

4 *Make sure that the snap ring is fully seated by using a screwdriver.*

5 *Install the upper D-shaped seal on the clutch drum hub. The rounded side of the seal should face toward the outside of the clutch drum. The flat side of the seal should face toward the drum hub.*

1-2-3-4 Clutch Piston

Install the 1-2-3-4 clutch piston into the clutch drum/1-2-3-4 housing. Install the 1-2-3-4 clutch Belleville return spring with the inside diameter tangs facing up. Lubricate and install the compensator/clutch dam piston with the tabs on the piston facing up and seal lips facing the housing. Lightly compress the compensator/clutch dam Belleville return spring using GM DT 38734 (or an equivalent) and a press tool. Install the snap ring.

Installing the 1-2-3-4 Clutch Piston into the Clutch Drum

1 *Install the 1-2-3-4 clutch piston into the clutch drum/1-2-3-4 housing. Install the 1-2-3-4 clutch Belleville return spring with the inside diameter tangs facing up.*

2 *Lubricate and install the compensator/clutch dam piston with the tabs on the piston facing up and the seal lips facing the housing.*

3 *Lightly compress the compensator/clutch dam Belleville return spring using GM DT 38734 (or an equivalent) and a press tool. Most kits supply a new snap ring for this location, as GM requires its technicians to replace it. Install the snap ring.*

Clutch Plate Installation

If the clutches are to be replaced, you will need to select the correct steel and friction plates from your overhaul kit. Check and compare the diameter, lug count, and thickness of the plates so that you can be certain you are selecting the correct components (many plates look similar).

1-2-3-4 Clutch Pack Installation

The 3-5-R/1-2-3-4 clutch drum is equipped with a set of blind splines. A common error when building the 6L units is for the technician to improperly position the wave plate, steel plates, apply/pressure plates, or snap ring in relation to the blind splines. This will result in a no-apply of that clutch pack, as the snap ring can pop out when the clutch applies, or the clutch will bind, resulting in a no-apply or dragging issues.

The wave plate and the steel plates must be installed with a large opening on the wave and steel plates positioned at the blind spline. The snap ring is then installed with the snap ring end butting up against the blind spline.

Proper Positioning

Make sure that you are properly positioning all the externally splined plates in relation to the blind spline. In addition, make sure that the friction surface of each clutch disc is next to the steel surface of the adjacent plate. You should never have friction-to-friction contact between any clutch discs. ■

If replacing the clutches, some technicians choose to soak them in Dexron VI transmission fluid prior to installing them in the clutch drum, while others install clutch discs dry. If you choose to install them dry, make sure when the vehicle is first started after the overhaul, it is operated in neutral at idle for a few minutes prior to putting the transmission in gear to provide lubrication to the clutches.

Clutch Installation

The 1-2-3-4 clutch pack consists of one wave plate, five internally splined plates, five externally splined plates, one backing plate (thicker than a steel plate), and one snap ring. The wave is installed first into the housing followed by an externally splined plate and then an internally splined plate. Alternate the externally and internally splined plates until all of the 1-2-3-4 clutches are installed. The thickest plate is the backing plate, and it will be installed on the top of the pack next to the drum snap ring.

Once the wave plate and all the friction and steel plates have been installed, install the backing plate. The backing plate is directional and three different designs have been used for the 6L80. Design 1 uses three "0" marks spaced 120 degrees from one another. On this design, the marks will face up in the drum. Design 2 utilizes an "UP" stamped on the plate that faces up in the drum when installed. Design 3 can be identified by the taper on the lug edge of the plate. The taper side of the plate faces the clutch pack.

The snap rings for the 3-5-R and 1-2-3-4 clutch packs have square-cut

The 3-5-R/1-2-3-4 clutch drum is equipped with a set of "blind" splines. A common build mistake on the 6L units is for the technician to improperly position the wave plate, steel plates, apply/pressure plates or snap ring in relation to the blind splines. This will result in a no apply of that clutch pack, as the snap ring can pop out when the clutch applies or the clutch will bind, resulting in a no apply or dragging issues.

The wave plate and the steel plates must be installed with a large opening on the wave and steel plates positioned at the blind spline. The snap ring is then installed with the snap ring end butting up against the blind spline.

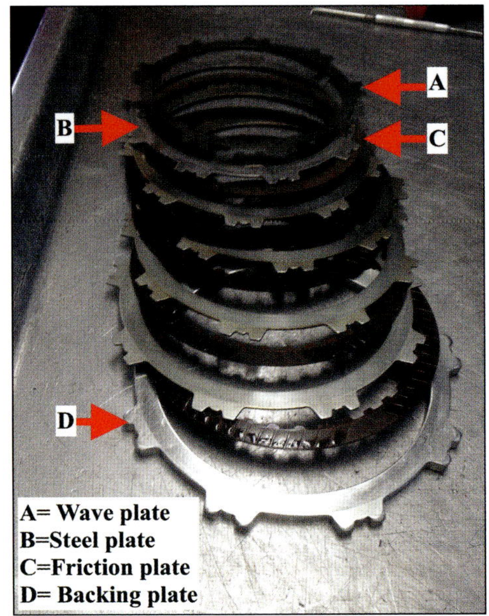

The 1-2-3-4 clutch pack consists of one wave plate, five internally splined plates, five externally splined plates, one backing plate (it is thicker than a steel plate), and one snap ring.

The wave is installed first into the housing and is followed by an externally splined steel plate and then an internally splined friction plate. Alternate the externally and internally splined plates until all of the 1-2-3-4 clutches are installed. The thickest plate is the backing plate, and it is installed on the top of the pack next to the drum snap ring.

ends, while the snap rings used for the low/reverse and 2-6 clutch packs have tapered ends. The 3-5-R snap ring and the 1-2-3-4 clutch packs have different thicknesses. Typically, the 3-5-R snap ring is thicker than the 1-2-3-4 clutch pack snap ring. The snap rings are selective to allow you to adjust for clutch pack travel issues.

Install the selective snap ring for the 1-2-3-4 clutch pack that was previously used in the drum. Refer to the selective snap ring chart if you think you may not know which snap ring is for the 1-2-3-4 clutch. Measure your snap ring and compare it to the chart if you are questioning which clutch pack it is for.

The wave is installed first into the housing and is followed by an externally splined steel plate and then an internally splined friction plate. Alternate the externally and internally splined plates until all of the 1-2-3-4 clutches are installed. The thickest plate is the backing plate, and it is installed on the top of the pack next to the drum snap ring.

The backing plate is directional, and three different designs have been used for the 6L80. Design 1 uses three "0" marks spaced 120 degrees from one another. On this design, the marks face up in the drum. Design 2 utilizes an "UP" stamped on the plate that faces up in the drum when installed. Design 3 can be identified by the taper on the lug edge of the plate. The beveled side of the plate faces the clutch pack.

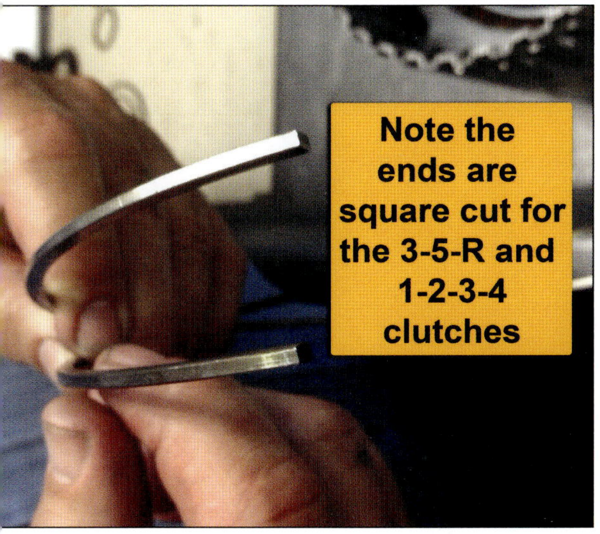

The snap rings for the 3-5-R and 1-2-3-4 clutch packs have square-cut ends, while the snap rings used for the low/ reverse and 2-6 clutch packs have tapered ends. The 3-5-R snap ring and the 1-2-3-4 clutch packs are different thicknesses. Install the selective snap ring for the 1-2-3-4 clutch pack that was previously used in the drum. Refer to the selective snap ring chart if you think you may not know which snap ring is for the 1-2-3-4 clutch.

Clutch Pack Travel

Measuring clutch pack travel is important. If the clutch-to-clutch clearance is too great, you may run out of piston travel as the clutch applies lead to flaring on the shift all the way to a slipping clutch issue. If the clearance is too tight, the clutch pack may drag when it is in the released position, leading to clutch damage and shift tie-up concerns.

Three methods can be used to check clutch travel on a 6L80 clutch: the factory method, an aftermarket method using air pressure, and an aftermarket method using measuring tools.

Factory Method (1-2-3-4 Clutch)

The GM factory method requires the use of a weight tool that is placed on the assembled clutch pack. A dial indicator is used to measure the stroke of the clutch as it is applied with air pressure. GM also has a tool for blocking the compensator ports to allow you to air test the compensator piston for proper operation.

The GM counterweight tool number is DT 47868-1, and an adaptor for the 1-2-3-4 clutch is DT 47868-3. Position the finished pump with the pump facing up on a workbench. Mount the 1-2-3-4/3-5-R drum onto the pump stator support. Mount a dial indicator and position the plunger onto the counterweight tool. Zero the dial indicator. Apply 60 psi of air pressure to the 1-2-3-4 and compensator feed holes in the pump while blocking the compensator holes in the pump stator support if needed. Read the clutch travel measurement registering on the dial

Selective Snap-Ring Thickness for 3-5-R Clutch		
Metric (mm)	**US (inch)**	**Color**
1.61 to 1.71	0.063 to 0.067	Gray
1.88 to 1.98	0.074 to 0.078	Light Green
2.15 to 2.25	0.085 to 0.089	Yellow
2.42 to 2.52	0.095 to 0.099	None
2.69 to 2.79	0.106 to 0.110	Purple

Selective Snap-Ring Thickness for 1-2-3-4 Clutch		
Metric (mm)	**US (inch)**	**Color**
2.42 to 2.52	0.095 to 0.099	None
2.69 to 2.79	0.106 to 0.110	Purple
2.96 to 3.06	0.117 to 0120	Light Blue
3.23 to 3.33	0.127 to 0.131	Orange
3.50 to 3.60	0.138 to 0.142	White

Measuring clutch pack travel is important. If the clutch-to-clutch clearance is too great, you may run out of piston travel as the clutch applies leading to flaring on the shift all the way to a slipping clutch issue. If the clearance is too tight, the clutch pack may drag when it is in the released position, leading to clutch damage and shift tie-up concerns. Three different methods can be used to check clutch travel on a 6L80 clutch: the factory method, an aftermarket method using air pressure, and an aftermarket method using measuring tools.

Mount a dial indicator and position the plunger onto the counter-weight tool. Zero the dial indicator. Apply 60 psi of air pressure to the 1-2-3-4 and compensator feed holes in the pump while blocking the compensator holes in the pump stator support if needed. Read the clutch travel measurement registering on the dial indicator. The clutch pack travel specification for the 1-2-3-4 clutch is 0.060 to 0.078 inch (1.53 to 1.99 mm). If the travel does not fall within the specification, you need to install a different selective snap ring.

Mount a dial indicator and position the plunger onto the clutch backing plate. Zero the dial indicator. Apply 60 psi of air pressure to the 1-2-3-4 and compensator feed holes in the pump while blocking the compensator holes in the pump stator support if needed. Read the clutch travel measurement registering on the dial indicator. The clutch pack travel specification for the 1-2-3-4 clutch is 0.083 to 0.105 inch (2.1082 to 2.667 mm). If the travel does not fall within the specification, install a different selective snap ring.

indicator. The clutch pack travel specification for the 1-2-3-4 clutch is 0.060 to 0.078 inch (1.53 to 1.99 mm). If the travel does not fall within the specifications, you will need to install a different selective snap ring.

Aftermarket Method Using Air Pressure (1-2-3-4 Clutch)

Position your finished pump with the pump facing up on a workbench. Mount the 1-2-3-4/3-5-R drum onto the pump stator support. Mount a dial indicator and position the plunger onto the clutch backing plate. Zero the dial indicator. Apply 60 psi of air pressure to the 1-2-3-4 and compensator feed holes in the pump while blocking the compensator holes in the pump stator support if needed. Read the clutch travel measurement registering on the dial indicator.

The clutch pack travel specification for the 1-2-3-4 clutch is 0.083 to 0.105 inch (2.1082 to 2.667 mm). If the travel does not fall within the specification, you need to install a different selective snap ring.

Aftermarket Method Using Measuring Tools (1-2-3-4 Clutch)

A little more crude but still fairly effective method that is used to measure clutch clearance is to use a feeler gauge or some other form of tool to measure the distance between the backing plate and the top friction disc. The specification is 0.057 to 0.065 inch (1.4478 to 1.651 mm).

3-5-R Clutch Pack Installation

Prior to the assembly, locate the drum blind splines.

If you choose to measure clutch travel with a feeler gauge, measure between the backing plate and the top friction disc. The specification is 0.057 to 0.065 inch (1.4478 to 1.651 mm).

Blind Splines

The 3-5-R/1-2-3-4 clutch drum is equipped with a set of blind splines. A common error when building the 6L units is for the technician to improperly position the wave plate, steel plates, apply/pressure plates, or snap ring in relation to the blind splines. This will result in a no-apply of that clutch pack as the snap ring can pop out when the clutch applies, or the clutch will bind, resulting in a no-apply or dragging issues.

The wave plate and the steel plates must be installed with a large opening on the wave and steel plates positioned at the blind spline. The snap ring is then installed with the snap ring end butting up against the blind spline.

If replacing the clutches, some technicians choose to soak them in Dexron VI transmission fluid prior to installing them in the clutch drum, while others install clutch discs dry. If you choose to install them dry, make sure that when the vehicle is first started after the overhaul, it is operated in neutral at idle for a few minutes prior to putting the transmission in gear to provide lubrication to the clutches.

Clutch Installation

The 6L80 3-5-R clutch pack consists of one wave plate, four internally splined plates, four externally splined plates, one backing plate (thicker than a steel plate), one apply ring, and one snap ring. The apply ring is installed first into the housing. Make sure that the legs of the apply ring make full contact with the 3-5-R piston and that it sits square in the housing. The wave is installed second into the housing and sits on the apply ring. It is followed by an externally splined plate and then an internally splined plate. Alternate the externally and internally splined plates until all of the 3-5-R clutches are installed. The backing plate will then be installed on the top of the pack next to the snap ring.

Once the wave plate and all the friction and steel plates have been installed, install the backing plate and snap ring. The snap rings for the 3-5-R and 1-2-3-4 clutch packs have square-cut ends, while the snap rings used for the low/reverse and 2-6 clutch packs have tapered ends. The 3-5-R snap ring and the 1-2-3-4 clutch packs are different thicknesses. Typically, the 3-5-R snap ring is thicker than the 1-2-3-4 clutch pack snap ring. The snap rings are selective to allow you to adjust for clutch pack travel issues.

Install the selective snap ring for the 3-5-R clutch pack that was previously used in the drum. Refer to the selective snap ring chart if you think you may not know which snap ring is for the 3-5-R clutch. Measure your snap ring and compare it to the chart if you are questioning which clutch pack it is for.

Installing the Clutch Pack

1 ***The apply ring is installed first into the housing. Make sure the legs of the apply ring are making full contact with the 3-5-R piston and that it sets square in the housing.***

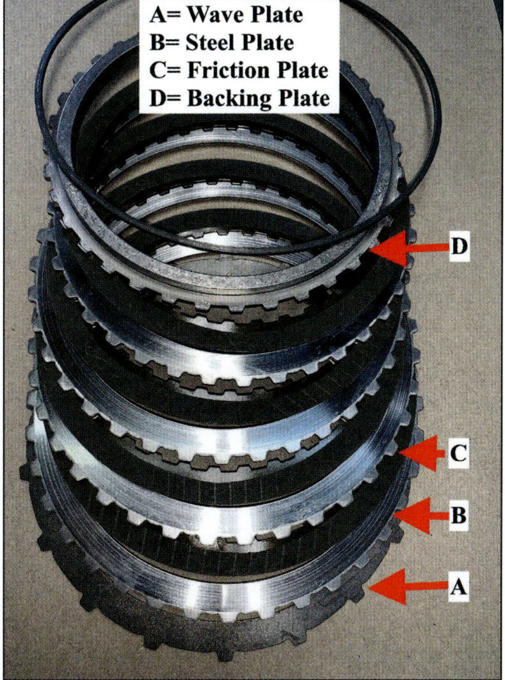

2 ***The 6L80 3-5-R clutch pack consists of one wave plate, four internally splined plates, four externally splined plates, one backing plate (thicker than a steel plate), one apply ring, and one snap ring.***

3 *The wave plate is installed second into the housing and sits on the apply ring, which is followed by an externally splined steel plate and then an internally splined friction plate.*

4 *Alternate the externally and internally splined plates until all of the 3-5-R clutch steel plates are installed.*

5 *Alternate the externally and internally splined plates until all of the 3-5-R clutch friction plates are installed.*

6 *Once the wave plate and all the friction and steel plates have been installed, install the backing plate and snap ring. The snap rings for the 3-5-R and 1-2-3-4 clutch packs have square-cut ends, while the snap rings used for the low/reverse and 2-6 clutch packs have tapered ends. The 3-5-R snap rings are available in selective thicknesses.*

Clutch Pack Travel

Measuring clutch pack travel is important. If the clutch-to-clutch clearance is too loose, you may run out of piston travel as the clutch applies lead to flaring on a shift all the way to a slipping clutch issue. If the clearance is too tight, the pack may drag when it is in the released position, leading to clutch damage and shift tie-up concerns.

Three methods can be used to check clutch travel on a 6L80 clutch: the factory method, an aftermarket method using air pressure, and an aftermarket method using measuring tools.

Factory Method (3-5-R Clutch)

The GM factory method requires the use of a weight tool that is placed on the assembled clutch pack. A dial indicator is used to measure the stroke of the clutch as it is applied with air pressure.

The GM counterweight tool number is DT 47868-1. Position your finished pump with the pump facing up on a workbench. Mount the 1-2-3-4/3-5-R drum onto the pump stator support. Mount a dial indicator and position the plunger onto the counterweight tool. Zero the dial

Here's the factory method: Mount the 1-2-3-4/3-5-R drum onto the pump stator support. Mount a dial indicator and position the plunger onto the counterweight tool. Zero the dial indicator. Apply 60 psi of air pressure to the 3-5-R feed hole in the pump. Read the clutch travel measurement registering on the dial indicator. The clutch pack travel specification for the 3-5-R clutch is 0.048 to 0.070 inch (1.21 to 1.79 mm). If the travel does not fall within the specification, you will need to install a different selective snap ring. Set the completed 1-2-3-4/3-5-R clutch assembly aside on your workbench for assembly at a later point.

Here's the aftermarket method using air pressure. Mount a dial indicator and position the plunger onto the clutch backing plate. Zero the dial indicator. Apply 60 psi of air pressure to the 1-2-3-4 and compensator feed holes in the pump while blocking the compensator holes in the pump stator support if needed. Read the clutch travel measurement registering on the dial indicator. The clutch pack travel specification for the 3-5-R clutch is 0.055 to 0.079 inch (1.397 to 2.066 mm). If the travel does not fall within the specification, you will need to install a different selective snap ring. Set the completed 1-2-3-4/3-5-R clutch assembly aside on your workbench for assembly at a later point.

indicator. Apply 60 psi of air pressure to the 3-5-R feed hole in the pump. Read the clutch travel measurement registering on the dial indicator. The clutch pack travel specification for the 3-5-R clutch is 0.048 to 0.070 inch (1.21 to 0.79 mm). If the travel does not fall within the specification, you will need to install a different selective snap ring.

Aftermarket Method Using Air Pressure (3-5-R Clutch)

Position your finished pump with the pump facing up on a workbench. Mount the 1-2-3-4/3-5-R drum onto the pump stator support. Mount a dial indicator and position the plunger onto the clutch backing plate. Zero the dial indicator. Apply 60 psi of air pressure to the 1-2-3-4 and compensator feed holes in the pump while blocking the compensator holes in the pump stator support if needed. Read the clutch travel measurement registering on the dial indicator.

The clutch pack travel specification for the 3-5-R clutch is 0.055 to 0.079 inch (1.397 to 2.066 mm). If the travel does not fall within the specification range, install a different selective snap ring.

Set the completed 1-2-3-4/3-5-R clutch assembly aside on your workbench for assembly at a later point.

Aftermarket Method Using Measuring Tools (3-5-R Clutch)

A little more crude but still fairly effective method that is used to measure clutch clearance is to use a feeler gauge or some other form of tool to measure the distance between the backing plate and the top friction disc. The specification is 0.057 to 0.065 inch (1.4478 to 1.651 mm).

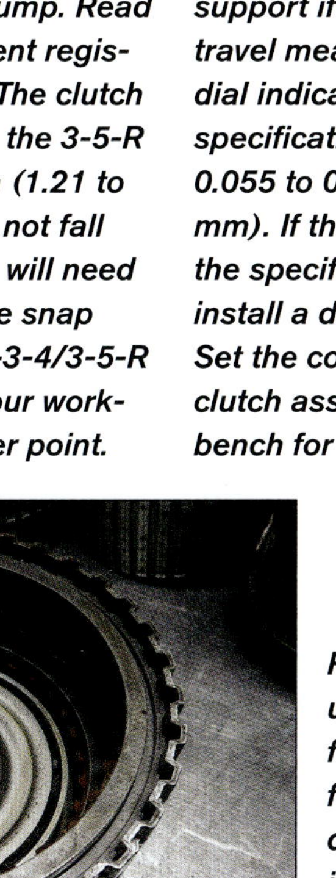

For the aftermarket method using measuring tools, use a feeler gauge or some other form of tool to measure the distance between the backing plate and the top friction disc. The specification is 0.057 to 0.065 inch (1.4478 to 1.651 mm).

4-5-6 Clutch Disassembly

Stand the 4-5-6 clutch assembly with the clutch facing the bench and the input (turbine) shaft facing up. Remove the input planetary carrier, sun gear, and sun gear bearing. Lay all of the components on a clean rag in the order in which they were removed for cleaning and inspection. Inspect and clean the planetary gears and bearing.

Rotate the 4-5-6 clutch assembly so that the input (turbine) shaft is facing down. A hole in your bench or a drum holder works well for this job. Remove the snap ring that retains the 4-5-6 clutch pack and remove the clutches. The 6L80 4-5-6 clutch consists of six internally splined plates, six externally splined plates, one wave plate, one backing plate, and one snap ring. The 6L90 uses one additional friction and one additional steel plate.

Using clutch compressor DT 43074 (or an equivalent), lightly compress the return spring and remove the snap ring. GM requires that this snap ring be replaced, so it is typically included in many seal kits.

With the snap ring removed, remove the 4-5-6 compensator piston, Belleville return spring, and 4-5-6 clutch piston. The 4-5-6 piston is a molded-design assembly, which is generally reused unless it is damaged. Typically, it is not included in a seal kit unless you order a kit that includes the molded pistons, so it will likely need to be purchased separately if needed.

With all the components removed, clean and inspect the drum and input (turbine) shaft for wear and damage. Inspect the input shaft closely for signs of twisting or cracks.

Disassembling the 4-5-6 Clutch

1 *Stand the 4-5-6 clutch assembly with the clutch facing the bench and the input (turbine shaft) facing up. Remove the input planetary carrier, sun gear, and sun gear bearing. Lay all the components on a clean rag in the order in which they were removed for cleaning and inspection. Inspect and clean the planetary gears and bearing. Now, rotate the 4-5-6 clutch assembly so that the input (turbine) shaft is facing down. A hole in your bench or a drum holder works well for this job. Remove the snap ring that retains the 4-5-6 clutch pack and remove the clutches.*

2 *Using clutch compressor DT 43074 (or an equivalent), lightly compress the return spring and remove the snap ring.*

3 *With the snap ring removed, remove the 4-5-6 compensator piston, Belleville return spring, and the 4-5-6 clutch piston.*

4 *The 4-5-6 piston is a molded-design assembly, which is generally reused unless it is damaged. Typically, it is not included in a seal kit unless you order a kit that includes the molded pistons, so it will likely need to be purchased separately if needed.*

Inspect the input shaft closely for signs of twisting or cracks.

4-5-6 Shaft Seal Replacement

The 4-5-6 clutch is fed via the input shaft. To seal the shaft, three solid Teflon seals are used. The seals require replacement. Use a knife to remove the old seals and then clean the seal grooves. The new seals included in your kit require the use of special tools to install and size the seals. GM as well as aftermarket tools are available to accomplish this task.

GM tool numbers DT 47768-1, DT47768-2, and DT47768-3 are used to install and size the seals. The DT47768-1 seal protector is adjustable to allow you to select which groove to install the seal. Install the bottom seal closest to the clutch drum first. Adjust the DT47768-1

Remove the old seals and install the new seals from your kit. The new seals that you are installing will require special tools to install and size them. GM and aftermarket tools or the use of a small engine ring compressor can be used to size the new seals. GM tool numbers DT 47768-1, DT47768-2, and DT47768-3 are used to install and size the seals. The DT47768-1 seal protector is adjustable to allow you to select which groove to install the seal. Install the bottom seal closest to the clutch drum first.

With the three seals installed in their grooves, the seals need to be properly sized. Lubricate the seals with transmission fluid. Lubricate the DT47768-3 sizer tool with transmission fluid. The sizer is tapered, and the tapered side is designed to slide over the seals. Install the sizer with the tapered side toward the seal and slowly move the sizer down over the seals. When the sizer has fully covered the seals, leave the tool in place for at least 5 minutes before removing it.

Lubricate the inside of the drum with transmission fluid. Lubricate the 4-5-6 piston and compensator pistons with transmission fluid, Transjel, or Vaseline. Install the 4-5-6 piston into the 4-5-6 clutch drum.

Install the compensator piston. Using clutch compressor DT 43074 (or an equivalent), lightly compress the return spring and install the new snap ring.

and install it over the shaft. The bottom of the tool should line up with the seal groove. Slide a new seal onto the tool.

DT47768-2 is used to push the seal down the seal protector and into place on the shaft. Once the seal is installed, adjust the tool for the second seal position on the shaft and install the seal. Repeat the process for the top seal.

With the three seals installed in their grooves, the seals need to be properly sized. Lubricate the seals with transmission fluid. Lubricate the DT47768-3 sizer tool with transmission fluid. The sizer is tapered, and the tapered side is designed to slide over the seals. Install the sizer with the tapered side toward the seal and slowly move the sizer down over the seals. When the sizer has fully covered the seals, leave the tool in place for at least 5 minutes before removing it.

If you are not able to find tools for this task, a small engine ring compressor may work to size the seals.

4-5-6 Clutch Assembly

Lubricate the inside of the drum with transmission fluid. Lubricate

Install the Belleville return spring with the inside diameter tangs facing up.

the 4-5-6 piston and compensator pistons with transmission fluid, Transjel, or Vaseline. Install the 4-5-6 piston into the 4-5-6 clutch drum. Install the Belleville return spring with the inside diameter tangs up. Install the compensator piston.

Using clutch compressor DT 43074 (or an equivalent), lightly compress the return spring and install the new snap ring.

4-5-6 Clutch Plate Installation

The 4-5-6 clutch is equipped with six internally splined plates, six externally splined plates, one wave plate, one backing plate, and one selective snap ring. If replacing the clutches, some technicians choose to soak them in Dexron VI transmission fluid prior to installing them in the clutch drum, while others install clutch discs dry. If you choose to install them dry, make sure that when the vehicle is first started after the overhaul, it is operated in Neutral at idle for a few minutes prior to putting the transmission in gear to provide lubrication to the clutches.

Install the wave plate into the clutch drum followed by an externally splined steel plate and an internally splined friction disc. Alternately install externally splined and internally splined plates until all of the plates are installed. Install the backing plate and drum snap ring.

Installing the 4-5-6 Clutch Pack

1 *The 4-5-6 clutch is equipped with six internally splined plates, six externally splined plates, one wave plate, one backing plate, and one selective snap ring.*

2 *Install the wave plate into the clutch drum. It is followed by an externally splined steel plate and then an internally splined friction disc.*

3 *Install the externally splined steel plate and then an internally splined friction disc.*

4 *Install the backing plate and drum snap ring.*

4-5-6 Selective Snap Ring Thickness		O.D. Color
1.60 to 1.70 mm	0.063 to 0.067 in	Yellow
2.02 to 2.12 mm	0.080 to 0.083 in	None
2.44 to 2.54 mm	0.096 to 0.100 in	Purple

Clutch Pack Travel

Three methods can be used to check clutch travel on a 6L80 clutch: the factory method, an aftermarket method using air pressure, and an aftermarket method using measuring tools.

Clutch pack travel is adjusted by changing the clutch pack selective snap ring.

Factory Method (4-5-6 Clutch)

The GM factory method requires the use of a weight tool that is placed on the assembled clutch pack. A dial indicator is used to measure the stroke of the clutch as it is applied with air pressure.

The GM counterweight tool number is DT 47868-1. Position the completed clutch drum with the clutch facing up on a workbench. Mount a dial indicator and position the plunger onto the counterweight tool. Zero the dial indicator. Apply 60 psi of air pressure to the input (turbine) shaft 4-5-6 clutch feed hole. Read the clutch travel measurement registering on the dial indicator. The clutch pack travel specification for the 4-5-6 clutch is 0.050 to 0.074 inch (1.28 to 1.89 mm). If the travel does not fall within the specification you will need to install a different selective snap ring.

Aftermarket Method Using Air Pressure (4-5-6 Clutch)

Position the completed clutch drum with the clutch facing up on a workbench. Mount a dial indicator and position the plunger onto the backing plate. Zero the dial indicator. Apply 60 psi of air pressure to the input (turbine) shaft 4-5-6 clutch feed hole. Read the clutch travel measurement registering on the dial indicator. The clutch pack travel specification for the 4-5-6 clutch is 0.060 to 0.084 inch (1.524 to 2.1336 mm).

Using the factory method, position the completed clutch drum with the clutch facing up on a workbench. Mount a dial indicator and position the plunger onto the counterweight tool. Zero the dial indicator. Apply 60 psi of air pressure to the input (turbine) shaft 4-5-6 clutch feed hole. Read the clutch travel measurement registering on the dial indicator. The clutch pack travel specification for the 4-5-6 clutch is 0.050 to 0.074 inch (1.28 to 1.89 mm). If the travel does not fall within the specification, install a different selective snap ring.

Using the aftermarket method, position the completed clutch drum with the clutch facing up on a workbench. Mount a dial indicator and position the plunger onto the backing plate. Zero the dial indicator. Apply 60 psi of air pressure to the input (turbine) shaft 4-5-6 clutch feed hole. Read the clutch travel measurement registering on the dial indicator. The clutch pack travel specification for the 4-5-6 clutch is 0.060 to 0.084 inch (1.524 to 2.1336 mm). If the travel does not fall within the specification, install a different selective snap ring.

If the travel does not fall within the specification, install a different selective snap ring.

Aftermarket Method Using Measuring Tools (4-5-6 Clutch)

A method that is still fairly effective but a little more crude to measure clutch clearance is to use a feeler gauge or some other form of tool to measure the distance between the backing plate and the top friction disc. The specification is 0.057 to 0.065 inch (1.4478 to 1.651 mm).

The aftermarket method for measuring clutch clearance that is little crude but still fairly effective is to use a feeler gauge or some other form of tool to measure the distance between the backing plate and the top friction disc. The specification is 0.057 to 0.065 inch (1.4478 to 1.651 mm).

Input Planetary Assembly

Set the 4-5-6 assembly with the ring gear and input (turbine) shaft facing up on your workbench. Install the input planetary Torrington bearing with the inside lip of the bearing race facing up. Install the plastic thrust washer onto the bottom of the input planetary carrier; retain it with Transjel. Install the input planetary carrier, meshing it with the ring gear. Install the input sun gear into the input planetary carrier assembly.

Set the completed 4-5-6 clutch assembly aside on your workbench for assembly at a later point.

Assembling the Input Planetary

1 ***Install the input planetary Torrington bearing with the inside lip of the bearing race facing up.***

2 ***Install the plastic thrust washer onto the bottom of the input planetary carrier, and retain it with Transjel.***

3 ***Install the input planetary carrier, meshing it with the ring gear.***

4 ***Install the input sun gear into the input planetary carrier assembly.***

Remove the 1-2-3-4 clutch hub (shell). Remove the 3-5-R/2-6 clutch hub (shell) and bearings. Make sure to keep all of the bearings properly positioned and oriented for direction, as this will save you time during reassembly. Clean the bearings and components.

Snap Ring Tension

Be careful removing the case snap ring because it has a lot of tension, and injury can occur. With the snap ring removed, grasp the center support with both hands and lift it straight up and out of the case. ■

Inspect the friction surface for evidence of wear and damage. Inspect the damper housing for signs of cracks. Inspect the hub bearing for wear and damage. Clean the damper assembly and parts. Reassemble the damper and reinstall the snap ring. Make sure that the snap ring is fully seated. Set the damper aside for transmission reassembly.

4-5-6 Damper, Center Support, Output Carrier, Output Shaft Removal, and Inspection

To remove the remaining transmission components, begin with the transmission output shaft facing down. Grasp the 4-5-6 clutch damper and remove it from the transmission. Make sure that you do not lose the damper Torrington bearing, which is located on the bottom side of the 4-5-6 damper/shaft assembly on top of the 1-2-3-4 clutch hub. Remove the 1-2-3-4 clutch hub (shell).

Remove the 2-6, 3-5-R clutch hub (shell) and bearings. The 2-6, 3-5-R clutch hub has Torrington bearings mounted on each side of the shell; do not lose them. Set all of the components on a clean cloth in the order in which they were removed. Inspect and clean all of the parts.

4-5-6 Damper Disassembly, Inspection, and Assembly

Stand the 4-5-6 clutch damper with the shaft facing up. Remove the damper snap ring and disassemble the damper. Inspect the friction surface for evidence of wear and damage. Inspect the damper housing for signs of cracks. Inspect the hub bearing for wear and damage.

Clean the damper assembly and parts. Reassemble the damper and reinstall the snap ring. Make sure that the snap ring is fully seated. Set the damper aside for transmission reassembly.

2-6 Center Support, Low/Reverse Clutch, and Low Sprag Removal

The 2-6 clutch, low/reverse clutch, and low sprag are housed in an assembly referred to as a center support. The center support assem-

The center support snap ring is shown along with giant snap-ring pliers.

Remove the center support snap ring.

Grasp the center support with both hands and lift it straight up and out of the case.

bly can be removed in conjunction with the output planetary gearsets and output shaft, as a single assembly, or by itself. Removing the support as a single unit is easier so that is the process I use here.

A giant tapered snap ring holds the center support assembly in the case. Giant snap-ring pliers are required to remove it from the case. GM snap-ring pliers J45126 or a good set of aftermarket giant snap-ring pliers, such as T6800AC from Adapt-A-Case tools, work well for this task.

Remove the case center support snap ring using a pair of giant snap-ring pliers.

2-6 Clutch Disassembly and Inspection

Remove the Torrington bearing from the hub/bushing area of the center support assembly. Remove the clutch snap ring and clutches from the support. The clutch pack consists of five internally splined plates, five externally splined plates, one wave plate, one apply plate, and one snap ring. The snap rings for the 3-5-R and 1-2-3-4 clutch packs have square-cut ends; the snap rings used for the low/reverse and 2-6 clutch packs have tapered ends.

Using the GM DT47761 clutch compressor tool (or an equivalent), compress the piston return spring. Compress the return spring far enough to remove the piston return spring snap ring. The piston return spring snap ring for the center support is mounted in the center support outer wall. If you do not have access to a clutch compression tool, the clutch can be disassembled with some assistance. Have an assistant place a large screwdriver on each side of the Belleville spring close to the snap ring. Have your assistant press down firmly on the screwdrivers while you pry out the snap ring with a small screwdriver and pick. Care must be taken if you are attempting to remove the snap ring in this manner.

With the piston return snap ring removed, remove the Belleville return spring and piston. You may need to use air pressure to help remove the piston. On the outside diameter of the center support housing are four round passages. With the housing sitting on your workbench and the piston facing up, blow air into the passage at the far left of the support to displace the 2-6 piston.

Inspect the bushings in the support for damage and position. The bushings sometimes walk out of the

Remove the Torrington bearing from the hub/bushing area of the center support assembly. Remove the clutch snap ring and clutches from the support.

Using GM tool DT47761 clutch compressor (or an equivalent tool), compress the piston return spring. Compress the return spring far enough to remove the piston return spring snap ring. If you do not have access to a compressor, you can pry the snap ring out of the support using a few screwdrivers. The piston return spring snap ring for the center support is mounted in the center support outer wall.

If needed, blowing air into the support feed passage will allow you to remove the piston.

housing. If the bushing is sticking out of the housing, replace the bushing or housing.

Lay all of the components on a clean cloth in the order in which they were removed.

Low/Reverse Clutch, Low Sprag Disassembly, and Inspection

Rotate the support so that the 2-6 clutch area is facing the workbench. The low/reverse clutch and low sprag will now be facing you so that they can be removed. Remove the clutch pack snap ring and remove the clutches from the center support assembly. The low/reverse clutch consists of five internally splined plates, five externally splined plates, one wave plate, one apply plate, and one snap ring. The clutch piston snap ring is mounted on top of the low sprag clutch. Using the GM 47779 tool (or an equivalent), compress the return spring and remove the low sprag snap ring from the hub of the center support.

With the center support hub snap ring removed, lift the low sprag from the center support and be sure to note which side of the sprag assembly is facing up. You may want to mark the top of the sprag to aid in reassembly. Remove the Belleville piston return spring, sprag O-ring, and piston from the center support housing.

Remove the low/reverse clutch pack snap ring and remove the clutches from the center support assembly. The clutch piston snap ring is mounted on top of the low sprag clutch. Using GM tool 47779 (or an equivalent), compress the return spring and remove the low sprag snap ring from the hub of the center support.

Compress the Sprag Inner Race

When compressing the low sprag, care must be taken not to damage the sprag spacer and thrust washer. The compressor should be pushing on the sprag inner race. ■

Remove the Belleville piston return spring, sprag O-ring, and low/reverse piston from the center support housing.

The center support has a series of lugs on its outside diameter. Lug damage is common, so inspect each lug carefully. Inspect the hub splines and internal splines for damage and wear. Replace the support if it is damaged or excessively worn.

You may need to use air pressure to help remove the piston. On the outside diameter of the center support housing are four round passages. With the housing sitting on your workbench and the piston facing down, blow air into the passage second from the left on the support to displace the low/reverse piston.

The low/reverse piston is a molded design and is typically not replaced if it is not damaged. Most kits do not include the molded pistons unless you order a kit that includes pistons.

Lay all the parts on a clean cloth in the order in which they were removed. Clean and inspect the center support for damage. The center support has a series of lugs on its outside diameter. Lug damage is common, so inspect each lug carefully. Inspect the hub splines and internal splines for damage and wear. Replace the support if it is damaged or excessively worn. Inspect the low/reverse piston seal for damage and replace as necessary.

Low Sprag Inspection and Sprag Assembly

The low sprag is used for first gear on the 6L80. If the sprag has failed, the symptom may be that the vehicle will launch in first gear, but as soon as it gets to approximately 2 to 3 mph, the transmission may drop to neutral. This is due to the low/reverse clutch being applied for launch but releasing as the vehicle starts to move. On some applications, the transmission may fail to move forward in the overdrive range but will move forward in manual ranges. Depending on the TCM software loaded, either may be a failure mode that is due to a faulty sprag.

A sprag element can be put into its races upside down or the complete assembly can be installed upside down on the hub. The sprag would then fail to lock in low gear but will lock in second gear when it was designed to freewheel, which will create a tie-up–related issue. To make your life easier, it just makes sense to keep the components oriented correctly so that you do not have to worry so much about reassembly of the sprag components.

To inspect the sprag, remove the inner sprag race. Lay the sprag on a clean cloth with the unit oriented as it was when splined to the center support hub. Remove the snap ring from one side of the outer race.

Clean and inspect the sprag, sprag races, and thrust washers for wear and damage. Inspect the inner and outer races for washboarding and roughness. There should be no discoloration on the inside diameter of the outer race or outside diameter of the inner race machined surfaces. Bluing or discoloration on the outside diameters of the races is normal and is due to the factory heat-treating process. Inspect each sprag element for wear or damage. If the sprag element is damaged or worn, it is available separate from the races through aftermarket parts suppliers. If a race is damaged or worn, the complete sprag assembly will need to be purchased.

If the sprag components are in good condition, reassemble the sprag in the order and with the parts oriented as they were prior to

Remove Snap Ring only from the Top Side

Do not remove both outer race snap rings; only remove the snap ring from the top side. Pull the sprag element and hardware from the outer race. Keep the sprag element, races, and thrust washers orientated in the same direction and position as they were removed when you clean and inspect the sprag. The same holds true with the inner and outer sprag races and other components. ■

Position the sprag assembly with the inner race groove facing up. Remove the snap ring retaining the sprag using a small screwdriver or pick. The sprag element and inner race can now be separated from the outer race.

disassembly. Lubricate all of the components with transmission fluid.

If the sprag components were somehow mixed up, lay the outer race on a workbench in the direction in which it was removed from the center support hub. Install the spacer, the thrust washer, and then the sprag element into the outer race. The sprag element is installed into the outer race with notches in the sprag cage facing up. Install the inner race by rotating it as you apply light downward pressure. Install the thrust washer, spacer, and snap ring into the outer race.

To test the sprag for an error during the rebuild, install it onto the center support hub splines with it oriented as it was previously assembled. Rotate the outer race. It should freewheel when rotated in the counterclockwise direction and lock when rotated clockwise. If does not rotate correctly, it is likely that it was not properly assembled and you will need to disassemble it and flip over the sprag element. Check for correct operation. Once it has been checked for proper assembly, remove the completed sprag assembly and set it aside so that the low/reverse clutch components can be installed.

Keep the sprag element, races, and thrust washers orientated in the same direction and position as they were when they were removed as you clean and inspect the sprag.

Clean and inspect the sprag, sprag races, and thrust washers for wear and damage. Inspect the inner and outer races for washboarding and roughness. There should be no discoloration on the inside diameter of the outer race or outside diameter of the inner race machined surfaces. Bluing or discoloration on the outside diameters of the races is normal; it is due to the factory heat-treating process. Inspect each sprag element for wear or damage. The sprag shown is worn and needs to be replaced.

Again, make sure to keep the sprag element, races, and thrust washers orientated in the same direction and position during sprag inspection. The sprag element is installed into the outer race with notches in the sprag cage facing up.

If the sprag components were somehow mixed up, lay the outer race on a workbench in the direction in which it was removed from the center support hub. Install the spacer, the thrust washer, and then the sprag element into the outer race. The sprag element is installed into the outer race with notches in the sprag cage facing up. Install the inner race by rotating it as you apply light downward pressure. Install the thrust washer, spacer, and snap ring into the outer race.

The outer race should freewheel when rotated in the counter-clockwise direction and lock when rotated clockwise.

Low/Reverse Clutch and Low Sprag Assembly into the Center Support

The low/reverse clutch piston and components are assembled prior to installing the sprag. Once the piston components and sprag have been installed, the low/reverse clutches can be installed.

To assemble the low/reverse clutch, lubricate the center support housing seal contact surfaces with transmission fluid. Lubricate the low/reverse piston with transmission fluid, Transjel, or Vaseline and install the piston into the center support. Install the sprag O-ring into the groove in the center support hub. GM has a seal protector tool for this operation, DT47780, or an equivalent tool can be used. If you do not have access to the tool, wrap the hub splines and snap-ring groove with black electrical tape. Coat the tape with transmission fluid. Roll the seal into position in the bottom groove.

Install the Belleville piston return spring with the inside tangs up. Install the sprag onto the center support hub.

The sprag and the center support are equipped with blank splines. These splines must be aligned with each other when the sprag is being installed. Failure to properly align the splines can result in lubrication failure.

Rotate the outer sprag race; it should freewheel when rotated counterclockwise and lock when rotated clockwise. Using the GM 47779 tool (or an equivalent), compress the return spring and install the low sprag snap ring onto the hub of the center support. The end of the snap ring must align with the blind sprag splines in the center support.

When compressing the low sprag, care must be taken to not damage the sprag spacer and thrust washer. The compressor should be applying force to the inner race.

Once the sprag has been installed the clutch plates can be installed. The low/reverse clutch is equipped with five internally splined plates, five externally splined plates, one wave plate, one backing plate, and one selective snap ring.

If replacing the clutches, some technicians choose to soak them in Dexron VI transmission fluid prior to installing them in the clutch drum; others install clutch discs dry. If you choose to install them dry, make sure that when the vehicle is first started after the overhaul, it is

Low/Reverse Selective Snap Ring Thickness		O.D. Color
1.85 to 1.95 mm	0.073 to 0.077 in	Yellow
2.26 to 2.36 mm	0.089 to 0.093 in	None
2.67 to 2.77 mm	0.105 to 0.109 in	Purple

operated in Neutral at idle for a few minutes prior to putting the transmission in gear to provide lubrication to the clutches.

Install the wave plate into the clutch drum, which is followed by an externally splined steel plate and an internally splined friction disc. Alternately install externally splined and internally splined plates until all the plates are installed. Install the backing plate and drum snap ring.

Assembling the Low/Reverse Clutch and Low Sprag into the Center Support

1 *Low/reverse clutch piston and components are assembled prior to installing the sprag. Lubricate the low/reverse piston with transmission fluid, Transjel, or Vaseline and install the piston into the center support.*

2 *Install the sprag O-ring into the groove in the center support hub. Install the Belleville piston return spring with the inside tangs facing up.*

3 *The blank splines on the sprag and the center support must be aligned with each other when the sprag is being installed. Failure to properly align the splines can result in lubrication failure.*

4 *The sprag is installed on the hub splines.*

5 *When compressing the low sprag, care must be taken not to damage the sprag spacer and thrust washer. The compressor should be applying force to the inner race. With the unit compressed, install the snap ring onto the hub groove.*

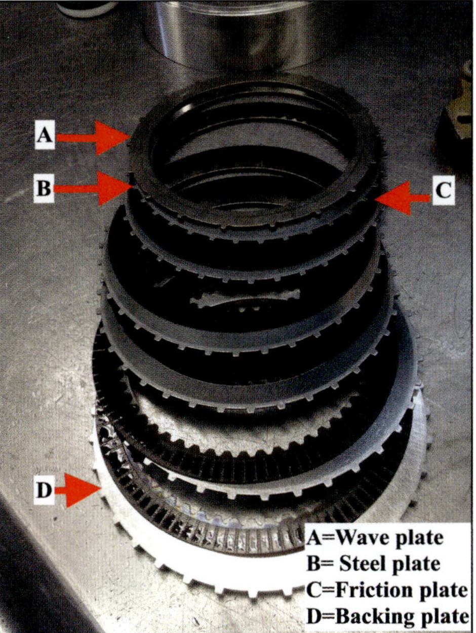

6 *The low/reverse clutch is equipped with five internally splined plates, five externally splined plates, one wave plate, one backing plate, and one selective snap ring.*

7 *Install the wave plate into the clutch drum followed by an externally splined steel plate and the internally splined friction disc. Alternately install externally splined and internally splined plates until all the plates are installed. Install the backing plate and drum snap ring. Install the Torrington bearings on each side of the support. The bearing on the L/R clutch side of the support is installed with the outside-diameter race facing the housing and the inner-diameter race facing away from the housing. Secure the bearing with Transjel.*

8 *Install the wave plate into the clutch drum followed by an externally splined steel plate and an internally splined friction disc.*

9 *Alternately install externally splined and internally splined plates until all the plates are installed.*

10 ***Install the backing plate and drum snap ring.***

A Common Error

Flipping the Belleville 2-6 clutch upside down is a common error during the rebuilding process and may lead to 1-2 shift feel–related complaints. ■

Clutch Pack Travel

Measuring clutch pack travel is important. If the clutch-to-clutch clearance is too great, you may run out of piston travel as the clutch applies lead to flaring on a shift all the way to a slipping clutch issue. If the clearance is too tight, the clutch pack may drag when it is in the released position, leading to clutch damage and shift tie-up concerns.

Two methods can be used to check Low-Reverse clutch travel on a 6L80 clutch: the factory method and an aftermarket method using measuring tools.

Clutch pack travel is adjusted by changing the clutch pack selective snap ring.

Factory Method (6L80 Clutch)

With the GM factory method, a dial indicator is used to measure the stroke of the clutch as it is applied with air pressure.

Position the completed clutch drum with the clutch facing up on a workbench. Install the GM counterweight tools: DT 47868-1 and DT47868-4 adapter. Mount a dial indicator and position the plunger onto the counterweight tool. Zero the dial indicator. Apply 60 psi of air pressure to the center support clutch feed hole. Read the clutch travel measurement registering on the dial indicator. The clutch pack travel specification for the low/reverse clutch is 0.051 to 0.081 inch (1.30 to

For the factory method, mount the tip of a dial indicator onto the counterweight tool, zero the dial on the indicator, and apply 60 psi of air pressure to the center support feed hole. The clutch travel will register on the indicator face. The travel specification for the low/reverse clutch pack is 0.051 to 0.081 inch (1.30 to 2.07 mm). If the travel does not fall within the specification you will need to install a different selective snap ring.

For the aftermarket method, use a wire-type feeler gauge to measure the clearance between the snap ring and the apply plate. The specification is 0.057 to 0.065 inch (1.4478 to 1.651 mm).

2.07 mm). If the travel does not fall within the specification, install a different selective snap ring.

Aftermarket Method Using Measuring Tools (6L80 Clutch)

Position the completed drum on the workbench with the clutch facing up. Using a wire-type feeler gauge, measure the clearance between the snap ring and the apply plate. The specification is 0.057 to 0.065 inch (1.4478 to 1.651 mm).

2-6 Clutch Assembly

Rotate the center support so the side that houses the 2-6 clutch is facing up. Lubricate and install the 2-6 clutch piston. Install the Belleville return spring with the center tangs facing down toward the center support.

The clutch pack consists of five internally splined plates, five externally splined plates, one wave plate, one apply plate, and one snap ring. Using the GM DT47761 clutch compressor tool (or an equivalent), compress the piston return spring. Compress the return spring far enough to install the piston return spring snap ring. The piston return spring snap ring for the 2-6 clutch is mounted in the center support outer wall. Install the 2-6 piston snap ring. The snap ring has a triangle shape.

If you do not have access to a clutch compression tool, the clutch piston can be assembled with some assistance. Have an assistant place a large screwdriver on each side of the snap ring. Have your assistant press down firmly on the screwdrivers while you pry the snap ring into the groove with a small screwdriver and pick. Care must be taken if you are attempting to install the snap ring in this manner.

If you replace the clutches, some technicians choose to soak them in Dexron VI transmission fluid prior to installing them in the clutch drum; others install clutch discs dry. If you choose to install them dry, make sure that when the vehicle is first started after the overhaul, it is operated in neutral at idle for a few minutes prior to putting the transmission in gear to provide lubrication to the clutches.

Install the wave plate into the clutch drum followed by an externally splined steel plate and an internally splined friction disc. Alternately install externally splined and internally splined plates until all the plates are installed. Install the backing plate and drum snap ring.

The snap rings for the 3-5-R and 1-2-3-4 clutch packs have square-cut ends; the snap rings used for the low/reverse and 2-6 clutch packs have tapered ends. Install the clutch pack snap ring with the end opening located 90 degrees from the clutch feed holes in the outside diameter of the center support. This means that with the support properly positioned in the transmission case, the end of the snap ring is at a 9 o-clock or 3 o-clock position.

Install the Torrington bearing #65 on the support. The bearing on the 2-6 clutch side of the support is installed with the outer race facing away from the housing; the inner bearing race is next to the housing. Secure the bearings with Transjel.

The 2-6 clutch does not have a factory method for adjusting clutch pack travel. The selective snap rings available for the 3-5-R clutch will work in the 2-6 clutch, which allows you to adjust the clutch pack travel. The 1-2 shift is the most difficult shift for the adapts to address, so adjusting the clutch pack travel has a major impact on how effective the adaptive strategies are in correcting shift-related issues.

Once the clutch pack travel has been checked, the center support can be set aside on the workbench for later assembly into the transmission.

Reassembling the 2-6 Clutch

1 *Lubricate and install the 2-6 clutch piston.*

2 *Install the Belleville return spring with the center tangs facing down toward the center support.*

3 *Compress the return spring far enough to install the piston return spring snap ring. If you do not have a compression tool, use a two screwdrivers to compress the spring, and with assistance, pry the snap ring into the groove. The piston snap ring has a triangular shape.*

4 *The clutch pack consists of five internally splined plates, five externally splined plates, one wave plate, one apply plate, and one snap ring.*

5 *Install the wave plate into the center support followed by an externally splined steel plate and an internally splined friction disc. Alternately install externally splined and internally splined plates until all the plates are installed.*

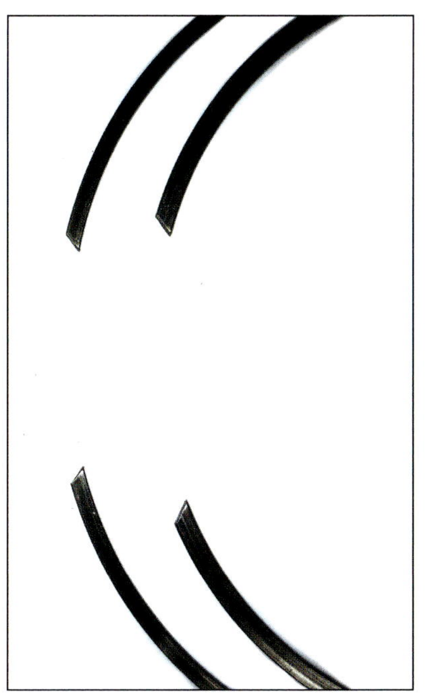

6 *The 2-6/L-R snap rings have tapered ends.*

7 *Install the snap ring in the 2-6 drum.*

8 *With the support properly positioned in the transmission case, the end of the snap ring is at the 9 o-clock or 3 o-clock position.*

9 *The bearing on the 2-6 clutch side of the support is installed with the outside-diameter race facing away from the housing; the inside-diameter bearing race is next to the housing. Secure the bearing with Transjel.*

Clutch Pack Travel

Measuring clutch pack travel is important. If the clutch-to-clutch clearance is too great, you may run out of piston travel as the clutch applies lead to flaring on a shift all the way to a slipping clutch issue. If the clearance is too tight the clutch pack may drag when it is in the released position, leading to clutch damage and shift tie-up concerns.

Two aftermarket methods can be used to check 2-6 clutch travel on a 6L80 clutch: a dial indicator and a feeler gauge. The 2-6 clutch does not have a factory method for adjusting clutch pack travel. The selective snap rings available for the 3-5-R clutch will work in the 2-6 clutch, which allows you to adjust the clutch pack travel.

Aftermarket Method Using a Dial Indicator (2-6 Clutch)

Mount a dial indicator making contact with clutch backing plate. Zero the dial indicator. Apply 60 psi of air pressure to the 2-6 clutch feed hole located in the center support. Read the value displayed on the meter to determine the clutch travel reading.

Using a feeler gauge, measure the clearance between the friction disc and the apply plate. The specification is 0.057 to 0.065 inch (1.4478 to 1.651 mm).

Aftermarket Method Using a Feeler Gauge (2-6 Clutch)

Position the completed drum on the workbench with the clutch facing up. Using a feeler gauge, measure the clearance between the friction disc and the apply plate. The specification is 0.057 to 0.065 inch (1.4478 to 1.651 mm).

The 2-6 clutch does not have a factory method for adjusting clutch pack travel. The selective snap rings available for the 3-5-R clutch will work in the 2-6 clutch, which will allow you to adjust the clutch pack travel. Mount a dial indicator making contact with clutch backing plate. Zero the dial indicator. Apply 60 psi of air pressure to the 2-6 clutch feed hole located in the center support.

Heavy Components

The output planetary components are quite heavy, so care must be taken. ■

Output Carrier and Output Shaft Removal and Inspection

The output planetaries and output shaft can be removed individually from the case, but it is much easier to pull the complete assembly from the case if you have access to a planetary removal tool for the 6L transmission. Using the GM DT 47786 lifting tool (or an equivalent), screw the tool into the planetary threaded hole in the center of the planetary. You can build you own tool by using a long metric bolt with the correct thread pitch and size. Weld a T-handle onto the bolt or bend the top of the bolt over at a 90-degree angle to provide a location to hold. Lift the complete planetary/output shaft assembly from the case and place it on a clean cloth on a workbench. The output shaft Torrington bearing is located in the bottom of the case.

Output Planetary Design Changes

Two types of output planetary designs are used in 6L80 applications: unigear and non-unigear. The update in gear design was implemented to reduce the amount of labor required at the assembly plant by combining some of the planetary components into one piece, known as a unigear. The update started to be implemented in mid-2012, but the update was not fully implemented across all vehicle lines and transmission models until late 2014. This means that between 2012 and late 2014 you may see either version of the planetary used.

Speed Sensor Design Changes

As a complete gearset, they are interchangeable, but the individual components are not interchangeable between a unigear and non-unigear design. In addition, the output speed sensor designs are also not interchangeable between a transmission equipped with a unigear and one equipped with a non-unigear planetary. If you try to interchange the two sensor designs, sensor failure and DTCs will result.

Make certain that you order the correct output speed sensor for your application and be sure to closely compare the new sensor to the old sensor before installing it onto the valve body. Once the planetary is on the bench, it can be disassembled and inspected by removing the snap ring on the top of the planetary.

The non-unigear planetary has a lot more parts compared to the unigear design. The unigear design is pretty straightforward, but the non-unigear can be a little confusing when attempting to service it. I am going to focus on the non-unigear design in this book, as it is much more of a challenge.

Non-Unigear Design Service

The non-unigear planetary consists of four Torrington bearings, one needle bearing, two snap rings, one planetary carrier, two sun gears, two ring gear/internal gears, one ring gear spacer, and one output shaft assembly. The needle bearing is the center support bearing, and GM recommends that it be replaced. To replace the needle bearing, use a slide hammer with a blind-hole puller. Also, a seal puller may work. Most quality kits include the new bearing. To install the new bearing, use GM bearing driver DT 47857 (or an equivalent). The side of the bearing race that is thickest faces up toward the front of the transmission.

One bearing is located on top of the planetary front sun gear, one is located between the sun gears, one is located under the planetary carrier between the lower sun gear and the output shaft, and one bearing is located between the output shaft and the transmission case. Both sun gears are directional. Each sun gear should be placed into the carrier with the inside champers facing up toward the front of the transmission.

One snap ring is located on the top of the planetary carrier and is used to hold the planetary carrier into the proper position with the output shaft. The other snap ring is used to hold the lower ring/internal gear and spacer in proper position with the output shaft.

If you are going to disassemble the planetary, make certain that you lay the parts on a clean cloth that is oriented in the same direction and position in which they were removed. Disassemble the planetary by removing the ring gear/carrier snap ring. Remove the planetary carrier. Remove the upper ring gear, making sure to lay it on your bench in the same direction it was removed. Remove the lower snap ring, ring gear spacer, and snap ring, making sure that the ring gear is placed on your bench as it was oriented when you took it out. Remove the sun gears and bearings.

Non-Unigear Bearing Positions

Inspect the bearings, bushings, gear teeth, gear splines, and planetary for damage. Clean and lubricate all the parts with transmission fluid. To assemble the planetary, install Torrington bearing #69, which sits between the planetary and output shaft, first with the inner race of the bearing with the large inner lip facing the output shaft. Torrington bearing #491 fits between the output carrier and the rear sun gear. It is installed with the large flat side facing front of the transmission and is not serviceable. If bearing #491 is damaged, the output carrier must be replaced.

The next Torrington bearing is #488, which fits between the top of the rear sun gear and the bottom of the front sun gear. It has a large lip on its inside-diameter race, which faces to the rear of the transmission and rear sun gear. Finally, Torrington bearing #486 fits on top of the front sun gear in the output carrier. It is positioned with the large outside-diameter lip facing the rear of the transmission and front sun gear.

When the planetary is complete, there should be four Torrington bearings and one needle bearing used. #491 goes below the rear sun gear and is not serviceable, #488 fits between the two sun gears, and #486 fits on top of the front sun gear. The other bearing used is #69, which fits between the output carrier and the output shaft. The needle bearing is pressed into the front of the output carrier and is sometimes replaced as part of your service as it is included in many kits.

Non-Unigear

Install the rear ring gear, spacer, snap ring, front ring gear, and the Torrington bearings in their proper locations and orientation. The rear ring gear is installed into the output shaft housing with the outside chamfer facing the output shaft. Then, the spacer, snap ring, and front ring gear with the flat side facing down are installed. Install

Twisted splines or cracked shaft issues can occur, especially in performance applications.

Bearing failures are not common, but they do occur. Generally, this is due to a lack of lubrication. If bearing damage is found, locate the cause; otherwise, the failure is likely to repeat itself.

To assemble the planetary, install Torrington bearing #69, which sits between the planetary and output shaft. Install the bearing with the inside-diameter race facing up and the outside-diameter race facing the output shaft.

Disassemble the planetary and inspect the components. Clean and then lubricate the components. Reassemble the lower ring, spacer, and snap ring. The lower ring gear chamfer faces the output shaft. The upper ring gear flat side faces the output shaft.

Assemble the ring gear and carrier and install the snap ring. Two methods can be used: 1) Assemble the ring gear onto the planetary and install the two components at one time into the output shaft and rear ring assembly. 2) Install the front ring gear and install the snap ring. Install the carrier. Unigear ring gears are part of the output shaft assembly. Simply install the planetary into the output/ring gears while rotating the planetary to align the teeth.

Rotate the gearset until it is assembled and install the upper ring gear snap ring.

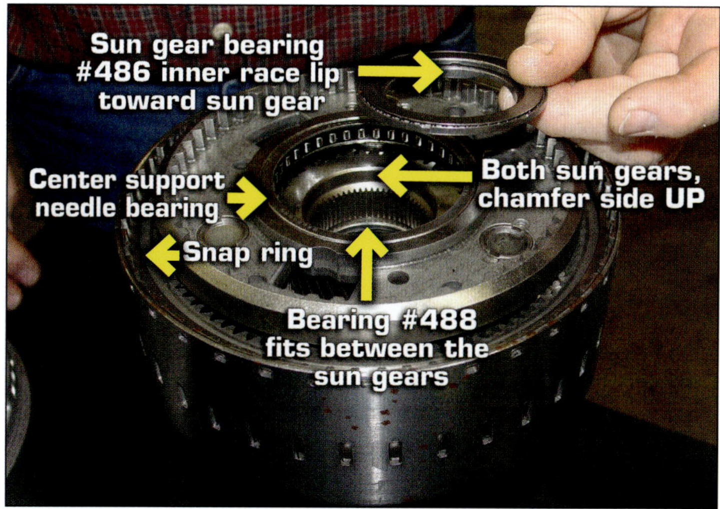

The carrier snap ring, front sun bearing #486, and sun gear direction are shown.

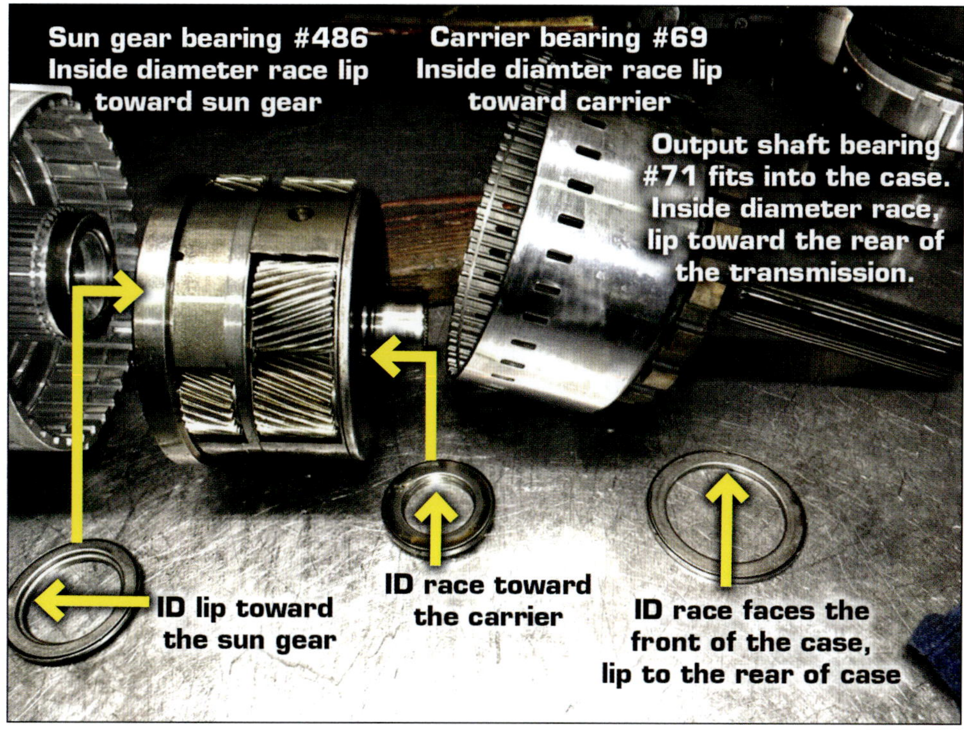

The installation direction is shown for bearings #486, #69, and #71. Be careful that the bearings are installed in their correct positions and directions. Laying out the bearings and components on the workbench in the exact position and order in which they were removed reduces the chance of making a mistake.

Two types of output planetary designs are used in 6L80 applications: unigear and non-unigear.

the planetary into the output shaft assembly and retain it with its snap ring. Install the sun gears and bearings. The sun gears are placed into the carrier with their champers facing up toward the front of the vehicle. Make sure that the front sun gear bearing #486 and the case bearing #71 are installed. Set the completed planetary on your bench for later assembly into the case.

Case Inspection, Service, and Output Seal Replacement

Clean the case. Inspect the internal case lugs for damage. Inspect the case for cracks and damage. Clean and inspect all of the threaded holes. On four-wheel-drive and all-wheel-drive applications, the output shaft

Inspect the internal case lugs for damage. Inspect the case for cracks and damage. Clean and inspect all the threaded holes.

seal is located in the rear of the transmission case. Remove the old seal with a seal puller. Clean the bore and install the new seal with the GM seal driver DT 38693 tool (or an equivalent). Lubricate the seal surface with Transjel or automatic transmission fluid.

Component Service Assembly

At this point, individual component assembly is complete. The individual components can now be assembled into the case as part of the transmission reassembly process. Two methods can be used to assemble the center support, output carrier, and output shaft into the transmission case: the factory method and aftermarket method. The method you choose depends on your preference as well as if you have access to a component lifting tool.

Factory Method

Install output shaft Torrington bearing #71 into the case with the side attached to the inner race, facing the front of the transmission case. At this point, the planetaries should be fully assembled and sitting on your bench.

Using a GM DT 47786 lifting tool (or an equivalent), screw the tool into the planetary threaded hole in the center of the planetary. You can build you own tool by using a long metric bolt with the correct thread pitch and size. Weld a T-handle onto the bolt or bend the top of the bolt over at a 90-degree angle to provide a location to hold. Double-check that you have no extra Torrington bearings on your bench that belong in the planetary assembly. Lift the completed assembly and install it into the case. Rotate the output shaft to make sure that the planetary is fully installed.

The front sun gear has a Torrington bearing #486, which should have been previously installed on the sun gear and properly oriented. Check to make sure it is installed correctly. Install the completed center support into the case while making sure the four holes in the support are aligned with the four holes in the valve body area of the case.

Center Support Snap Ring

A giant snap ring holds the center support assembly in the case. Giant snap-ring pliers are required to remove it from the case. GM snap-ring pliers J45126 or a good set of aftermarket giant snap-ring pliers, such as T6800AC from Adapt-A-Case, work well for this task.

The tapered center support snap ring is installed into the case with the flat side of the snap ring facing the rear of the case. The snap ring opening should be located at the 9 o-clock position in relation to the bottom of the transmission when it is installed. Install the case center support snap ring using a pair of giant snap-ring pliers. Fully seat the snap ring into the case.

Be careful when installing the case snap ring because it has a lot of tension and injury can occur.

Install the 2-6/3-5-R clutch hub/shell #65 bearing onto the center support with the race side equipped with a lip. The bearing race with the lip should face the center support previously installed.

Aftermarket Method

The aftermarket method is a little more time-consuming process compared to the factory process. This process can be used if you do not have access to the factory special tools.

Installing Bearing #71

If you do not have access to planetary loading tools, the components can be loaded into the case individually. Install the output shaft Torrington bearing #71 into the case with the side attached to the inner race, facing the front of the transmission case.

Installing Planetary Components

Install the output shaft/ring gear assembly into the case. Install bearing #69 with the inside race facing the carrier. Install the carrier and rotate the carrier so that the pinion teeth mesh with the ring gear teeth. Install bearing #486 onto the sun gear with the inside diameter lip/race facing the sun gear.

Installing the Center Support and Snap Ring

Install the completed center support into the case while making sure that the four holes in the support are aligned with the four holes in the valve body area of the case.

A giant snap ring holds the center support assembly in the case. Giant snap-ring pliers are required to remove it from the case. GM snap-ring pliers J45126 or a good set of aftermarket giant snap-ring pliers, such as T6800AC from Adapt-A-Case, work well for this task.

The tapered center support snap ring is installed into the case with the flat side of the snap ring facing the rear of the case. The snap ring opening should be located at the 9 o-clock

The factory method installs the planetary and output shaft as an assembly. Using GM DT 47786 lifting tool (or an equivalent), screw the tool into the planetary threaded hole in the center of the planetary. Lift the completed assembly and install it into the case. Rotate the output shaft to make sure that the planetary is fully installed.

If you do not have access to planetary loading tools, the components can be loaded into the case individually, using the aftermarket method. Install the output shaft Torrington bearing #71 into the case with the side attached to the inner diameter race, facing the front of the transmission case. Install the output shaft/ring gear assembly into the case. Install bearing #69 with the inside race facing the carrier.

Install the output shaft Torrington bearing #71 into the case with the side attached to the inner race, facing the front of the transmission case.

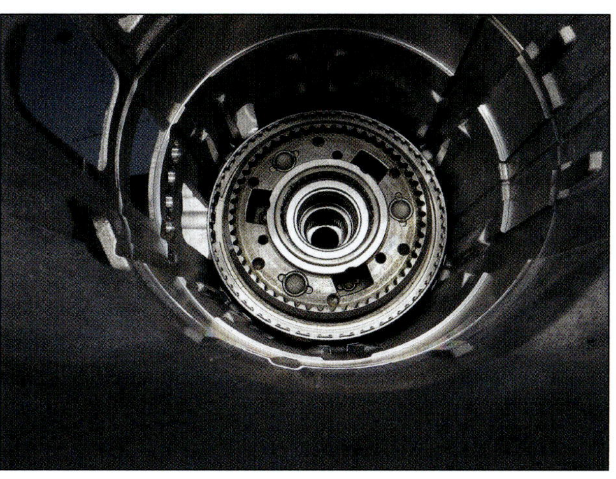

Install the carrier and rotate the carrier so that the pinion teeth mesh with the ring gear teeth. Install bearing #486 onto the sun gear with the inside-diameter lip facing the sun gear.

Install the completed center support into the case while making sure the four holes in the support are aligned with the four holes in the valve body area of the case. You may need to rotate the output shaft to get the support to fully drop into position. The tapered-center support snap ring is installed into the case with the flat side of the snap ring facing the rear of the case. The snap-ring opening should be located at the 9 o-clock position in relation to the bottom of the transmission when it is installed. Install the case center support snap ring using a pair of giant snap-ring pliers. Fully seat the snap ring into the case.

position in relation to the bottom of the transmission when it is installed. Install the case center support snap ring using a pair of giant snap-ring pliers. Fully seat the snap ring into the case.

Install the 2-6/3-5-R clutch hub/ shell #65 bearing onto the center support with the inner-diameter race side toward the support. The bearing inside-diameter race should ride on the center support that was previously installed.

Be careful when installing the case snap ring because it has a lot of tension and injury can occur.

Installing Bearing #65

Install the 2-6/3-5-R clutch hub/ shell #65 bearing onto the center support with the inner race side facing the support. The bearing ID race should ride on the center support previously installed.

2-6/3-5-R Clutch Hub/Shell, 1-2-3-4 Clutch Hub/Shell, 4-5-6 Clutch, and Input Planetary Installation

Several components are installed individually as we start to assemble the upper portion of the transmission. These include the 2-6/3-5-R clutch hub, the 1-2-3-4 clutch hub, the 4-5-6 clutch and input shaft assembly, and the input planetary assembly. Make sure that all of the appropriate bearings are installed in their correct locations as the components are assembled.

Hub/Shell Installation (2-6/3-5-R Clutch)

Install the large 2-6/3-5R clutch hub/shell into the planetary gearset, and rotate the clutch hub to align the clutch hub splines with the planetary gear splines. The hub should drop down and ride against the center support Torrington bearing #65 that you previously installed. With the clutch hub installed, install the 1-2-3-4 shaft/hub bearing #63 onto the 2-6/3-5-R clutch hub with the side of the bearing equipped with the inner lip facing the 2-6/3-5-R clutch hub.

Hub/Shell Installation (1-2-3-4 Clutch)

Install the 1-2-3-4 clutch hub/ shell, rotating it to make sure that it is fully engaged in the planetary splines. The 1-2-3-4 hub shell is slightly smaller than the shell that you previously installed, and it has round holes cut into it. Install the 1-2-3-4 clutch hub/shaft Torrington bearing #59 onto the 1-2-3-4 shell with the side equipped with the large inner lip facing the 1-2-3-4 shell/hub and the open side of the bearing facing up.

Clutch Damper Installation

Install the previously completed 4-5-6 clutch damper with the shaft engaging the planetaries and clutch hubs/shells. Rotate the 4-5-6 damper until it engages with the splines and the damper assembly sits down against the previously installed bearing #59 on the 1-2-3-4 clutch hub/ shell. Install the input (turbine) shaft Torrington bearing #57 onto the snout of the 4-5-6 clutch damper. The bearing should be installed with the outside tangs facing up on the snout of the 4-5-6 damper.

4-5-6 Clutch Drum, Input Shaft, and Front Planetary Installation

Install the previously completed 4-5-6 clutch drum and front planetary assembly. The 4-5-6 clutch drum has the input (turbine) shaft and front planetary ring gear attached to the drum. Install the assembly with the input (turbine) shaft facing up. Rotate the shaft until all of the clutches are aligned and the shaft/drum assembly drops fully in place in the transmission. Typically, you will need to do a lot of rotating in both directions and wiggling to get the clutches to properly align.

If the front planetary was not previously installed when you assembled the 4-5-6 drum, install the input sun gear Torrington bearing #54 over the input (turbine) shaft and down onto the drum. The inner-race lip of the bearing mounts to a lip on the shaft/drum. The bearing is installed with the inner race lip facing up. This allows the bearing to rotate while the bearing inner race is held by the shaft lip.

Install the input planetary carrier. Make sure that the carrier thrust washer you previously mounted to

Install the large 2-6/3-5-R clutch hub/shell into the planetary gearset and rotate the clutch hub to align the clutch hub splines with the planetary gear splines. The hub drops down and rides against the center support Torrington bearing #65 that was previously installed. Install the 1-2-3-4 shaft/hub bearing #63 onto the 2-6/3-5-R clutch hub with the outside-diameter race next to the 2-6/3-5-R clutch hub.

Install the 1-2-3-4 clutch hub/shell, rotating it to make sure that it is fully engaged in the planetary splines. Install the 1-2-3-4 clutch hub/shaft Torrington bearing #59 onto the 1-2-3-4 shell with the open side of the bearing facing up.

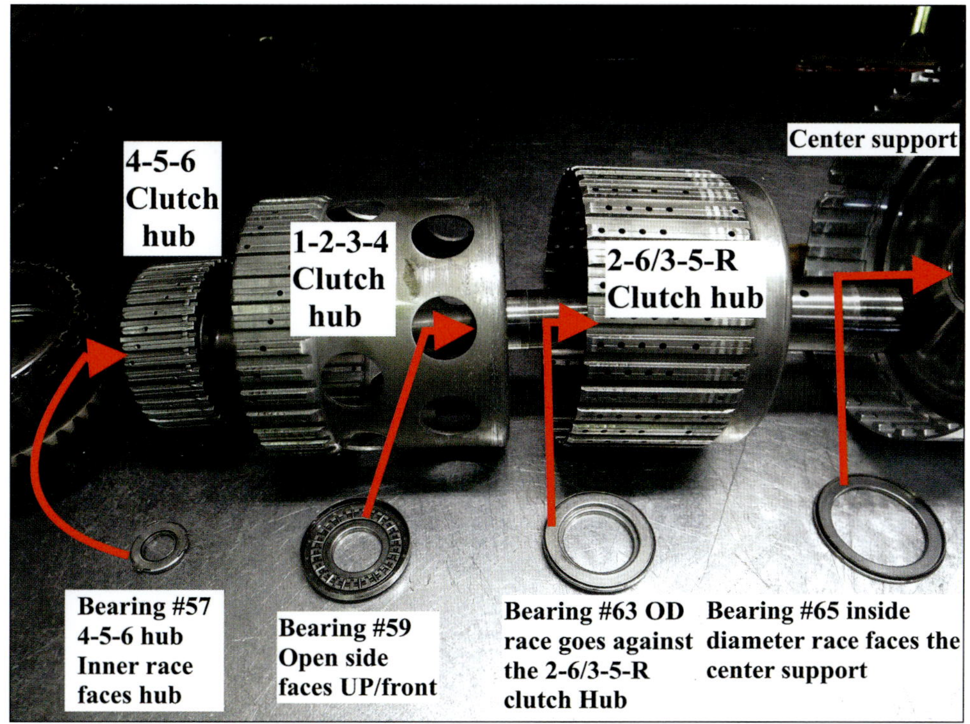

Here's the clutch hub installation and bearing layout.

Install the previously completed 4-5-6 clutch damper with the shaft engaging the planetaries and clutch hubs/shells.

Install the turbine shaft Torrington bearing #57 onto the snout of the 4-5-6 clutch damper. The bearing should be installed with the outside tangs facing up on the snout of the 4-5-6 damper.

If the front planetary was not previously installed when you assembled the 4-5-6 drum, install the input sun gear Torrington bearing #54 over the input (turbine) shaft and down onto the drum. The inner side diameter race of the bearing mounts to a lip on the shaft/drum. The bearing is installed with the inner-diameter lip facing up and the inside-diameter race next to the housing.

Two methods can be used when installing the 4-5-6 drum: installing the parts individually (the factory method) and installing all the components as an assembly (the aftermarket method).

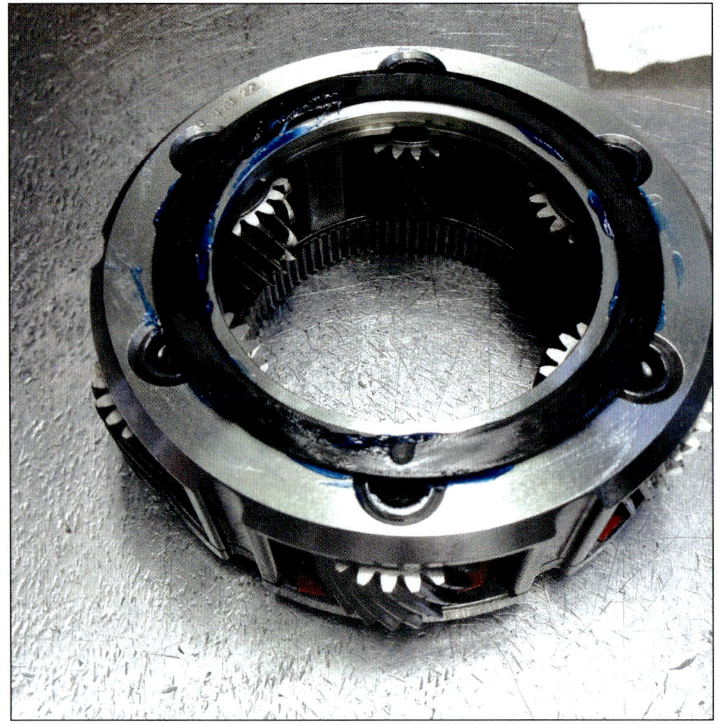

If not previously installed, install the thrust washer onto the carrier. Retain the washer with Transjel.

Install the input planetary carrier with the inside lip up and install the sun gear. Make sure that the carrier thrust washer you previously installed is still in place.

the carrier is still in place. The carrier is installed in the ring gear with the thrust washer facing the 4-5-6 clutch drum (down), while the inside-diameter lip on the carrier splines face up. Rotate the carrier to get it to engage with the teeth on the planetary ring gear. Install the planetary sun gear and rotate it to engage the teeth on the sun gear with the teeth on the planetary carrier.

Factory Method: Installing the 1-2-3-4/3-5-R Clutch

Installation of the 1-2-3-4/3-5-R clutch drum with the use of factory or aftermarket clutch drum holding tools makes the process very easy. The drum can be installed without the use of special tools, but the process is more time consuming.

Drum Installation Tools

Install the previously completed 3-5-R/1-2-3-4 clutch drum into the case. Tool DT 47781 (or an equivalent) will make the job much easier, although it can be accomplished without the tool if you have a lot of patience and time. You can make a homemade tool from an old THM 400 band and a hanger that you can purchase from a hardware store. A pair of C-clamp Vise-Grips can then be used to clamp the band around the drum. The tools grab the drum, making it easy to lift, hold, and rotate the drum as you rotate the input shaft to align the two sets to clutch discs as well as the drum-to-clutch hub splines. Rotate and wiggle the drum until the splines and clutch discs are fully aligned and the drum drops into place in the transmission. Make sure that the components are fully installed into the case. Inspect the component position from the valve body side of the case.

Aftermarket Method: Installing the 1-2-3-4/3-5-R Clutch, 4-5-6 Clutch, and Front Planetary as an Assembly

If you do not have access to a 1-2-3-4/3-5-R clutch drum loading tool, another method can be used to load the completed clutch drums and planetary as an assembly. If the front planetary was not previously installed when you assembled the 4-5-6 drum, install the input sun gear Torrington bearing #54 over the input (turbine) shaft and down onto the drum. The inner lip of the bearing mounts to a lip on the shaft/drum. The bearing is installed with the inner-race lip facing up. This will allow the bearing to rotate while the bearing inner race is held by the shaft lip.

Input Carrier

Install the input planetary carrier. Make sure that the carrier thrust washer you previously mounted to the carrier is still in place. The carrier is installed in the ring gear with the thrust washer facing the 4-5-6 clutch drum (down), while the inside-diameter lip on the carrier splines will face up. Rotate the carrier to get it to engage with the teeth on the planetary ring gear. Install the planetary sun gear and rotate it to engage the teeth on the sun gear with the teeth on the planetary carrier.

Clutch Drum Installation

With the input (turbine) shaft facing up, install the 1-2-3-4/3-5-R completed clutch drum onto the front planetary/4-5-6 clutch assembly. Rotate and wiggle the drum until

Installing the components individually is easier using a 3-5-R drum installation tool that can be built or purchased.

Install the 3-5-R/1-2-3-4 drum. Rotate and wiggle the drum until it drops into place.

If you do not have access to a drum installation tool, install the components as an assembly. Install the front planetary and bearings into the 4-5-6 drum as previously described. Install the 3-5-R/1-2-3-4 drum onto the 4-5-6 drum with the components on the bench. Make sure that the clutches are fully seated.

Install the completed assembly into the case by rotating and wiggling the assembly.

When the components are fully seated in the case, it will appear as shown here.

the clutches fully engage the housing splines.

Grab the input shaft and lift the completed 3-5-R/1-2-3-4, 4-5-6 front planetary assembly into the case while rotating the assembly to align the housing splines. To be sure the components are fully installed, inspect the housing position from the valve body side of the case.

Installing the Pump/Bellhousing Assembly

The pump and bellhousing assembly can be installed after all of the main transmission components have been installed in the case. As with other components, the pump/bellhousing assembly needs to be positioned correctly so that the bolts will line up properly.

Bellhousing Seal Installation

Rotate the previously completed bellhousing/pump assembly with the pump facing up on the bench. Check to make sure that you previously installed the large-diameter seal onto the bellhousing and pump assembly. Lubricate the seal with transmission fluid, Transjel, or Vaseline. Rotate the assembly with the pump facing the workbench and make sure that the front seal was properly installed and lubricated.

Bellhousing and Pump Installation

Lift the housing and place it over the input (turbine) shaft. Lower the housing onto the transmission case while wiggling and applying light downward pressure until the housing is mounted flush onto the case. If the housing will not fully drop onto the case, it is likely that a clutch disc or some other part is out of position and you will need to locate and address the issue prior to attempting to reinstall the housing. After tightening the bolts, make sure that the input shaft will turn and that there is some end play present by pulling the

Be Careful!

Do not force or pull the housing into position using the bolts, as damage can occur. ■

If not previously installed, install the large-diameter bellhousing/pump seal.

shaft up and down. If not, something is not properly aligned, positioned, or meshed.

Bellhousing Bolts and Torque Sequence

Install the nine bellhousing bolts. Torque the bolts to 53 ft-lbs (72 Nm) in the proper sequence. Install the input (turbine) shaft, place the TCC O-ring seal onto the input (turbine) shaft, and lubricate the seal with transmission fluid.

Unit End Play

If the pump was replaced with a remanufactured unit or if the pump was machined, check the unit end play. GM does not use an end-play specification, as it only replaces the pump/bellhousing with a new assembly. In the aftermarket, this is not generally the case. So, you will need to check the input shaft end play after the unit has been reassembled. The specification target is 0.004 to 0.006 inch (0.102 to 0.152 mm); typical end play on a 6L80 generally runs between 0.006 and 0.035 inch

Lift the housing and place it over the input (turbine) shaft. Lower the housing onto the transmission case while wiggling and applying light downward pressure until the housing is mounted flush onto the case. You may have to rotate the turbine shaft as you are installing the bellhousing to align the components.

After tightening the bolts, pull the shaft up and down to make sure the input shaft will turn and that there is some end play present. If not, something is not properly aligned, positioned, or meshed.

Install the nine bellhousing bolts. Torque the bolts to 53 ft-lbs (72 Nm) in the proper sequence.

Install the turbine/input shaft, place the TCC O-ring seal onto the input (turbine) shaft, and lubricate the seal with transmission fluid.

With the bellhousing bolts installed and torqued, mounted a dial indicator to the end of the turbine/input shaft. Move the shaft up and down to measure the end play.

If the pump was replaced with a remanufactured unit or if the pump was machined, check the unit end play. GM does not use an end-play specification because they only replace the pump/bellhousing with a new assembly. In the aftermarket, this is not generally the case, so check the input shaft end play after the unit has been reassembled. The specification target is 0.004 to 0.006 inch (0.102 to 0.152 mm); typical end play on a 6L80 generally runs between 0.006 and 0.035 inch (0.152 and 0.889 mm). Aftermarket shims are available from Superior Transmission products to address input end play issues.

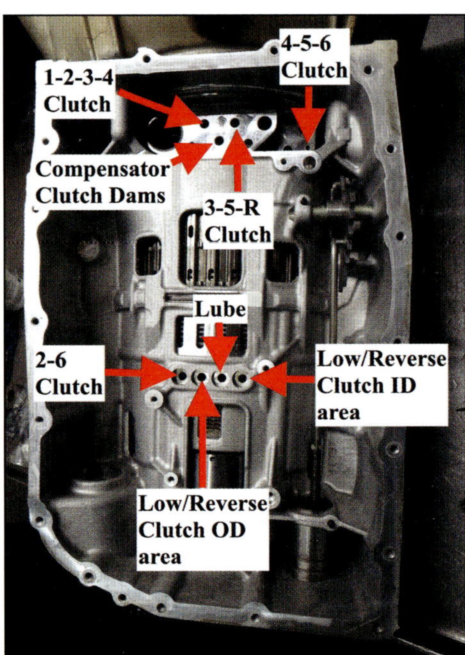

Using shop air pressure that is regulated to 50 psi, apply air pressure to the pump passages and to the passages in the case center support. If you are air testing a clutch, you will hear the clutch make a "thump" type of noise. When air testing the large-diameter low/reverse clutch circuit, it is normal to hear air coming from the low/reverse small-diameter seal circuit. If you are testing a compensator/clutch dam circuit, simply listen for an excessive air leak.

(0.152 and 0.889 mm). Aftermarket shims are available from Superior Transmission products to address input end play issues.

Air Testing

Once the transmission has been completed, prior to installing the valve body and TEHCM, air test the clutches to make sure that a seal was not damaged during installation. Using shop air pressure regulated to 50 psi, apply air pressure to the pump passages and to the passages in the case center support. If you are air testing a clutch, you should hear the clutch make a "thump" type of noise. When air testing the large-diameter low/reverse clutch circuit, it is normal to hear air coming from the low/reverse small-diameter seal circuit. If you are testing a compensator/clutch dam circuit, listen for an excessive air leak. If the clutches and compensator circuits appear to be working, you are now ready for the valve body/TEHCM service and installation, which is covered in Chapter 4.

Manual Shaft Inspection

Some 6L80 applications have issues with the park rod not being properly hardened, which can lead to the vehicle popping out of Park. The park rod and parking pawl should be inspected for wear and damage. GM has updated parts designed to address this issue. Remove the two roll pins that hold the park rod assembly. The components can then be removed

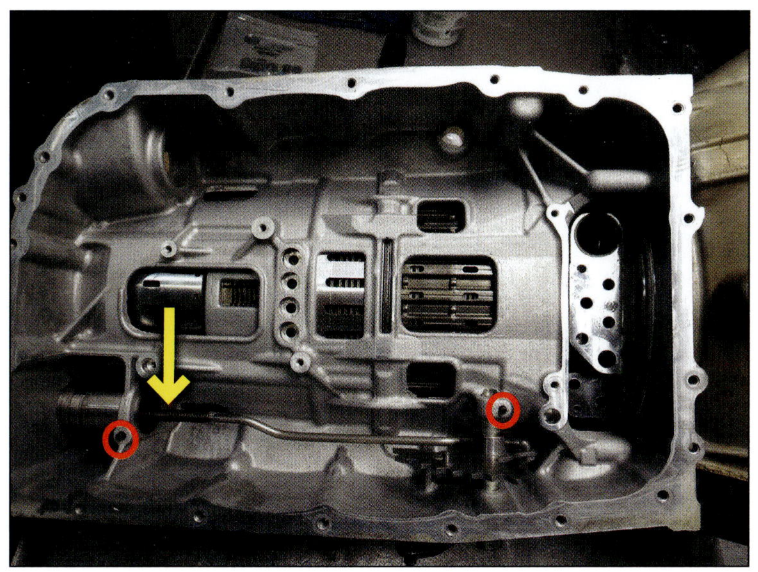

It is important to remove and inspect the manual shaft and park pawl for wear and damage. Two roll pins retain the components. GM has updated parts to address the wear issue. If worn, the transmission can pop out of Park.

Using the DT 45201 seal remover (or an equivalent), extract the old seal from the bore. This process can be done without special tools if you remove the manual linkage. If you do not have access to the tools, service the seal when you have the park rod removed for inspection.

and fully inspected. Reinstall the components in the reverse order. Two O-rings are used on the actuator guide that should be replaced as well, as GM recommends that the roll pins be replaced (they are typically included in most kits).

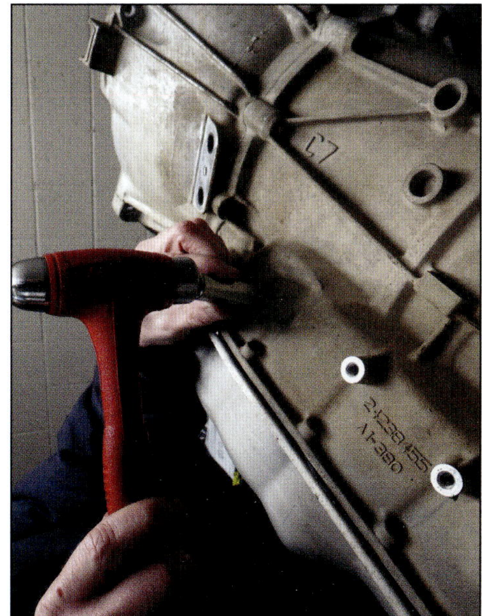

Using the DT 47770 seal installer (or an equivalent), install the new seal over the shaft and into the bore. This process can be done without special tools if you remove the manual linkage.

Manual Shaft Seal Replacement

The manual shaft seal can be removed and installed without special tools, although the tools make the job much easier. Using DT 45201 (or an equivalent seal remover), extract the old seal from the bore.

Using DT 47770 (or an equivalent seal installer), install the new seal over the shaft and into the bore. If you do not have the proper tools, service the seal when you have the park rod and linkage removed for inspection.

Extension Housing Installation

If not previously installed, install the output-shaft dust seal. Install the large housing-to-case seal onto the extension housing. Install the extension housing and torque the bolts to 41 ft-lbs (55 Nm) using a crossing pattern.

If not previously installed, install the output-shaft dust seal. Install the large housing to the case seal onto the extension housing. Install the extension housing and torque the bolts to 41 ft-lbs (55 Nm) using a crossing pattern.

TEHCM Inspection and Testing

The transmission electrical hydraulic control module (TEHCM) controls the operation of the 6L80. The TEHCM houses the following:

- The shift and pressure control solenoids
- The transmission temperature sensor
- Four clutch pressure switches
- The TCM (transmission control module), which acts as the computer that controls transmission operation

If the TEHCM is going to be replaced, replacement TEHCMs are available as remanufactured units and as new units. In either case, the replacement TEHCM must be programmed to function properly. Keep in mind that multiple TEHCM part numbers are available for the 6L80 application. If you are replacing the TEHCM, make sure that you have the correct one for your application.

If you plan to reuse your TEHCM, consider testing it to make sure that it is functioning before it is reinstalled on the transmission.

GM Factory Method

GM developed a test plate to allow you to conduct static tests of the solenoids. A static test will find a solenoid that is stuck open or closed, but it will not determine if the flow rate from the solenoid is correct at various commanded positions. The test plate can be used any time you have the TEHCM removed from the vehicle. This means that when the unit is out of the vehicle, such as when you are conducting a rebuild, you can test the TEHCM for proper operation. The vehicle will be required to complete this test as the scan tool interface with the TEHCM still relies on the vehicle data bus for communication. The process is the same for both the rear-wheel-drive and the front-wheel-drive 6-speed applications, although the harness interface part numbers vary with the application.

GM uses a special tool (DT47825) to test the operation of the 6L family TEHCM. The tool requires that the TEHCM be removed from the transmission. The TEHCM is then separated from the valve body and the tool is bolted onto the TEHCM. The TEHCM and tool are then connected through an umbilical cord tool (DT47825-10) and to the vehicle harness that plugs into the transmission. Air pressure is then applied to the tool and a pressure gauge is used to read the pressure available at each solenoid port on the tool. The TEHCM is then actuated through the use of a scan tool using its output override commands. As the solenoids are turned on and off by the scan tool, the pressure is read at each of the tool's pressure ports to determine if the TEHCM solenoids are functioning or not.

The process of using the tool is as follows:

1. Remove the TEHCM from the transmission. Flip the TEHCM over to allow any trapped fluid to drain prior to attaching the tool. Separate the TEHCM from the valve body by removing the attaching bolts.
2. Install tool DT47825 onto the TEHCM with the filter plate installed between the TEHCM and the test tool. Torque the

attaching bolts to 44 in-lbs (5 Nm). Apply regulated shop air (90 to 100 psi) to the tool.

3. Connect the scan tool to the TEHCM through the DT47825-10 jumper harness and pass-through connector. When attaching the harness to the TEHCM, make sure that you connect the vehicle harness pass-through sleeve from the transmission to the TEHCM prior to connecting the jumper harness. This ensures that the pins from the harness are properly connected to the correct pins at the TEHCM. Failure to use the pass-through sleeve from the transmission may result in the pins in the jumper harness being connected to the wrong pins at the TEHCM, which can cause damage to the TCM. Attach the other end of the DT47825-10 jumper harness to the transmission vehicle harness.
4. Key-on using your scan tool and command the solenoid on/off. Air pressure should be present on the gauge, and then it should exhaust as the solenoid is cycled. If the solenoid is malfunctioning, the gauge pressure will not change as you cycle the solenoid. If a malfunction is determined to be present, replace the complete TEHCM. To prevent the solenoid from overheating, do not operate a solenoid for longer than 2 minutes.
5. If the solenoid test was passed, install the gauge on another solenoid port and command that solenoid on/off with the scanner to repeat the process.

GM developed test plate DT47825 to allow you to use shop air pressure to conduct static tests of the solenoids. A static test will find a solenoid that is stuck open or closed, but it will not determine if the flow rate from the solenoid is correct at various commanded positions. Refer to the chart in this chapter to determine which solenoid is being tested.

TEHCM Solenoid Test Chart

Component	Test Plate, Test Port
PCS 1	G
PCS 2	C
PCS 3	A
PCS 4	B
PCS 5	F
TCC	E
SS1	H
SS2	D

Aftermarket Method

GM limits bench diagnosis of the solenoids to the use of the test plate. With a digital volt ohmmeter (DVOM), you can bench test the electrical operation of the solenoid just as you would any other solenoid.

Lay the TEHCM on the bench and inspect the solenoid terminals on the TEHCM for any debris that may be bridging the terminal welds. If debris is found, this may be your problem. If no debris is present, use your meter to connect to the solenoid that you wish to test.

Resistance Testing the Solenoids

To measure the solenoid resistance, a high-impedance DVOM will need to be used. With the meter set to measure OHMs, connect the leads across each solenoid terminal. The meter will display the resistance value of the solenoid. Repeat the process for each solenoid. Compare the meter readings to the specifications for the solenoid. The six PWM pressure control solenoids should measure between 3 and 8 ohms. The two

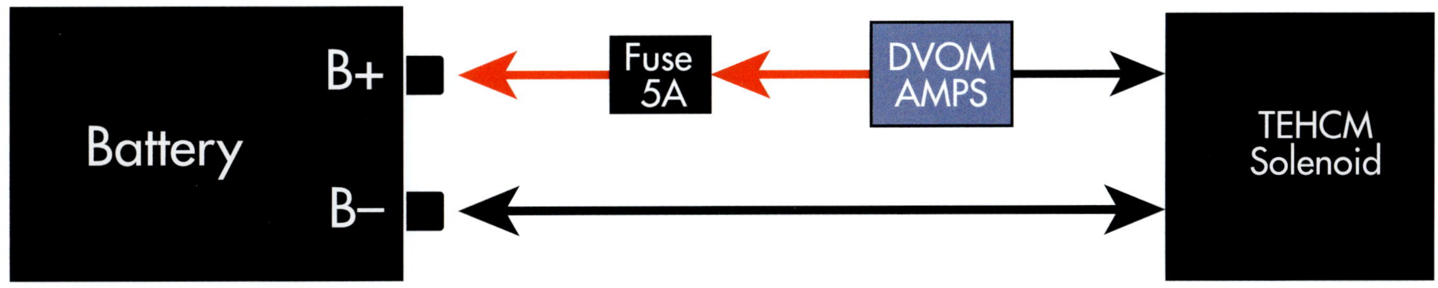

on-off shift solenoids should measure 20 to 40 ohms.

Solenoid Current Flow Testing

You can also check the current flow through the solenoids. This is not recommended for PWM solenoids by the manufacturer, but it can be done in a safe manner if you limit how long you leave the current flowing through the solenoid. Do not leave the solenoid energized for longer than 1 to 2 seconds when testing because solenoid damage may occur.

- Connect one DVOM meter lead to the solenoid terminal and the

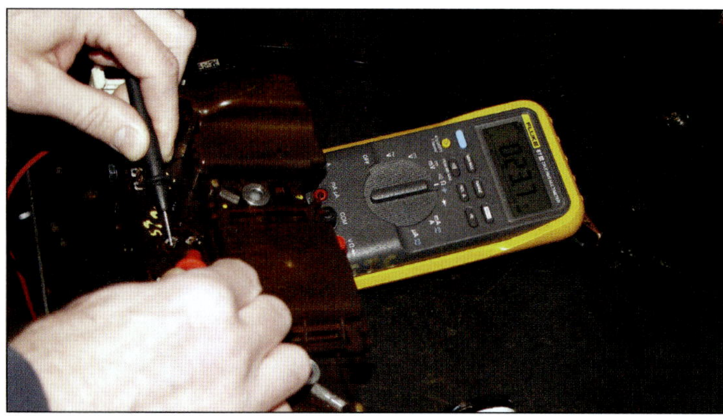

Testing the resistance of the two shift solenoids can be accomplished with the use of a high-impedance ohmmeter DVOM. Connect the meter leads across the solenoid you wish to test. The specification is 20 to 40 ohms.

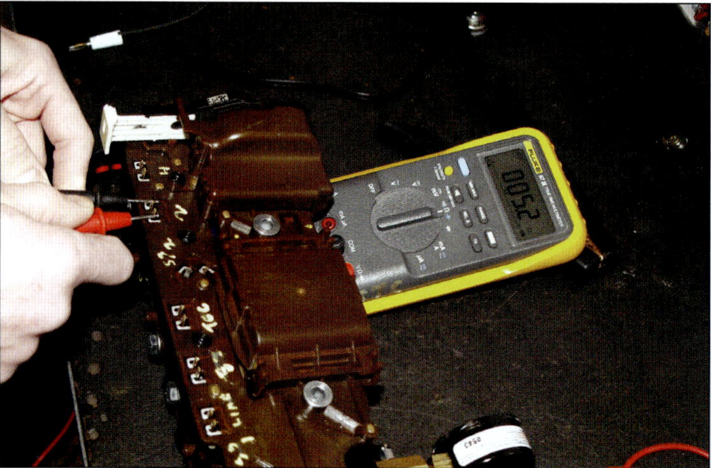

Connect the meter leads across the solenoid that you wish to test. The specification is 3 to 8 ohms.

Connect the meter leads in "series" to the solenoid that you wish to test (as shown). Connect one meter lead to the solenoid terminal and the other meter lead to a fused jumper that is connected to a voltage supply. Connect the other solenoid terminal to your voltage supply ground (do not leave the solenoid energized longer than 1 or 2 seconds). Read the amperage on your meter. Normal amperage based at normal solenoid resistances and a measured 12-volt supply should be: Shift Solenoids (SS, on/off solenoid) 0.3 to 0.7 amps at 12 volts. If the measured amperage values are incorrect, the solenoid has failed and the TEHCM requires replacement.

Testing the current flow (amperage) of the six pressure control solenoids can be accomplished using a high-impedance ohmmeter DVOM. Connect the meter leads in "series" to the solenoid that you wish to test as shown in the graphic. Connect one meter lead to the solenoid terminal and the other meter lead to a fused jumper that is connected to a voltage supply. Connect the other solenoid terminal to your voltage supply ground (do not leave the solenoid energized longer than 1 to 2 seconds). Read the amperage on your meter. Normal amperage based at normal solenoid resistances and a measured 12-volt supply should be: PCS PWM solenoids 1.5 to 4 amps at 12 volts. If the measured amperage values are incorrect, the solenoid has failed and the TEHCM requires replacement.

TEHCM TFT sensor can be tested with the use of a high-impedance ohmmeter DVOM by connecting the meter across the sensor. The resistance of the sensor will vary with temperature. If the meter displays "OL" or 0 ohms, the sensor is faulty and the TEHCM requires replacement. No specifications are available for this sensor based on temperature, so all you can do with an ohmmeter is determine if the sensor is shorted or open. You can also use a blow dryer to vary the temperature to make sure that the TFT sensor is capable of changing resistance.

other meter lead to a fused jumper connected to a voltage supply.

- Connect the other solenoid terminal to the voltage supply ground (do not leave the solenoid energized for too long).
- Read the amperage on your meter. Normal amperage based at normal solenoid resistances and a measured 12-volt supply should be the following: Shift Solenoids (SS, on/off solenoid) 0.3 to 0.7 amps at 12 volts; Shift Solenoids (PCS PWM solenoid) 1.5 to 4 amps at 12 volts.

If the measured amperage values are incorrect, the solenoid has failed and the TEHCM requires replacement.

The four fluid pressure switches can be tested with the use of a high-impedance ohmmeter DVOM. Connect an ohmmeter to the switch circuit on the TEHCM assembly body. Using a pencil eraser, push on the switch membrane to push the switch into the opposite position. With the switch open, the meter should read "OL," as the circuit should indicate no continuity.

TEHCM Transmission Temperature Sensor Bench Testing

The TEHCM fluid temperature sensor is integrated into the TEHCM assembly. The transmission fluid temperature sensor is an NTC-type thermistor. The resistance of the sensor can be tested with an ohmmeter. If the sensor is faulty, the TEHCM needs to be replaced.

TEHCM Fluid Pressure Switch Bench Testing

Four fluid pressure switches are used by the TEHCM to determine when a clutch is receiving pressure and when that pressure is being exhausted. The fluid pressure switches can be tested with the use of an ohmmeter and a pencil eraser. Connect an ohmmeter to the switch circuit on the TEHCM assembly body. Using a pencil with an eraser, push on the switch membrane to push the switch into the opposite position. The meter should measure less than 10 ohms when the switch is closed. With the switch open, the meter should read "OL" because the circuit should indicate no continuity. If the meter does not indicate the correct values, remove the membrane and clean the switch. Retest the switch. If it still indicates an issue, the TEHCM needs to be replaced.

The meter should measure less than 10 ohms when the switch is closed. If the meter does not indicate the correct values when open or closed, remove the membrane and clean the switch. Retest the switch. If it still indicates an issue, the TEHCM needs to be replaced.

TEHCM Fluid Pressure Sensors Membrane Replacement

TransGo and Sonnax sell replacement membrane repair kits for the TEHCM pressure switches. TransGo kits require only a small screwdriver to replace the membrane and the rubber. Sonnax includes an installation tool to install the rubber on the switch. Remove the old rubber, membrane, and switch disc from the switch then clean the bore with electric circuit board cleaner. Install the switch disc, membrane, and rubber. Lubricate the rubber with Trans-jel when completed.

Replacing the TEHCM Fluid Pressure Sensors

1 *Sonnax and TransGo have pressure switch service kits available. The Sonnax kits include installation tools for the rubber seals (shown).*

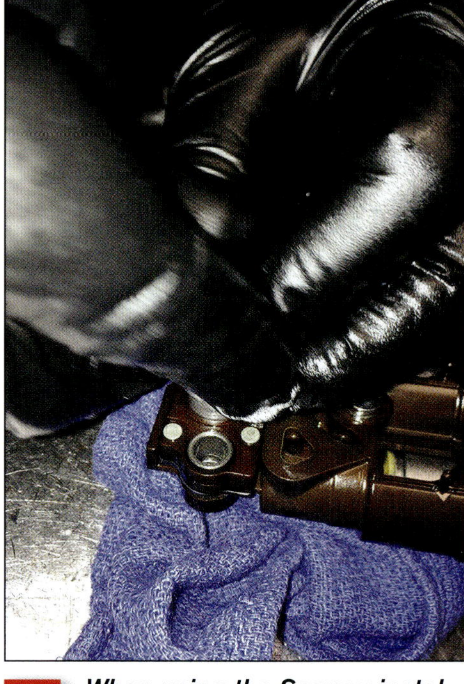

2 *When using the Sonnax installation tool, the disc is installed into the switch first, followed by the plastic membrane and, finally, the rubber seal. The rubber seal is loaded into the tool and then it is installed into the pressure switch hole. Make sure that the seal is properly positioned and fully installed.*

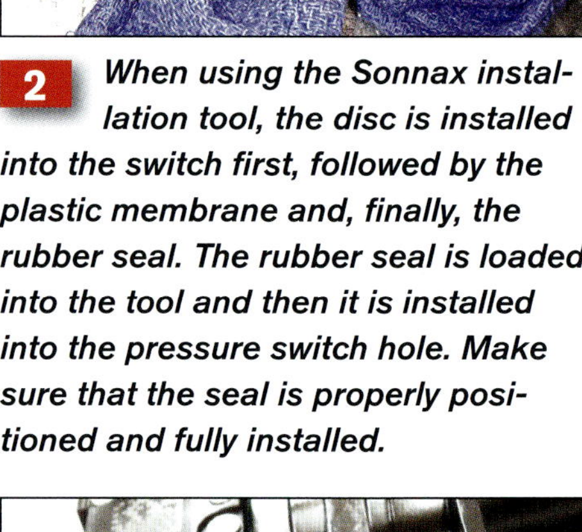

3 *The TransGo pressure switch kits do not require any special tools—simply a small screwdriver and pick. First, install the disc; then, install the plastic membrane.*

4 *Install the rubber seal using a small screwdriver or pick. Make sure that the seal is properly positioned and fully installed.*

5 *Fully lube all four pressure switch rubber seals with Transjel or clean transmission fluid.*

IMS Bench Testing

Diagnosis of the IMS can be accomplished with your scan tool prior to transmission disassembly by monitoring the IMS values outlined in Chapter 2. If the values do not match the chart, either the IMS or the TEHCM are likely defective. The IMS can be bench tested using an ohmmeter.

It is easiest if the IMS is tested prior to removing the valve body and IMS from the transmission. Disconnect the sensor connector from the TEHCM. Using a terminal probing tool or a paper clip, attach an ohmmeter to the appropriate leads at the connector you just disconnected. Move the shift lever that is located on the driver's side of the transmission through the ranges. As the shifter is moved, the meter should display a resistance reading of less than 10 ohms or "OL" (open circuit) depending on which range selected. As it is moved through the ranges, the reading will show some ranges with continuity while other ranges will indicate and open circuit. All you are looking for is that the switch is capable of closing and opening. If the meter stays locked on OL or if it shows continuity in every range (it stays locked in one position), the IMS is faulty. If the first circuit tests as being good, move to the other circuits and repeat the process.

- Connect one meter lead to pin A (Gray) and the other to pin B (Black) on the IMS
- Connect one meter lead to pin A (Gray) and the other to pin C (Yellow) on the IMS
- Connect one meter lead to pin A (Gray) and the other to pin D (Red) on the IMS
- Connect one meter lead to pin A (Gray) and the other to pin E (Green) on the IMS
- Connect one meter lead to pin A (Gray) and the other to pin F (White) on the IMS

IMS Continuity Testing

Range Selected	IMS Pin E	IMS Pin D	IMS Pin C	IMS Pin B
Park	Continuity	OL	OL	Continuity
P to R	Continuity	Continuity	OL	Continuity
Reverse	Continuity	Continuity	OL	OL
R to N	OL	Continuity	OL	OL
Neutral	OL	Continuity	OL	Continuity
N to D	OL	Continuity	Continuity	Continuity
Drive 6	OL	Continuity	Continuity	OL
Drive 6 to Drive 4	Continuity	Continuity	Continuity	OL
Drive 4	Continuity	Continuity	Continuity	Continuity
Drive 4 to Drive 3	Continuity	OL	Continuity	Continuity
Drive 3	Continuity	OL	Continuity	OL
Drive 3 to Drive 2	OL	OL	Continuity	OL
Drive 2	OL	OL	Continuity	Continuity

Diagnosis of the IMS can be accomplished with your scan tool prior to transmission disassembly by monitoring the IMS values outlined in Chapter 2. If the values do not match the chart, either the IMS or the TEHCM are likely defective. An ohmmeter can be used to bench test the IMS. Test the IMS prior to removing it from the valve body. With the sensor disconnected from the TEHCM, probe the terminals with a paper clip or probing tool. Attach the ohmmeter to the probes connected to the IMS connector. Shift the transmission through the ranges using the shifter located on the driver's side of the transmission. The meter display should read either "OL" (open circuit) or less than 10 ohms in each range depending on the shifter position.

If the meter reads "OL" all the time, the IMS is faulty.

Speed Sensor Assemblies

Two different-design speed sensor assemblies are available that fit 6L80 applications. The sensor design that is used is based on the output shaft tone ring and planetary design (unigear or non-unigear). The sensor designs are not interchangeable, and failure will occur if you install the incorrect-design assembly. Compare your new/old parts before installing the sensor assembly. ■

Speed Sensor Testing, Input Speed Sensor, and Output Speed Sensor

Speed sensors can only be tested prior to the removal of the transmission from the vehicle, but the speed sensor TECHM input can be tested by using a signal generator that is connected to the speed sensor connector at the TEHCM to provide a speed signal to the TCM. The signal generator is set to provide an 8-volt square wave to the TCM as a substitute for the speed sensor signals.

GM has an umbilical cord special tool (DT 47825-10) that attaches to the TEHCM/valve body with the assembly removed from the transmission. The cord is attached to the TEHCM/valve body assembly and the vehicle transmission harness connector. A scan tool is then attached to the vehicle so that you can monitor speed inputs.

With input from the signal generator, you should see a speed signal on your scan tool. If the signal is now present on your scan tool, but the sensor did not function during normal vehicle operation, the sensor assembly requires replacement. If the scan tool registers 0 rpm, the TEHCM is faulty and requires replacement.

To test or replace the speed sensors requires the TEHCM/valve body assembly to be removed from the transmission (see Chapter 2). This requires that it be unbolted (six bolts) from the case. With the assembly on the bench, flip it over to expose the speed sensors. Install the new sensors and connector and reinstall the assembly. Torque the six attaching bolts to the specification of 106 in-lbs (12 Nm).

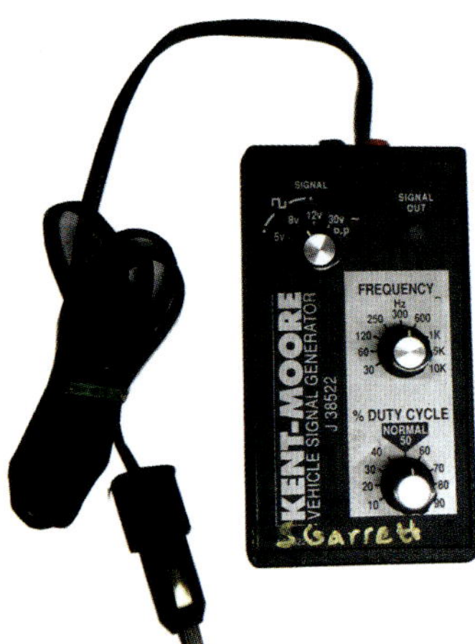

Bench testing of the speed sensors can be accomplished with the use of a signal generator to act as a substitute for the sensor signal to the TEHCM. The TEHCM is removed and umbilical cord tool DT47825-10 is attached to the TEHCM and vehicle harness. The sensor connector is then disconnected. Then, the signal generator is set to provide and 8-volt square-wave signal to the TEHCM ISS or OSS terminal. The sensor connector is then unplugged from the TEHCM and the signal generator is attached to the TEHCM sensor connection. With a scan tool connected to the vehicle, monitor the speed sensor values as you change the signal frequency. If the scan tool indicates a speed value, the TEHCM is functioning, which indicates a problem with the sensors. If the scan tool indicates 0 speed input, the TEHCM is faulty.

The speed sensors are sold as one assembly and are retained to the top of the valve body with two bolts. When installing a new sensor, the bolt torque specification is 106 in-lbs (12 Nm).

Valve Body Identification, Disassembly, and Inspection

The 6L family of transmissions use specific valve bodies based on the application. The various valve bodies cannot be interchanged. If you need to replace your valve body, it is imperative that you replace it with the same configuration. If an incorrect valve body assembly is installed, major transmission operational issues can result.

The GM plant identifies the valve body application by machining flat a casting boss on the top of the valve body. The bosses are cast into the top surface of the valve body. Depending on which letter boss is machined flat, the machined boss lettering indicates at which valve body you are looking. The bosses are lettered A through E.

Letter	Representation
A	6L45
B	6L50
C	6L80
D	6L90
E	6L80 2010 model
S	Stop/Start equipped

Valve Body, Pump, Valve Disassembly, and Inspection

Cleanliness is the most important attribute to have when it comes to servicing the valving in the valve body and pump. Flip the valve body over and allow the fluid to drain. Just as when working on the other portions of the transmission, you should wear disposable gloves, safety glasses, and a mask for protection from the solvents that you will be using to clean the parts.

Using brake cleaner or solvent, spray off the valve body castings. Air dry the castings. This will make valve body/pump valve service much more pleasant.

Valve Body and Pump Valve Removal and Disassembly

The valves are held in position with retainers and clips, so you will need a small screwdriver, picks, and a small pair of needle-nose pliers to help with disassembly and reassembly of the valve body. Make sure to wear safety glasses. Prepare a clean surface on your workbench where the components can be laid out in the order in which they were removed. Depress the valve that you want to remove, remove the retainer holding in the valve, and remove the valvetrain (valve, valves, spring, springs, and end plug). Tipping the valve body on end and lightly tapping it on your workbench may help to get the valves to move in the bore. If necessary, use a pick to lightly push on the edge of a valve land to get the valve to move. In some instances, you may need to use your small pair of needle-nose pliers to grab the end of a valve plunger to remove the valve. Do not grab the valve land, as damage can occur. Be careful that you do not damage a valve land or the valve bore when removing the valves.

The valve body and its valves are the heart of the hydraulic system in today's automatic transmissions. Valves are used to control how much pressure each component receives as well as when and where that pressure will travel within the transmission. To operate correctly, the valves need to have a specific clearance between the valve and its bore. Typically, the manufacturer will run a valve-to-bore clearance between 0.0006 and 0.0016 inch (.0127 and 0.040 mm). In comparison, a human hair is approximately 0.0034 inch (0.086 mm) wide and a sheet of paper is about 0.0045 inch (0.114 mm) wide.

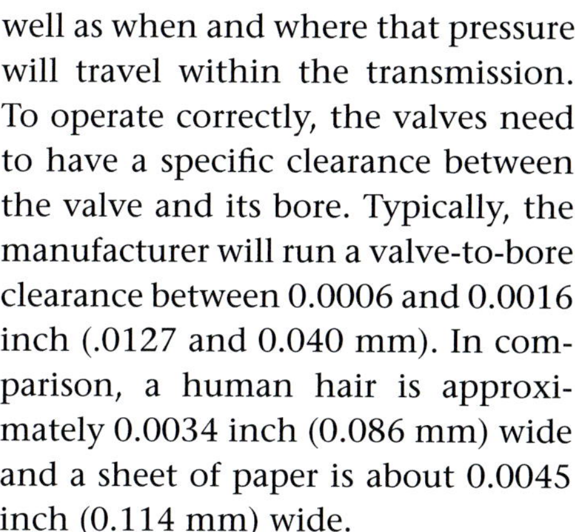

If the clearance is too tight, the valve may stick. If the clearance is too loose, valve leakage may occur. Valve issues can result in symptoms including a transmission failing to make a shift, all the way to flares, bumps, slippage, tie-up, and clutch damage issues.

Valve and Valve Bore Inspection

Inspect the valves for burrs, nicks, and wear. Valve wear is typically due to valve side loading, which occurs on many valve bodies due to the valve body pressures exerting more force on one side of a land than on the other side of the land. This is generally due to the design of the castings. Spring pressure also has an effect on valve side loading as the spring may be exerting side load pressure rather than just fore and aft pressure on the valve. The use of PWM-design solenoids as well as poor-quality casting materials also lead to accelerated valve and bore wear in today's transmissions.

Valve and Bore Testing

In addition to valve wear, the valve bores can also wear. This is typically due to the same forces that can cause valve wear. Beyond visual inspection, the valves and bores can be inspected by using any of the following methods.

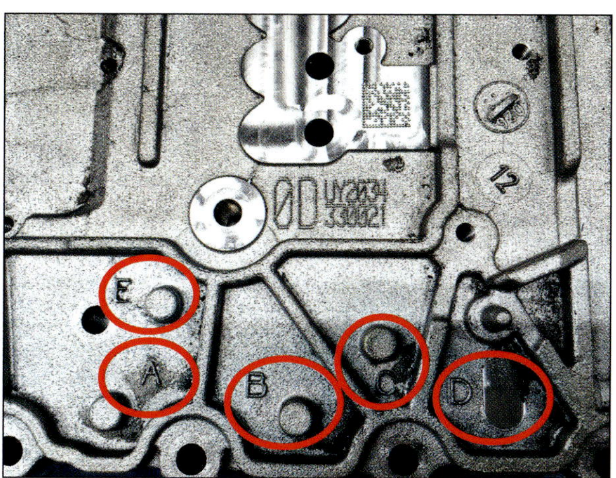

The GM plant identifies the valve body applications by machining flat a casting boss on the top of the valve body. Four, five, or six bosses are cast into the top surface of the valve body. Depending on which letter of boss is machined flat, the machined boss lettering indicates at which valve body you are looking. The 6L family of transmissions uses different valve bodies based on the application, and they are not interchangeable from application to application (6L45, 6L50, 6L80, and 6L90).

- Vacuum testing
- Light testing
- Air testing
- Wiggle testing
- Bore/valve measurements
- Sag/deflection measurements

Vacuum testing is the most effective form of valve wear testing, but it requires a vacuum test tool, which is not generally used except by a transmission repair shop. Light and wiggle testing are the most common processes used by the average technician.

Light testing typically utilizes a small flashlight. The clean valve is installed into the clean bore with the valves in their normal resting position. Place the light onto the valve body casting with light facing one side of the valve land that you want to inspect. Look at the other side of the valve land for any light escaping the land. If light can be seen, the valve/bore are worn.

The wiggle test is just as the name indicates. The valve is placed into the bore in the position in which it normally rides. Wiggle the valve sideways and up/down and note the amount of movement.

Valve Function

The 6L80 uses multiple valvetrains housed in the pump and valve body assembly. The lower valve body houses five valves; the upper valve body houses eight different valvetrains. The pump houses three valvetrains and one pressure-relief blow-off ball. The 16 various valvetrains that are used in the 6L80 provide six forward speeds, one reverse, and neutral range for the transmission. Each valvetrain consists of one or more spool valves and one or more springs to control the valve operation.

Oil Pump Valves

The oil pump houses three valvetrains and one pressure-relief ball assembly. The pump valving controls the transmission oil pressure (line pressure) and the some of the torque converter functions.

Pressure Regulator

The pressure regulator is responsible for controlling the transmission pressures. The regulator valve receives supply oil from the oil pump. The valve regulates that flow and its output becomes the transmission line pressure. Line pressure is used to apply the clutches as well as feed other regulator valves within the transmission, which then reregulate the pressure for several functions. Pressure regulator wear is common on this application and should be addressed.

Isolater valve

The isolator valve helps to control the position of the pressure regulator valve by controlling the pressure regulator valve spring tension. The TEHCM pressure control solenoid (PCS) applies fluid pressure to the isolator valve, which then compresses the regulator valve spring, leading to increased line pressure. This allows the transmission line pressure to rise and fall based on engine torque.

Torque Converter Clutch Control valve

The torque converter clutch (TCC) control valve controls the application and release of the TCC. The TCC control valve is operated by the TEHCM TCC solenoid. The TCC control valve also regulates the oil cooler flow and ultimately the transmission lubrication pressure.

Converter Limit Valve

This valve controls the amount of torque converter and lubrication pressure when the TCC is in the off position.

Lower Valve Body Valves

The lower valve body houses five valvetrain assemblies. These valves

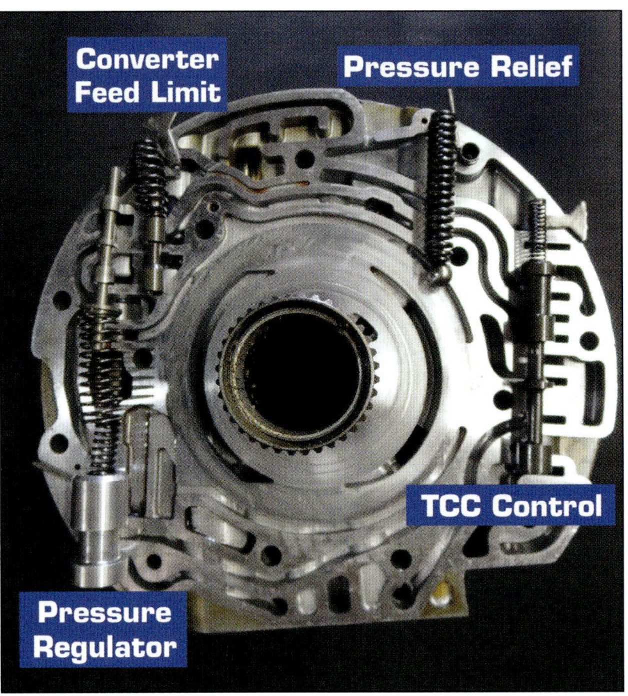

The oil pump houses four valves, a pressure regulator, an isolator valve, TCC control, and the converter limit. Pressure regulator wear is very common and must be addressed. Inspect the valves and bores for wear and damage. Always wear safety glasses when servicing the pump valving.

are designed to control clutch operation, manual range selection, and torque converter operation.

Clutch Select Valve 2

This valve routes fluid to the clutch select 3 valve to control the operation of the 4-5-6 clutch. Clutch select valve sticking issues are common on this application.

Clutch Select Valve 3

This valve controls the operation of the 3-5-Reverse clutch and the 4-5-6 clutch. Clutch select valve sticking issues are common on this application.

Clutch Dam Regulator

This regulator feeds compensator fluid to the clutch piston compensators for the 1-2-3-4, 3-5-Reverse, and 4-5-6 clutches. This pressure is used to assist the clutch return springs to help with release of the clutches. In addition, it helps to control shift feel by controlling the stroke rate of the clutch pistons.

TCC Regulator

This regulator uses 1-6 apply pressure to control the amount of oil pressure being fed to the torque converter during apply. Since this is an EC3-design system, the TEHCM not only controls the apply and release of the TCC but also controls the amount of TCC slippage and the TCC apply and release feel. TCC regulator valve wear should always be inspected.

Manual Valve

This valve is fed by line pressure and controlled by the driver shift lever, as with other applications. The manual valve controls the transmission range and whether the transmission will select forward or reverse.

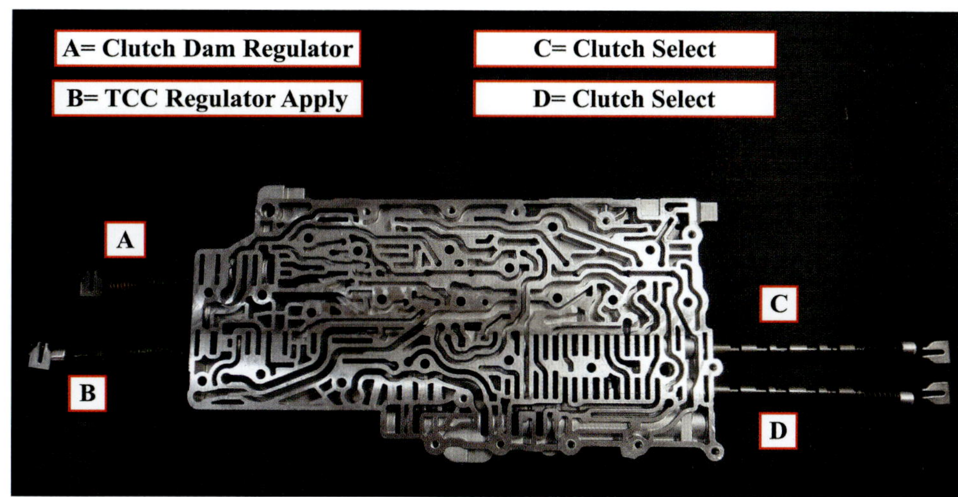

Always wear safety glasses when servicing the valve body valving. The lower valve body houses four valves: "A" is the clutch dam regulator, "B" is the TCC regulator apply, "C" is the clutch select #3, and "D" is clutch select #2. The manual valve is not shown. Wear and sticking issues are common with the TCC regulator and the clutch select valves.

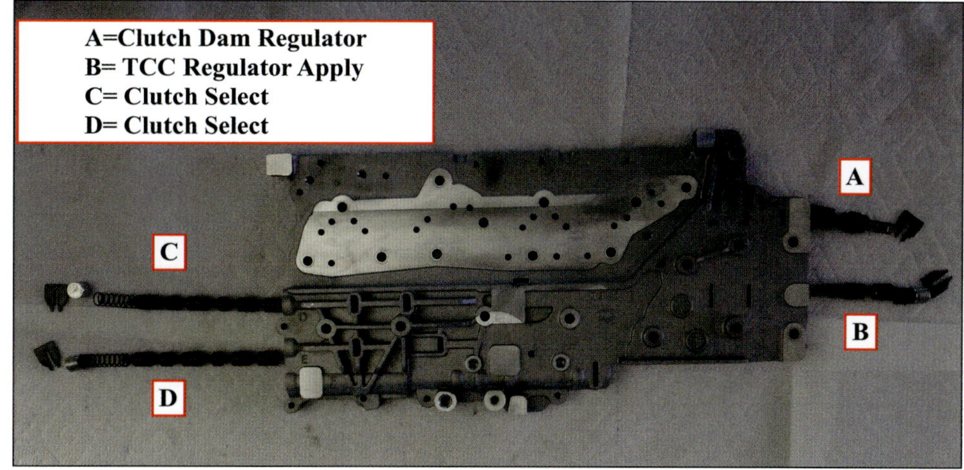

If the valve body is flipped over, the valve position will be reversed. Some technicians prefer to work on the valve body in this position because you can see the casting letters (A, B, C, and D).

Upper Valve Body Valves

The upper valve body houses eight valvetrain assemblies. These valves are designed to control clutch operation, solenoid feed oil pressure, and some of the transmission default actions.

The actuator feed limit valve regulates the pressure that is fed to the solenoids. This action controls the amount of pressure available to the solenoids no matter how high line pressure becomes. Wear on this valve is common on this application, and the valve should always be inspected for wear.

The CBR1/C456 clutch regulator valve regulates CBR1/4-5-6 clutch feed pressure during P-R-N-1st-4th-5th-6th. The pressure from this valve is also routed to pressure switch #5.

4-5-6 Boost Valve

This valve controls the pressure going to the CBR1-456 regulator valve to control boost pressure to the 4-5-6 clutch. PSI is boosted when solenoid pressure reaches 684 kpa. This increases clamp load after the clutch has applied. This process prevents clutch slippage during rapid torque changes.

2-6 Cutch Regulator and Gain Valves

These valves regulate the 2-6 clutch feed during second and sixth gear. Pressure also controls pressure switch #3.

3-5 Reverse Boost

This controls the position of the 3-5 regulator valve to control boost for the 3-5 reverse clutch. PSI is boosted when solenoid pressure reaches 684 kpa. This increases clamp load after the clutch has applied. This process prevents clutch slippage during rapid torque changes.

3-5 Reverse Clutch Regulator

This regulates the amount of pressure available to the 3-5-Reverse clutch. It also controls pressure switch #1.

1-2-3-4 Clutch Regulator

This regulates the amount of pressure available to the 1-2-3-4 clutch. It also controls pressure switch #4.

1-2-3-4 Clutch Shuttle

This shuttle is located on the end of the 1-2-3-4 clutch regulator valve. This is a safety valve in case a failure occurs, this valve inhibits all gears except P-N-R-third or fifth. It controls the position of the 1-2-3-4 regulator valve to control boost for the 1-2-3-4 clutch. PSI is boosted when solenoid pressure reaches 684 kpa. This increases clamp load after the clutch has applied. This process prevents clutch slippage during rapid torque changes.

In this image, "1" is the actuator feed limit, "2" is the first/reverse/4-5-6 clutch regulator, "3" is the clutch boost valve, "4" is the 2-6 clutch regulator, "5" is the clutch boost, "6" is the 3-5-R clutch regulator, "7" is the 1-2-3-4 clutch regulator, and "8" is the clutch boost. Wear issues are common with the actuator feed limit valve.

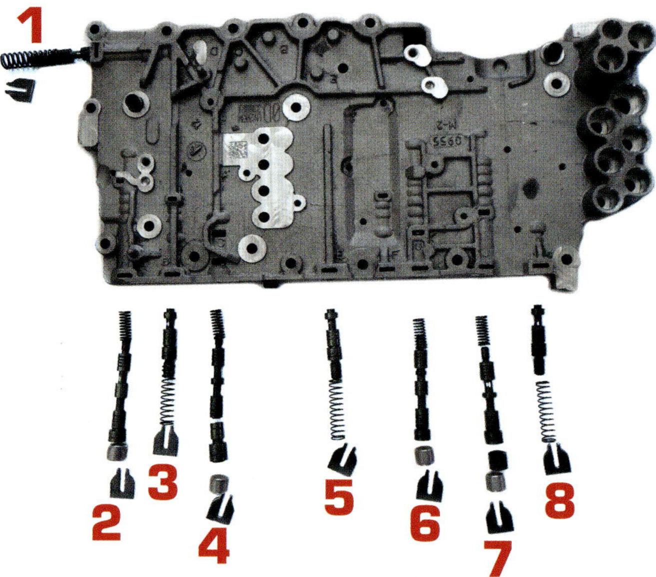

If the valve body is flipped over, the valve position will be reversed. Some technicians prefer to work on the valve body in this position because you can see the casting letters (A, B, C, D, E, F, G, H, and J).

Valve Body Assembly and TEHCM Installation

The valve body and TEHCM are installed as a single assembly. All of the bolts must be correctly torqued.

Component Installation

The assembly of the valve body is the reverse of the disassembly. Once the valve body has been cleaned and inspected, the valves/springs can be lubricated and reinstalled into their correct bores. Lubricate the bores and valves with clean transmission fluid. Insert the valves/springs in their correct orientation into the bores. Install the end plug (if used) and the retainer/clip for the valve that you are servicing. (Caution: always wear safety glasses and disposable gloves.)

Check Balls

Once the valves/springs have been installed into their proper locations, it is time for the check balls to be installed into their appropriate locations. Seven or eight check balls are used in the 6L80 depending on year. In 2014, a change was made that added an updated spacer plate and the #8 check ball to the valve body. Check ball wear is common with the 6L series of transmissions, so replacement of all of the check balls is always a good idea. Most quality kits contain new check balls. Retain the check balls in their locations by using Transjel to hold them in position.

Replace the spacer plate or the gaskets. GM bonds the gaskets to its spacer plates, so if you plan on reusing the spacer plate, the old gaskets need to be removed from the spacer plate. The new gaskets can be held in place on the spacer plate by using a thin layer of Transjel. Several methods can be used to remove the gaskets, including chemical treatments such as TranTec's Gasket Wizard, CRC, or Permatex Gasket Removers. If you choose, a new plate with the bonded gasket already installed can be purchased from GM.

> **TECH TIP**
>
> **Valve Body/TEHCM Bolts**
>
> The two M5x53 bolts must be installed on the side of the valve body/TEHCM. Installing longer bolts in these locations will damage the valve body and may cause issues with third and reverse gear operation. ■

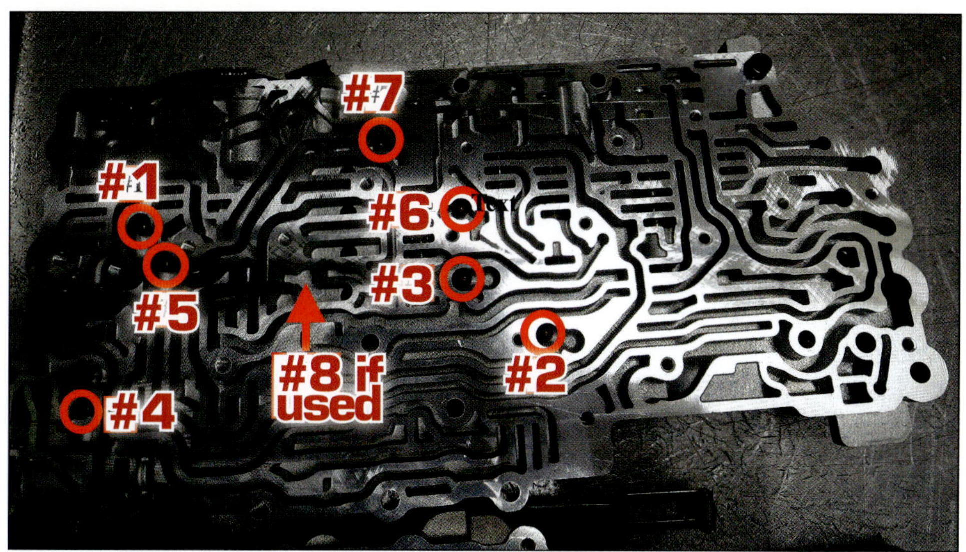

Always replace the check balls because check ball wear is very common on this application. The most common ball to wear is #1. Install the check balls in the locations shown. If you choose, retain them with Transjel. Installing a ball into an incorrect location will cause issues. The balls control the following: #1 drive 1-6, #2 shift solenoid 1, #3 shift solenoid 2, #4 pressure switch 4, #5 drive 1-6, #6 2-6 clutch/1-2-3-4 clutch feed, #7 3-5-Reverse clutch feed, #8 reverse/first clutch feed. The #8 ball may or may not be used depending on the model year of the transmission.

With the check balls installed, place the spacer plate and gaskets onto one half of the valve body. Place the other valve body half on top of the spacer plate and the other valve body half. Make sure that the spacer plate and gaskets are properly aligned. Install the five lower-to-upper valve body bolts (M5x45) and one M5x55 bolt and lightly tighten.

TEHCM Attachment

The TEHCM can now be attached to the valve body assembly. Install a new filter plate between the TEHCM and the valve body. Install the 11 bolts attaching the TEHCM to the valve body (two M5x53, four M5x55, and five M5x45).

Install the IMS and 1 IMS attaching bolt while making sure to align the IMS plunger with the valve body manual valve. Tighten the 12 valve body bolts, 1 IMS bolt, and 11 TEHCM attaching bolts to 71 in-lbs (8 Nm) using the proper torque sequence. The 2 TEHCM side-mount heat-sink bolts should be torqued last. Visually inspect the heat sink area. The TEHCM must be pulled tight against the valve body, otherwise TEHCM thermal shut down will

Install the spacer plate and gaskets. GM uses bonded gaskets. If you are using the gaskets supplied in your kit rather than buying a new spacer plate/ bonded gasket, use some alignment bolts to properly position the valve body and spacer plate/gaskets.

Properly align the upper valve body, spacer plate and gaskets, and the lower valve body halves. Then, install the bolts.

Finger-tighten the five M5x45 and one M5x55 bolts to retain the valve body halves.

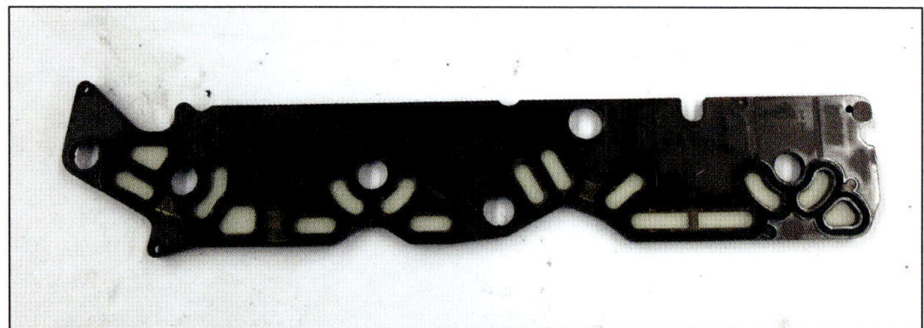

Install a new filter plate; do not reuse this component.

Install the new filter plate onto the TEHCM.

Install the two M5x53 bolts connecting the TEHCM to the valve body. Note that the use of the incorrect bolts in this location can lead to valve body damage and operational issues. Finger tighten the bolts. There should be no gap between the TEHCM heat sink and the valve body. If a gap exists, the parts are not properly aligned and will need to be addressed.

Install the four M5x55 and five M5x45 TEHCM bolts into their holes in the valve body and TEHCM. Finger tighten the bolts. Place all of the bolts into their holes prior to tightening any bolts. Look at the amount of the bolt that is protruding from the VB/TEHCM; they should all protrude about the same amount. If that is not the case, swap the bolt positions until they all protrude the same amount.

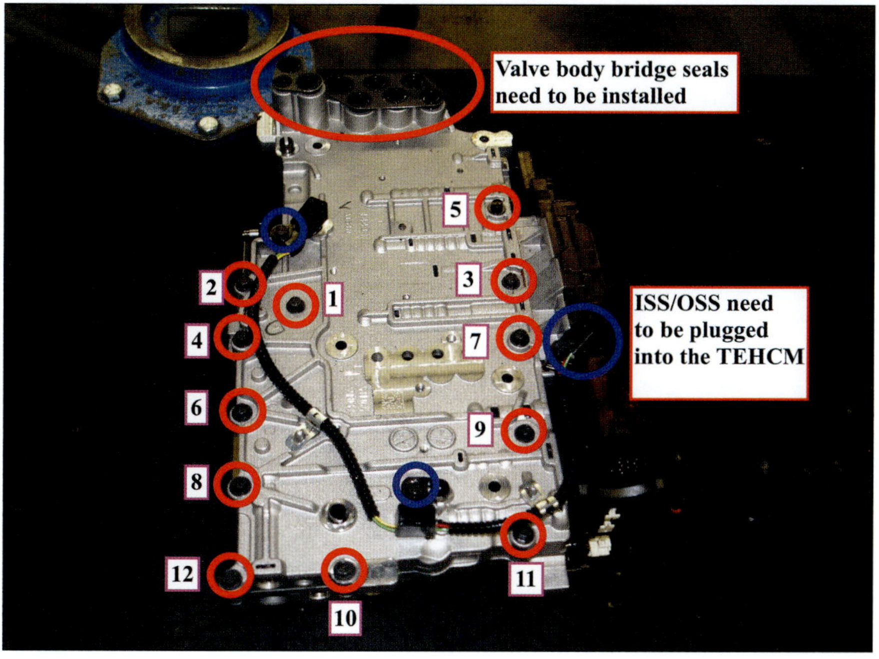

Flip over the valve body and install all 12 of the M5x36 upper-to-lower valve body bolts. Finger tighten the bolts. Torque the bolts following the sequence shown to 71 in-lbs (8 Nm). Install the speed sensor assembly onto the upper valve body and clips and torque the two M6x20 speed sensor bolts to 106 in-lbs (12 Nm). Attach the speed sensor connector to the TEHCM connection. Install the valve body bridge seals into the valve body.

Install the case-to-valve body bridge seal into the case. The bridge seals used in the 6L45/6L50 are not interchangeable and should not be used on a 6L80/6L90 application; otherwise, failure will result. Lube the seals with clean transmission fluid.

occur. Torque bolts #1 through #18 in the proper sequence to 71 in-lbs (8 Nm) prior to installing the valve body/TEHCM on the transmission.

Install the ISS/OSS assembly to the upper valve body. Two M6x20 bolts are used and should be torqued to 106 in-lbs (12 Nm). Connect the ISS/OSS connector to the TEHCM. Attach the IMS connector to the TEHCM.

Valve Body/TEHCM Installation

Once the valve body/TEHCM assembly is complete, it can be installed into the transmission. Install the bridge seals onto the valve body and a set of bridge seals into the case center support. Install the assembly onto the transmission and install the six attaching bolts (M5x70). Torque the bolts to 71 in-lbs (8 Nm). Double-check the bolt torque for bolts #1 through #16 and #19 through #24. Install the electrical pass-through connector into the case and TEHCM.

Valve Body, Pump Valve Repair Kits, and Additional Components

The 6L series of transmissions are quite popular, so several companies have repair kits to address issues with valve wear as well as other prob-

Install new O-rings and seal on the pass-through connector. Install the pass-through connector into the case with the tab at the 12-o clock position. Make sure that it is locked into position. If needed, the DT47715 tool (or an equivalent) can be used to assist with the installation. Lock the connector TEHCM white locking tab in the down position. The locking tab is located on the TEHCM.

Attach the valve body to the TEHCM with two M5x53 (heat sink) bolts, five M5x55 bolts and five M5x45 bolts. The lower valve body is attached to the upper valve body with five M5x45 and one M5x55 bolt. The IMS needs to be aligned with the manual valve. All 18 bolts are torqued to 71 in-lbs (8 Nm) in the sequence shown. The heat-sink bolts are torqued last when attaching the TEHCM to the valve body. Install the valve body/TEHCM assembly into the case while aligning the detent manual valve link. Install the remaining six 5x73 valve body-to-case attaching bolts identified as #19–24 here and torque them to 71 in-lbs (8 Nm).

lems. The most popular companies are TransGo (transgo.com), Superior (superiortransmission.com), and Sonnax (sonnax.com). Most of the TransGo and Superior products are designed to be a drop-in component, while many of the Sonnax repairs require valve body or pump bore reaming for updated valve installation.

Instructions for the installation and use of each of the aftermarket products are typically included with the products or are available on the aftermarket manufacturer's website.

Aftermarket Service and Performance Parts Available	
Trans Go Products	**Part Number**
Shift reprogramming kit	SK 6L80
Pump pressure regulator kit	6L8-VL-PR3
Boost valve kit	6L8-BOOST-OES
Clutch select and TCC regulator kit	6L8 CS-TCC
TEHCM pressure switch repair kit	PSR-5

Oil Filter and Oil Pan Installation

The filter seal should have been previously installed, but if for some reason it was not, the seal can be installed now. Install the seal using tools DT47848 and J42183. If you do not have access to the GM tools, you can fabricate a flat tool to allow you to evenly drive the seal in place. Lubricate the seal with transmission fluid or Transjel and install the filter. Install the reusable pan gasket and the pan. Install the 18 pan bolts. The bolts should be torqued to 80 in-lbs

Some Sonnax replacement components require that the worn bores be machined oversize. To accomplish this in a shop environment, Sonnax developed a reaming fixture to hold and guide the reamers used to machine the worn bore. Most transmission shops have the reaming fixture, so if your bore is severely worn, contact your local shop to have the machining done or replace the valve body/pump with a remanufactured pump or valve body.

The aftermarket has multiple kits available to help you to repair worn valve and bore issues, which are common on the 6L family of transmissions. TransGo, Sonnax, and Superior are the most common brands used in the industry. Some kits are available as drop-in components while others require that the valve body or pump bore is machined so that an oversized valve can be installed. A full list of the valve components as well as other products for each company are highlighted in this chapter. (Photos Courtesy TransGo)

(9 Nm) in a crossing sequence starting from the middle and working outward.

Fluid, Capacity, Checks, and Operation

The filler tube (dipstick) seal and dipstick should have previously been installed; if not, install both of the items now. Make sure that the seal and the tube are fully seated into the case. (Note that not all applications use a dipstick or filler tube.)

Fluid

The 6L80 uses Dexron VI fluid. Dexron VI is far superior to Dexron III, which it replaced. Major improvements in wear control, film strength, friction durability, and oxidation stability were achieved. Clutch-to-clutch shift transmissions, such as the 6L/6T series, require a much more robust fluid compared to previous automatic transmission designs. Companies currently licensed to produce Dexron VI include Mobil, Chevron, Shell, SK Lubricants, and Valvoline. Using Dexron III in this application can lead to clutch failure, so always use the correct fluid.

Fluid Capacity

The 6L80 has five different oil pans available depending on the application. It is imperative that you have the correct oil pan on your application. Either overfilling or underfilling the transmission can result in transmission clutch failure. Two different pan designs are used:

- Equipped with a standpipe (various standpipe heights are used).
- Equipped with a dipstick, no standpipe used.

Fluid capacity is strictly dependent on the vehicle application in which the transmission is used because the pan part number is dependent on the body type. So, when it comes to fluid capacity, reference the owner's manual for the capacity for your application.

Fluid Level

How the fluid level is checked varies depending on whether your pan is equipped with a standpipe or if the unit has a dipstick.

Superior Transmission Products	Part Number
End play washers	K0146
Valve body update kit	STL6L80
Cooler bypass repair kit	STL010
Pump upgrade kit	STL012

Sonnax Transmission Products	Part Number
Boost valve kit	104520-12K
Line pressure booster kit	6L80-LB1
Oversized converter feed limit valve	104520-11
Oversized pressure regulator kit	104520-07K
Pressure regulator kit	104520-14K
Pump slide spring	104534-HD
Pump vane	76742
Pump thrust washer selective	33452A
Actuator feed limit valve kit	104740-47K
Center support seal kit	104740-14K
Check balls	10000-08
Clutch select valve spring kit	104740-02K
Compensator feed valve kit	104740-09K
End plugs with O-rings	104740-23K
Oversized actuator feed limit valve	104740-12
Oversized clutch boost valve kit	104740-01
Oversized TCC regulator valve kit	104740-07K

Sonnax Transmission Products	Part Number
TCC regulator valve kit	104740-46K
TCC regulator spring	104740-45K
Valve body ZIP kit	6L80-ZIP
Extension housing bushing	104066A
TEHCM pressure switch repair kit	124740-TL30
4-5-6 clutch backing plate	104140-01A
4-5-6 clutch steel plate (0.090 inch)	104120-02
4-5-6 clutch steel plate (0.078 inch)	104120-01
Bearing kit	SBK-G80
Extreme-duty 4-5-6 clutch hub and shaft	104680-45
Heavy-duty 1-2-3-4 piston	104984-01
Heavy-duty 4-5-6 clutch piston kit	104960-01K
Heavy-duty 4-5-6 clutch hub and shaft	104680-36
High-capacity 3-5-R apply ring	104548-01
High-capacity 4-5-6 clutch piston kit	104960-10K

Replace the fluid seal any time the filter is replaced. Use a pair of snap-ring pliers, a screwdriver, or a seal puller to remove the seal. Install the new seal with a seal driver or an appropriately sized socket or flat tool. Lubricate the seal before installing the filter with Transjel or clean transmission fluid. Wiggle the filter as you apply pressure to the filter to engage the filter seal. Install the pan gasket and pan. Tighten all of the bolts evenly.

Dexron VI is the only approved fluid for the 6L applications. Do not use Dexron III or other fluids in this application! Dexron VI made major improvements in oxidation resistance, lubrication capabilities, and temperature ranges compared to Dexron III. Dexron VI is licensed by several manufacturers, including Valvoline, which manufactures the NAPA fluid that is shown. Fluid capacities are listed in this chapter.

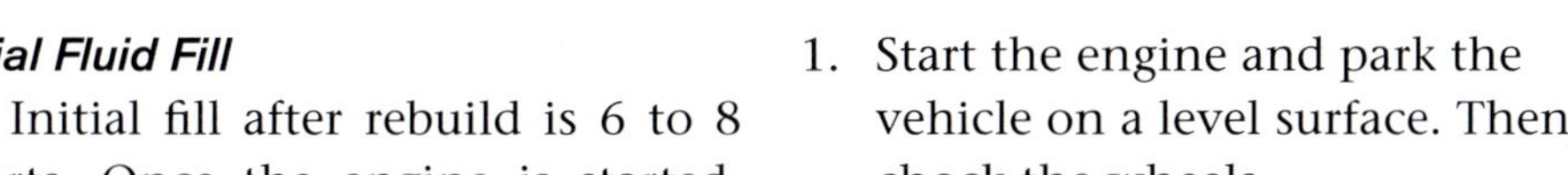

Initial Fluid Fill

Initial fill after rebuild is 6 to 8 quarts. Once the engine is started, the shifter is moved between all of the ranges, pausing as the transmission engages in each range. The fluid level should then be checked. Add fluid as required to get the fluid to the correct level on the dipstick or standpipe.

Dipstick Applications

Before checking the fluid level, perform the following:

1. Start the engine and park the vehicle on a level surface. Then, chock the wheels.
2. Apply the parking brake and vehicle brake and place the shift lever in Park. Move the shifter to each forward gear range as well as reverse, pausing for 3 seconds in each range. Place the vehicle in Park.
3. Allow the engine to idle for a few minutes.
4. Observe the transmission fluid temperature (TFT) using the Driver Information Center (DIC), a scan tool, or by using a temperature gun to measure the oil pan temperature.

Capacity Will Vary Based on Application (2008 Suburban Shown)	Specification	
	Metric	English
Pan Removal and Filter Replacement, Approximate Capacity	5.7 liters	6.0 quarts
Rebuild, Approximate Capacity	9.9 liters	10.5 quarts
Initial fill after rebuild is 6 to 8 quarts. Once the engine is started and the shifter is moved between all the ranges, pausing as the transmission engages in each range, the fluid level should be checked. Add fluid as required to get the fluid to the correct level on the dipstick or standpipe.		
Complete Transmission System, Approximate Capacity	11.5 liters	12.2 quarts
Complete Transmission System (Heavy-Duty Cooling), Approximate Capacity	11.7 liters	12.4 quarts

Cold Fluid Check Procedure

Use the following cold-check procedure to check fluid level when the transmission fluid temperature is between 80 and 90°F (27 and 32°C). Note that it is not as accurate as the hot-check procedure.

1. Locate the dipstick, flip the handle, pull out the dipstick, and wipe it with a clean rag.
2. Install the dipstick, pushing it back in all the way. Wait a few seconds, and pull it out.
3. Check both sides of the dipstick, and use the lower level.
4. Inspect the color of the fluid and its condition.
5. If the fluid level is below the "COLD" mark (lower), add only enough fluid through the dipstick tube as is needed to bring the level up to the mark.
6. If the fluid level is correct, push the dipstick back in all the way. Then, flip the handle down to lock the dipstick in place.
7. Perform a hot check once the transmission has reached operating temperature.

Hot Fluid Check Procedure

Use this procedure to check the transmission fluid level when the transmission fluid temperature is between 160 and 200°F (71 and 93°C):

1. Locate the dipstick, flip the handle, pull out the dipstick, and wipe it with a clean rag.
2. Install the dipstick, pushing it back in all the way. Wait a few seconds, and pull it out.
3. Check both sides of the dipstick, and use the lower level.
4. Inspect the color of the fluid and its condition.
5. If the fluid level is below the "HOT" mark (upper), add only enough fluid through the dipstick tube as is needed to bring the level up to the mark.
6. If the fluid level is correct, push the dipstick back in all the way. Then, flip the handle down to lock the dipstick in place.

Standpipe Applications

Use this procedure to check the transmission fluid level when the transmission fluid temperature is between 86 and 122°F (50 and 80°C):

1. Start the engine and park the vehicle on a level surface, block the wheels.
2. Apply the vehicle brake and parking brake, and place the shift

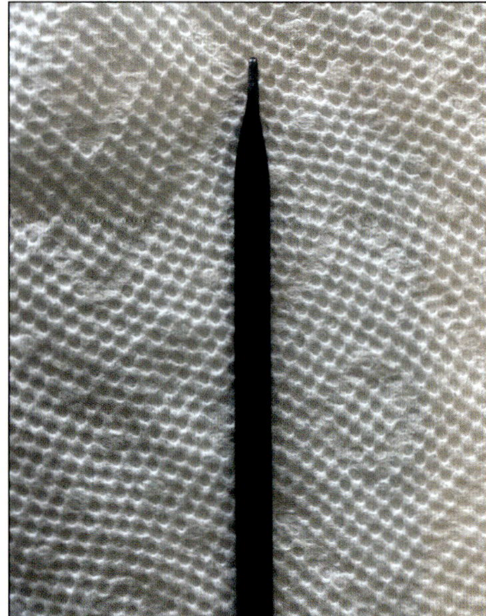

Some 6L applications use a dipstick to check the transmission fluid level. The dipstick includes hot and cold levels.

Some 6L applications are equipped with standpipes rather than a dipstick to check the fluid level. Fluid temperature is critical when checking fluid level via a standpipe. To check the fluid level, a 6L transmission must be between 86 and 122°F (50 and 80°C); otherwise, you can underfill or overfill the transmission because the reading will not be accurate. With the transmission filled with fluid and in park, the engine running, and the wheels chocked and on level ground, remove the standpipe plug. Fluid should drip from the plug when the level is correct. If fluid runs out or no fluid is present, the unit is overfilled or underfilled.

lever in Park. Move the shifter to each forward gear range as well as reverse, pausing for 3 seconds in each range. Place the vehicle in Park.
3. Allow the engine to idle for a few minutes.
4. Observe the transmission fluid temperature (TFT) using the Driver Information Center (DIC), a scan tool, or by using a temperature gun to measure the oil pan temperature.
5. With the engine running, remove the standpipe plug located in the transmission oil pan.
6. If oil runs out of the standpipe, allow it to drain until it is only dripping. Install the plug and torque it to 18 ft-lbs (25 Nm).
7. If oil fails to drip or run out, add fluid through the standpipe hole or the fill port on the passenger's side of the transmission.

On-Vehicle Repairs and Adjustments

Once the transmission has been installed into the vehicle, it may be necessary to perform on-vehicle adjustments for the transmission to perform properly. Some of the adjustments are mechanical in nature, such as adjusting the shift cable, while others will require the use of a scan tool to perform.

Shifter Cable Adjustments

If the shifter cable was simply removed from the transmission during the rebuild, you should not need to adjust the cable. However, if the cable requires replacement or you find that the cable was adjusted incorrectly, the cable will need to be adjusted.

Two shifter cable designs are used on the 6L80: one-piece and two-piece. The biggest difference is that the socket on the two-piece design must be unbolted from the transmission shift linkage because it will be damaged if you try to pry it off the attaching ball.

If the cable was removed during disassembly, it is likely that it will not need to be adjusted and can simply be reinstalled. If the cable was somehow adjusted incorrectly or was replaced, it will require adjustment. To adjust, place the transmission in park and chock the wheels. Grab the cable, pull back the white cover to expose the natural-colored lock. Insert a flat-blade screwdriver under the lock ramp on the top of the lock. This will release the cable adjustment. Release the transmission end of the cable, allowing the spring to adjust the cable. Push down the natural-colored lock to lock the cable into position. Clip the white cover into position. Check each range position to make sure that you performed the adjustment correctly. If any ranges are not available, repeat the process.

Adjustment Procedure

1. Place the shift lever in the Park position with the wheels chocked.
2. Place the transmission manual shaft lever in the Park position.
3. Open the white cable cover using a screwdriver to unlock the cable locking tab (natural colored). Grasp the shift cable shifter end in your left hand and the shift cable transmission end in your right hand. Align the two ends and slide them together. Once you slide the two-piece cable together, it will no longer come apart, as it locks permanently into position.
4. Release the transmission end; this will allow the spring to apply tension to the cable.
5. Open the white cover on the shifter end of the cable. Push down the natural-colored lock button. This will engage the locking teeth on the transmission end of the cable.

Adaptive Learning

Clearing and relearning the adaptive values stored in the TEHCM memory requires the use of a scan tool. Not all scan tools are capable of performing these functions, so refer to your scan tool manufacturer's literature to determine if your scanner will be able to perform the required resets.

The 6L80 software is equipped with a feature known as adaptive learning. This is designed to ensure that the transmission shifts and operates the same at 100,000 miles as it did at 100 miles. Multiple different types of adaptive learning are used, but the most common type is the upshift/downshift adapt.

The 6L80 TCM has the ability to learn the shift times of all the transmission upshifts and downshifts; this is known as shift adapts. This effectively allows the TCM to determine if a shift is too hard or too soft and make adjustments for the shift feel issue.

The TCM measures the clutch apply/release rates to determine the shift time. This is accomplished by the TCM monitoring the shift command, the ISS and OSS frequencies during the shift. The TCM commands a shift and then monitors for a change in the ISS frequency. By measuring the time between when the solenoid was commanded to make a shift and the time when it sees an ISS change showing that the shift is complete, the TCM can determine the shift time.

The measured shift time is then compared to the desired shift time by the TCM for that vehicle load and shift. If the shift time was too short, the TCM will command less pressure the next time that particular shift is commanded again. If the shift time was too long, the TCM will increase the pressure when that particular shift happens again. The corrected shift pressure offset positive and negative values are stored in the TCM memory to be used on the next shifts. While the system is very sophisticated, the TCM is monitoring the shift times for all of the upshifts and downshifts at various throttle openings and storing that information in the TCM memory for use on the next shift that meets that criteria.

The shift adapt pressure offset values are learned and stored in the TCM memory for each shift. If repairs are performed on the transmission that can affect shift times, it is important that the shift adapt stored values are reset and relearned.

Clearing and Relearning Adapts

The shift adapts should be cleared and relearned if any of the following occur:

- The transmission was replaced
- The transmission was rebuilt
- The valve body was replaced or repaired
- Any repair that could impact shift times was performed, including replacing or reprogramming the TEHCM TCM

Clearing the adaptive memory is accomplished with a quality scan tool. The reason that the adapts must be cleared is because you were likely repairing the transmission because of an issue with the transmission. The TCM will have learned and attempted to correct for the issues present within the transmission.

For example, if the seal for the 2-6 clutch is worn, the 1-2 and/or 5-6 shifts may flare up. The TCM will learn the shift time and provide a positive pressure offset in an attempt to correct for the worn seal on the next adaptable shift. Then, you repair the transmission and install new seals so that the leakage is no longer present. However, the TCM does not know that you repaired the transmission. So, it will shift the transmission using the pressure offsets that were stored for the worn transmission. This can cause transmission damage as well as an upset driver because it takes many shifts at various throttle openings and temperatures relearn the correct values for the repaired transmission.

Clearing the adapts clears all the adaptive memories. Clear all DTCs prior to clearing the adapts. Follow the instructions on your scan tool to clear the adapts. Once the adapts are cleared, new transmission adapts need to be relearned. Some scan tools have the ability to perform a "fast learn," which shortens the length of time that it takes to relearn the adapts. Once the fast learn has been performed, a road test should be performed, upshifting and downshifting the transmission through all of gears at various different throttle openings.

If your scan tool does not have the ability to perform a fast learn, perform a very extensive road test, operating the vehicle through all the upshifts and downshifts at various throttle openings and temperatures. On late-model applications, a scan tool parameter is available, indicating when the adapt up dates are complete.

Fast learn capabilities are not available on some models or model-year applications. The 1-2 and 3-2 shifts are the most difficult to learn for the 6L80 application, so it is likely that it will take some extended driving, while cycling through those shifts, to attain and acceptable shift feel for the driver.

Road Testing

Road testing is used to test the transmission for proper operation as well as to allow the adapts to relearn

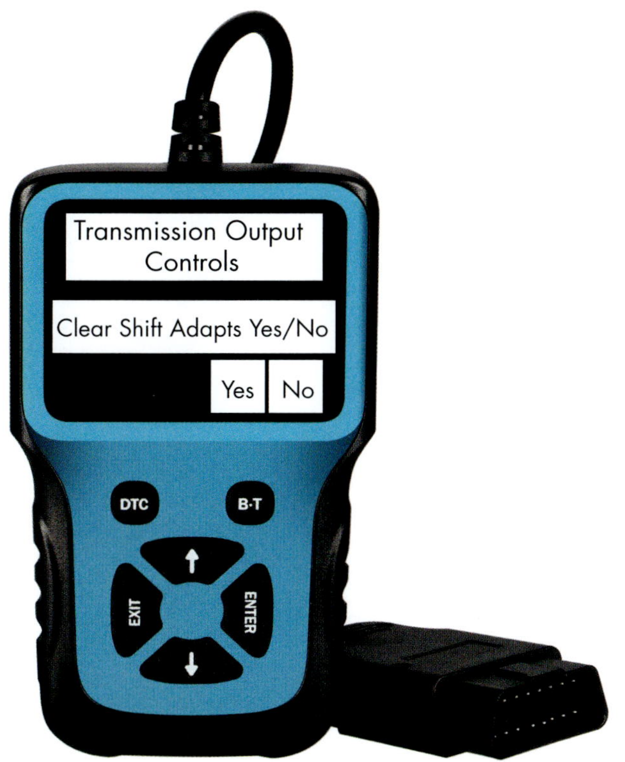

the transmissions shift characteristics. With the scan tool attached, the road test needs to be thorough and complete. This includes scan tool checks, TCC operation, upshift and downshift operation, and garage shift operation.

Scan Tool Checks

Perform the following procedure to ensure that the electronic transmission components are functioning properly. If these components are not checked, a simple electrical condition could be misdiagnosed.

1. Connect the scan tool.
2. Ensure that the gear selector is in Park and that the parking brake is set.
3. Start the engine. Scan for DTCs and address any current DTCs set before moving to the next step.
4. Verify that the following scan tool data parameters can be obtained and that they are functioning properly. The parameters include engine speed, transmission ISS, transmission OSS, vehicle speed, IMS, commanded gear, gear ratio, line PC Sol, pressure command, brake switch, ECT, TFT, TCM temperature, calculated throttle position, actual throttle position, ignition voltage, TFP Switch 1, TFP Switch 3, TFP Switch 4, TFP Switch 5, PCS 2 Pressure Command, PCS 3 Pressure Command, PCS 4 Pressure Command, PCS 5 Pressure Command, Shift Solenoid 1, Shift Solenoid 2, TCC PCS Duty Cycle, and TCC Slip Speed.

Monitor the data values at key-on, engine off, and engine running and compare the values to the service manual standards or data from another known good vehicle.

Garage Shifts

- Set the parking brake. Start the engine and allow the transmission to warm up. With the engine running, apply the brake pedal.
- Move the gear selector through each gear range: P/R, R/P, R/N, N/R, N/D, D/N, D/M, and M/D. (M stands for manual.)
- Pause 2 to 3 seconds in each gear position. Verify that the gear engagements are not delayed (engagements should take less than 2 seconds) and should not be harsh. Monitor the engagement with your scan tool by observing the ISS/turbine shift speed sensor value. ISS should drop to 0 showing when the engagement is complete.

Harsh engagement may be caused by high engine idle speed, incorrect line pressure, or high line pressure resulting from a DTC being set or incomplete adaptive learning.

Delayed engagement may be caused by low idle speed, low fluid level, incorrect line pressure, the TFT being too cold, the shift selector linkage being out of adjustment, or incomplete adaptive learning.

TCC and Shift Controls

The TCM calculates the upshift/downshift points based on MAP, MAF, TFT, ECT, throttle position, and vehicle speed. The TCM compares the values to those stored in a shift-point table located in the vehicle software set. When it is appropriate for the vehicle to make an upshift or downshift, the TCM commands the appropriate pressure control solenoid to turn on or off.

The key parameters to monitor for shift control operation include the gear ratio, TCC slip, PCS 2, PCS 3, PCS 4, PCS 5, TCC PCS commands and feedback values, and engine RPM to determine if a shift has occurred and if the clutch is slipping.

The TCC system that is used in 6L80 applications is an EC3 design. This design makes it difficult to feel the TCC apply because it uses a pulse width modulated control system to control TCC apply and release. EC3 systems are also designed to slip at steady load and steady throttle openings, which should be considered normal. Normal TCC slip rates vary from 0 to 100 rpm while on flat roads with steady throttle and TCC commanded on. Excessive slip rates indicate an issue with the system, such as a faulty torque converter or TCC apply valve, a TCC regulator valve that is stuck or worn, a TCC circuit hydraulic leakage, or a faulty TCC PCS.

Downshifts

1. Attach your scan tool and monitor the commanded gear shift time parameters. Accelerate the vehicle in drive range at light throttle (5 to 15 percent) until third gear is just achieved.
2. Quickly increase throttle angle until the commanded gear position indicates that a downshift to second gear was commanded. Note the shift feel and shift time. Repeat this process for each shift (4 to 3, 5 to 4, and 6 to 5).
3. Note any harsh, soft, or delayed shifts or slipping conditions. Note any noise or vibration.
4. The same process should be conducted using manual shift control either with the shift lever or by using the driver shift controls on the steering wheel.

Using a 6L80 in a Non-GM Application or GM Application Not Originally Equipped

The 6L series of transmissions are equipped with an internally mounted TCM known as a TEHCM. The TEHCM controls all of the transmission functions and also communicates/interacts with many different controllers on the vehicle. The other controllers share information via the CAN data bus with the TEHCM, which is vital to TCM operation. Without the correct input from those controllers, the TEHCM will be unable to operate the transmission. Installing a 6L transmission into a vehicle not previously equipped with a 6L application will result in major transmission operational issues.

If you want to use a 6L80 in a non-OEM application, you must use an aftermarket controller to provide the required information to the TEHCM. Two companies have products already released or products that will be released shortly to allow the conversion:

- Powertrain Control Solutions (powertraincontrolsolutions.com) from Ashland, Virginia, has a product referred to as the TCM2650 Mechatronic Transmission Controller that can operate the GM 6L, GM 6T, and Allison transmissions. In addition, the TCM2650 can also be used to operate the ZF 6HP generation II or the VW DSG dual-clutch applications. The TCM2650 is programmable, which allows you to select upshift/downshift schedules and TCC application schedules based on your needs.
- HGM Electronics (hgmelectronics.com) from Torrance, California, home of the Compushift, is in the process of developing a stand-alone controller for the 6L80 application.

Other Aftermarket Products and Non-Internal Components

Internal aftermarket components, such as valve body kits, shafts, and drums, were covered earlier in this chapter. Non-internal aftermarket components include:

- The Rostra harness repair kit (part number 104445) is a replacement pigtail for your vehicle harness. Simply remove the old harness connector and splice in the new harness.
- The Motion Race Works cooler installation kit (part number 1600004) allows you to bypass the factory cooler configuration so that an aftermarket standalone cooler may be installed.
- The Earl's cooler bypass kit (part number 1128ERL) eliminates the cooler bypass valve and provides threaded fittings for the use of braided cooler lines. The part number 1133ERL kit allows the attachment of braided lines to the factory cooler bypass valve.
- The ICT Billet cooler bypass kit (part number 551121-8AN) eliminates the cooler bypass valve and provides threaded fittings for the use of braided cooler lines.
- Bower Performance Transmissions offers a cooler bypass kit (part number 6L80CMA-01).
- Performance torque converters are available from multiple

companies, including ProTorque, RevMax, TCI, Hughes, and more.
- Shifters are available from Lokar (part numbers ES6L80EM and ES6L80FM) and Pace Performance (part number GMP-7613).
- B&M (part number 22168) is a flexible dipstick assembly.
- A bellhousing adapter from QuickTime (part number RM 7051) allows the 6L80/90 to be installed behind the Cadillac 3.0L engine.
- Transfer case adapter kits are available from Advance Adapters that allow the 6L80 to be coupled to non-GM transfer cases, such as the Toyota Land Cruiser (part numbers 50-9612, 50-9611, and 50-9610), Jeep Dana 300 (part number 50-9620), Jeep NP241 (part number 50-9940), Land Rover (part number 6245-027), and GM NP205 (part number 50-9552B).
- G-force cross members allow the 6L80 to be installed in non-OEM applications, such as the 1975–1981 Camaro/Firebird (part number RCF2L-6L80), 1970–1974 Camaro/Firebird (part number RCF2E-6L80), 1967–1969 Camaro/Firebird (part number RCF1-6L80), Nova/Chevy II 1962–1967 (part number RCNV-6L80), 1982–2005 S-10 (part number RCS-10-6L80), 1969–1970 B-Cars (part number RCBE-6L80), 1977–1990 B-Cars (part number RC83-6L80), 1964–1972 A-Cars (part number RCAE-6L80), 1973–1977 A-Cars (part number RCAL-6L80), 1982–2005 Blazer (part number RCS-108-6L80), 1978–1988 G-Cars (part number RCG-6L80), and 1968–1981 Corvette (part number RCC3-6L80).
- B&M part number 70392 is a billet deep pan for the 6L80.
- The HGM Electronics part number 6L80 is a deep PML.

Diagnostic Pointers

Always start your diagnosis by inspecting the battery, power, and ground circuits for issues. Using a scan tool, check for any DTCs that are stored in the various controllers. DTC default actions may be what is keeping your transmission from working correctly, so they need to be addressed prior to condemning the transmission.

Keep in mind that slippage issues are typically due to low clutch-apply pressure, while hard engagement issues are typically due to high clutch-apply pressures. If you have slippage or hard/slipping shift issues, always verify that you have the correct line pressure as a starting point. Again, many hard shift–related issues are created by the default actions that the TCM takes when some DTCs are set.

Below is a list of issues with diagnostic advice.

Issue	Potential Reason
Vibration or Noise that Changes with Speed	Torque converter bolts; bearings #55, #57, #65, #69, #71, #63, and #57 damaged; planetary carrier teeth damaged; TCC shudder; engine misfire; U-joint worn; or driveshaft damaged.
Noise/Vibration in 1st and/or Reverse	Center support, low/reverse clutch, low sprag, output carrier damaged, or splines stripped.
Noise/Vibration in 1st, 2nd, 3rd, 4th, 5th, and Reverse	Input carrier or sun gear damaged/worn, 1-2-3-4 or 3-5-R clutch damaged/worn.
Noise/Vibration in 1st, 2nd, 6th, or Reverse	Center support or output carrier bearings #458, #460, or #485 damaged/worn; worn output carrier or sun gear.
Noise/Vibration in 2nd and/or 6th Gear	Worn 2/6 clutch components, worn sun gear bushings.
Noise/Vibration in 4th and/or 5th and/or 6th	4-5-6 clutch hub damaged, 4-5-6 clutch damaged, 4-5-6 clutch damper damaged, worn/damaged bearings #55 or #57.
Shift Indicator Displays the Wrong Range	Shift cable out of adjustment, worn manual valve detent, faulty IMS.
No Movement	Low on fluid, low pressure, faulty pump, stuck pressure regulator valve, plugged filter, shift cable adjustment, broken input/output shaft, valve body or check ball issue, worn/stuck clutch select valve, the #2 check ball missing.

Issue	Potential Reason
No Park	Shift linkage out of adjustment, park pawl system worn/damaged, broken output shaft or Park gear, worn manual valve detent.
Harsh Garage Shift	Adaptive learning values not reset or relearned, engine speed too high, high line pressure, worn/stuck pressure regulator valve or isolator valve, TFT sensor faulty, line pressure control solenoid faulty, 1-2-3-4 or 3-5-R clutch-apply issue due to incorrect clutch clearance/travel. (Note that it is normal for the shifts to be more aggressive when the transmission fluid temperature is cold).
No 1st Gear	Worn/damaged/improperly assembled 1-2-3-4 clutch, damaged/improperly assembled low sprag, broken/cracked 1-2-3-4 piston, worn/stuck clutch select 2 or 3 or 1-2-3-4 clutch regulator valves, center support seals damaged or incorrect seals installed, worn or missing check balls #1 and/or #2 and/or #3, low pressure, incorrect fluid level, worn pump or pressure regulator valve, shaft splines damaged, worn or incorrectly installed low sprag, adapts not properly reset or relearned.
1st and/or Reverse Harsh/Soft/ Slipping	Center support seals incorrect or leaking, 1R/4-5-6 pressure regulator worn/sticking, clutch select valves 2 and/or 3 worn or sticking, low/reverse clutch damaged or incorrectly assembled, low sprag failing, fluid level incorrect, filter plugged, low fluid pressure, check balls worn or missing, leaking 1-2-3-4 or 3-5-R clutch seals, cracked 3-5-R drum or 1-2-3-4 piston, adapts not properly reset or relearned.
No 2nd and/or 6th or Harsh/Soft/Slipping 2nd and/or 6th Gear	Sticking/worn 2-6 clutch regulator valve, incorrect or damaged center support seals, worn or damaged 2-6 clutch seals or clutches, pressure control solenoid #4 faulty, #6 check ball missing or worn, adapts not properly reset or relearned.
No 3rd and/or 5th and/or Reverse or Harsh/Soft/Slipping 3rd and/or 5th and/or Reverse	Sticking or worn 3-5-R clutch regulator valve or clutch select valve #3, missing/worn #7 check ball, worn/damaged 3-5-R clutch seals, stator support seal rings, cracked 3-5-R clutch drum, pressure control solenoid #2 faulty, adapts not properly reset or relearned.
No 4th and/or 5th and/or 6th or Harsh/Soft/Slipping 4th and/or 5th and/or 6th	Sticking or worn 4-5-6 clutch regulator valve or clutch select valve 2, missing/worn check ball #3, #4, damaged turbine shaft seals, worn/damaged 4-5-6 clutch seals, cracked/broken 4-5-6 clutch drum or shaft, pressure control solenoid #3 faulty, adapts not properly reset or relearned.
No Reverse	Missing/worn #5 check ball, worn/stuck 3-5-R and/or 1R4-5-6 clutch regulator valves, incorrect or damaged center support seals, fluid level incorrect, low line pressure, plugged filter, incorrectly assembled or leaking low/reverse clutch seals, incorrectly assembled or leaking 3-5-R clutch seals, cracked 3-5-R drum, leaking stator support seal rings, stripped shaft splines.
No TCC Apply	Sticking/worn TCC apply valve, converter limit valve or TCC regulator valve, TCC solenoid faulty, turbine shaft seal leakage, damaged stator support, faulty torque converter.
No TCC Release	Stuck/worn TCC control valve, TCC apply valve, TCC limit valve, faulty TCC solenoid.
Low Line Pressure	Sticking/worn pressure regulator valve, actuator feed-limit valve, clutch boost valve, pump pressure-relief valve, worn isolator valve, low fluid level, plugged filter, worn pump, leaking filter plate.
High Line Pressure	Sticking/worn pressure regulator valve, actuator feed-limit valve, clutch boost valve.

MAJOR MECHANICAL COMPONENTS

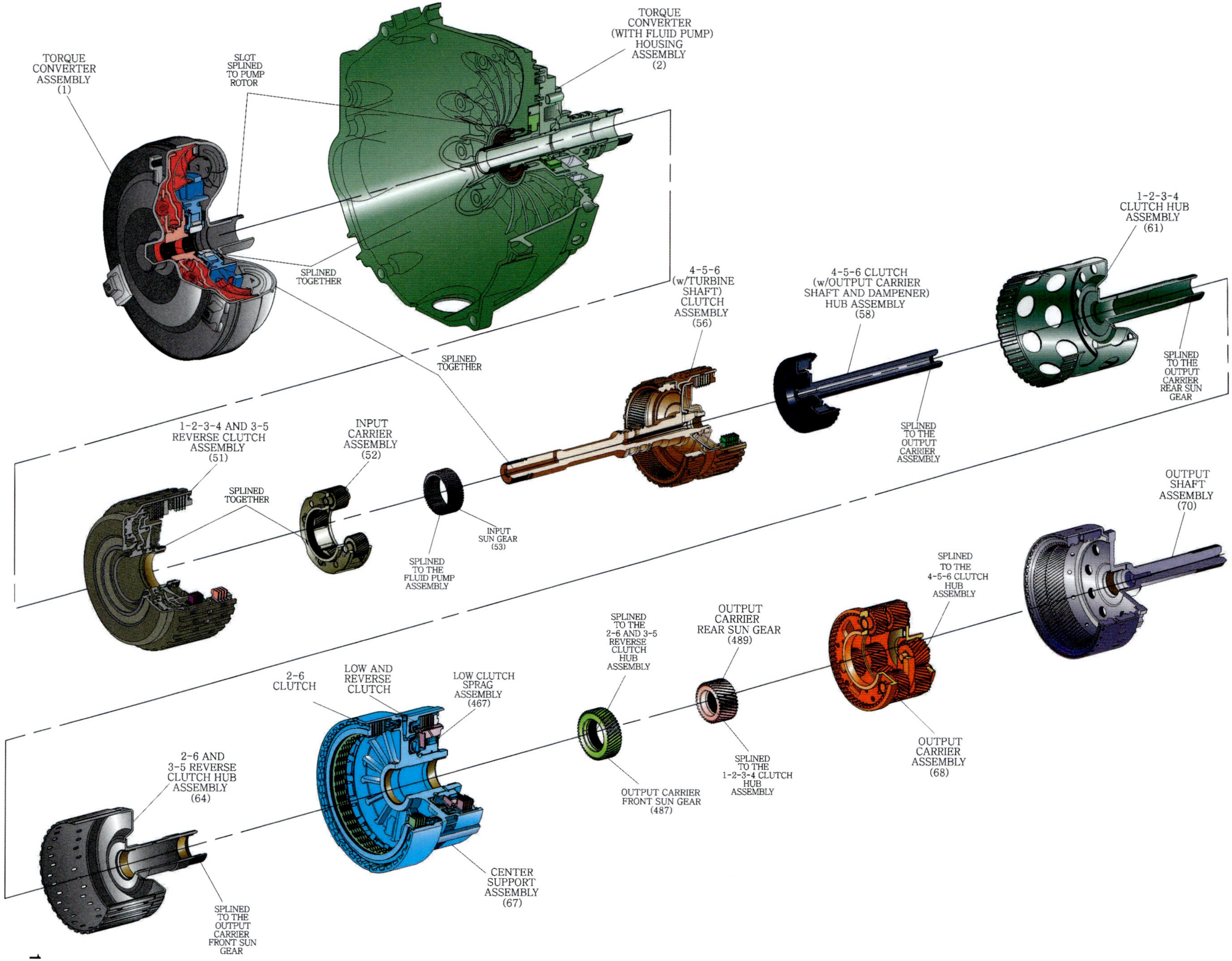

TORQUE CONVERTER ASSEMBLY (1)

SLOT SPLINED TO PUMP ROTOR

TORQUE CONVERTER (WITH FLUID PUMP) HOUSING ASSEMBLY (2)

SPLINED TOGETHER

SPLINED TOGETHER

4-5-6 (w/TURBINE SHAFT) CLUTCH ASSEMBLY (56)

4-5-6 CLUTCH (w/OUTPUT CARRIER SHAFT AND DAMPENER) HUB ASSEMBLY (58)

1-2-3-4 CLUTCH HUB ASSEMBLY (61)

SPLINED TO THE OUTPUT CARRIER REAR SUN GEAR

SPLINED TO THE OUTPUT CARRIER ASSEMBLY

1-2-3-4 AND 3-5 REVERSE CLUTCH ASSEMBLY (51)

SPLINED TOGETHER

INPUT CARRIER ASSEMBLY (52)

INPUT SUN GEAR (53)

SPLINED TO THE FLUID PUMP ASSEMBLY

OUTPUT SHAFT ASSEMBLY (70)

SPLINED TO THE 4-5-6 CLUTCH HUB ASSEMBLY

OUTPUT CARRIER ASSEMBLY (68)

OUTPUT CARRIER REAR SUN GEAR (489)

SPLINED TO THE 1-2-3-4 CLUTCH HUB ASSEMBLY

SPLINED TO THE 2-6 AND 3-5 REVERSE CLUTCH HUB ASSEMBLY

OUTPUT CARRIER FRONT SUN GEAR (487)

2-6 CLUTCH

LOW AND REVERSE CLUTCH

LOW CLUTCH SPRAG ASSEMBLY (467)

CENTER SUPPORT ASSEMBLY (67)

2-6 AND 3-5 REVERSE CLUTCH HUB ASSEMBLY (64)

SPLINED TO THE OUTPUT CARRIER FRONT SUN GEAR

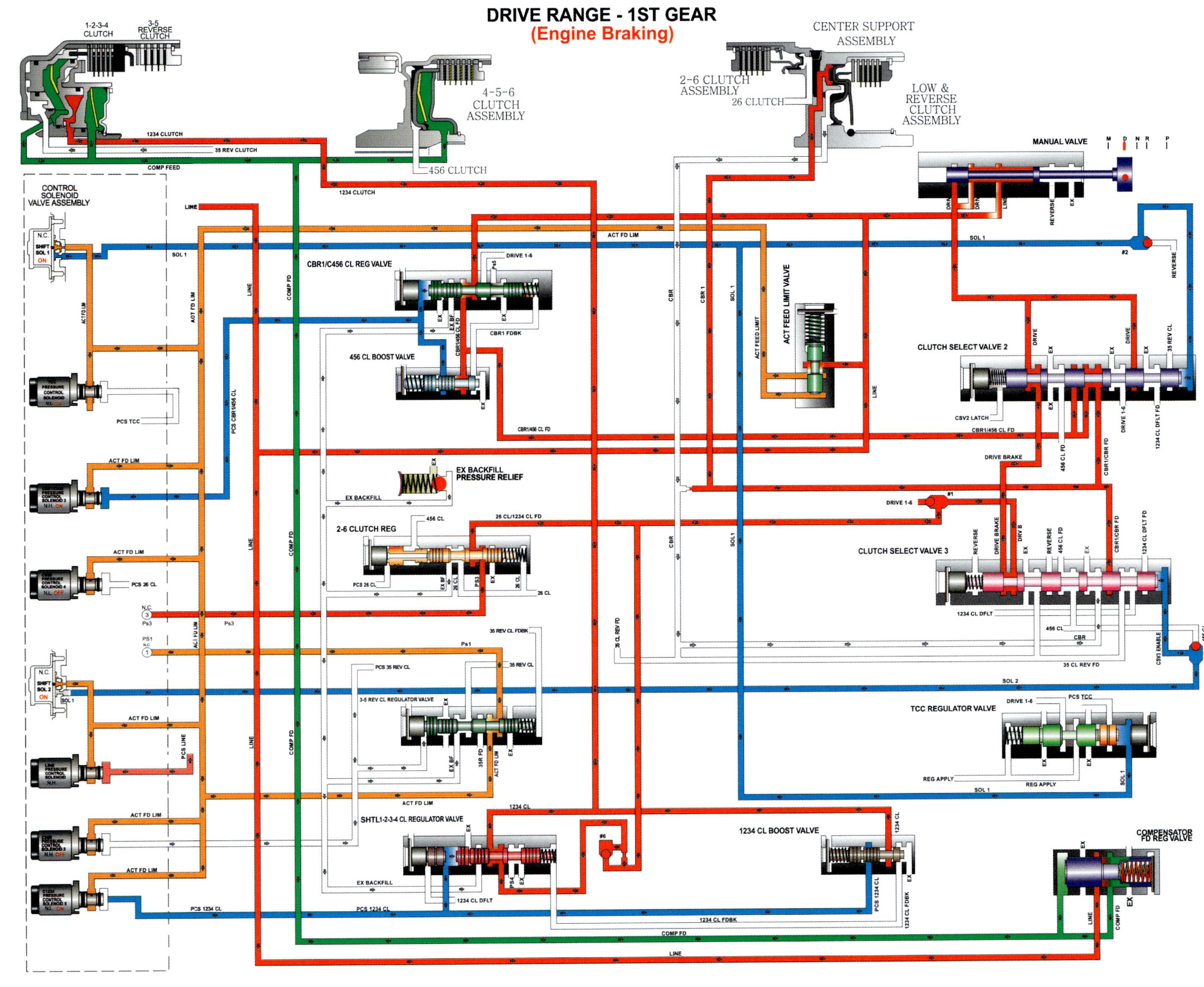
DRIVE RANGE - 1ST GEAR
(Engine Braking)
1-2-3-4 CLUTCH
3-5 REVERSE CLUTCH
4-5-6 CLUTCH ASSEMBLY
456 CLUTCH
CENTER SUPPORT ASSEMBLY
2-6 CLUTCH ASSEMBLY
26 CLUTCH
LOW & REVERSE CLUTCH ASSEMBLY
MANUAL VALVE
CONTROL SOLENOID VALVE ASSEMBLY
CBR1/C456 CL REG VALVE
456 CL BOOST VALVE
ACT FEED LIMIT VALVE
CLUTCH SELECT VALVE 2
EX BACKFILL PRESSURE RELIEF
2-6 CLUTCH REG
CLUTCH SELECT VALVE 3
TCC REGULATOR VALVE
SHTL1-2-3-4 CL REGULATOR VALVE
1234 CL BOOST VALVE
COMPENSATOR FD REG VALVE
1234 CLUTCH
35 REV CLUTCH
COMP FEED
LINE
ACT FD LIM
SOL 1
SOL 2
CBR
CBR 1
COMP FD

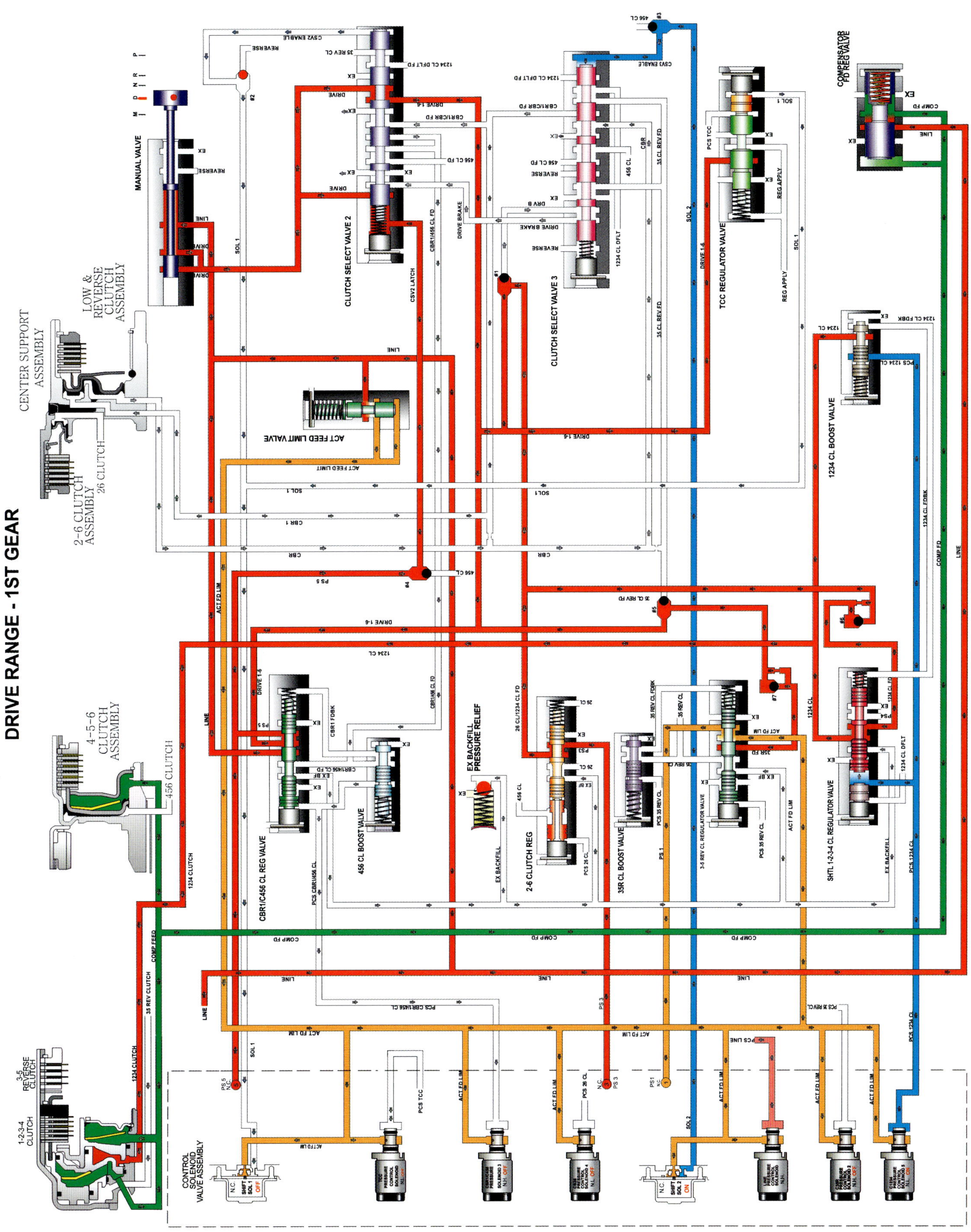
DRIVE RANGE - 1ST GEAR
MANUAL VALVE
CLUTCH SELECT VALVE 2
CLUTCH SELECT VALVE 3
TCC REGULATOR VALVE
COMPENSATOR FD REG VALVE
ACT FEED LIMIT VALVE
1234 CL BOOST VALVE
CENTER SUPPORT ASSEMBLY
LOW & REVERSE CLUTCH ASSEMBLY
2-6 CLUTCH ASSEMBLY
26 CLUTCH
4-5-6 CLUTCH ASSEMBLY
456 CLUTCH
CBR1/C456 CL REG VALVE
456 CL BOOST VALVE
EX BACKFILL PRESSURE RELIEF
2-6 CLUTCH REG
35R CL BOOST VALVE
3-5 REV CL REGULATOR VALVE
SHTL 1-2-3-4 CL REGULATOR VALVE
3-5 REVERSE CLUTCH
1-2-3-4 CLUTCH
CONTROL SOLENOID VALVE ASSEMBLY

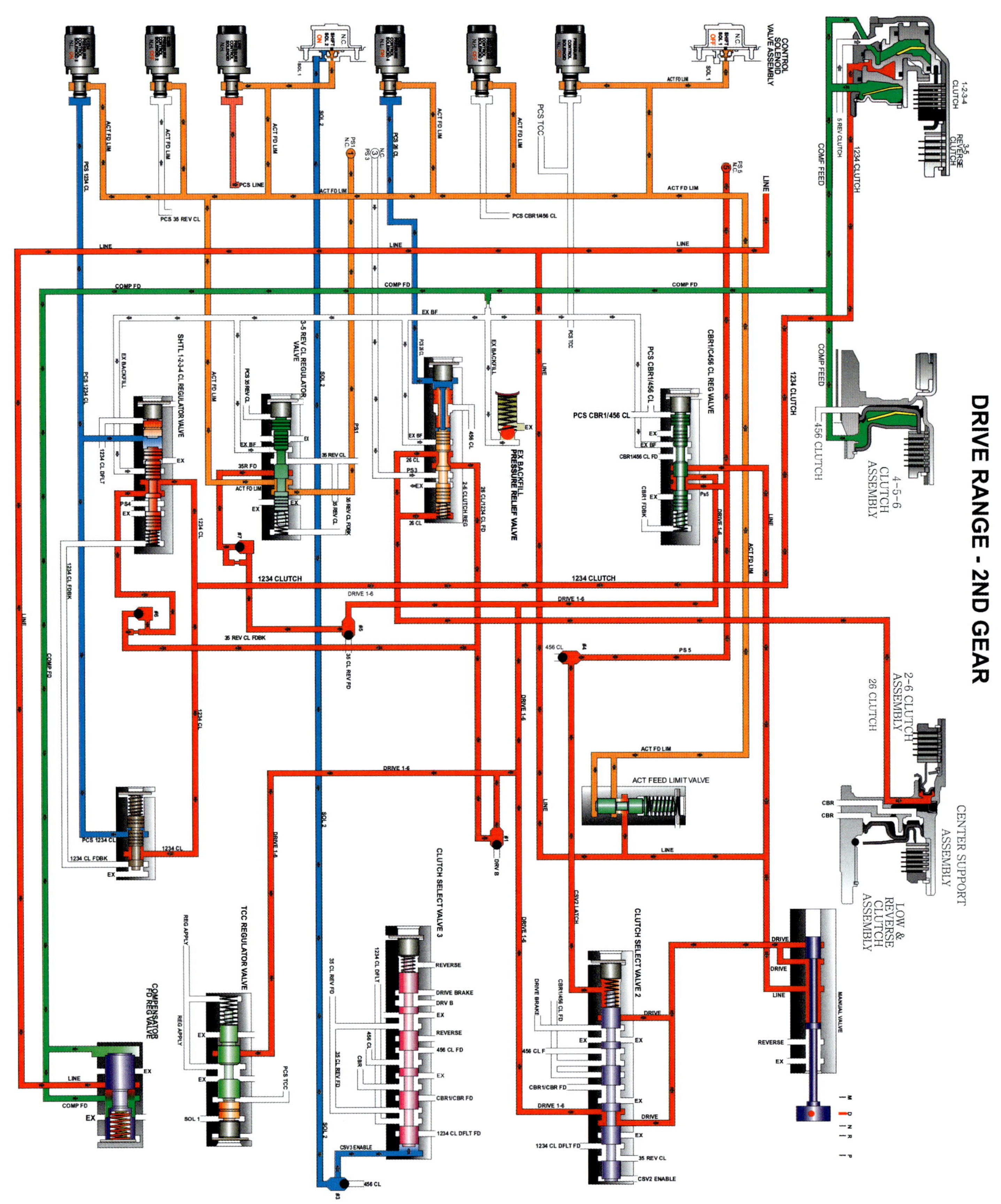

DRIVE RANGE - 2ND GEAR
CONTROL SOLENOID VALVE ASSEMBLY
1-2-3-4 CLUTCH
3-5 REVERSE CLUTCH
456 CLUTCH
4-5-6 CLUTCH ASSEMBLY
2-6 CLUTCH ASSEMBLY
26 CLUTCH
CENTER SUPPORT ASSEMBLY
LOW & REVERSE CLUTCH ASSEMBLY
ACT FEED LIMIT VALVE

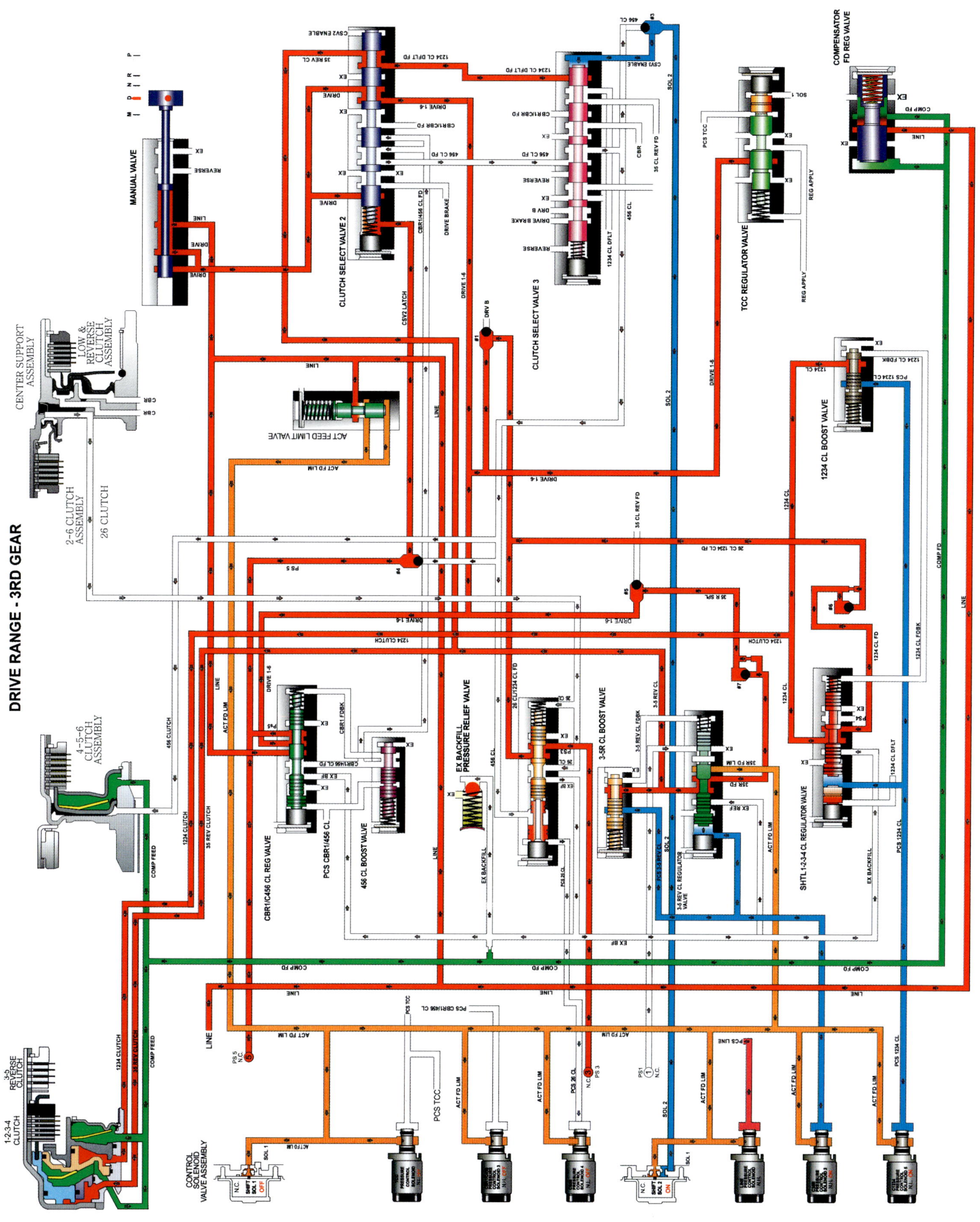
DRIVE RANGE - 3RD GEAR
MANUAL VALVE
CLUTCH SELECT VALVE 2
CLUTCH SELECT VALVE 3
TCC REGULATOR VALVE
COMPENSATOR FD REG VALVE
CENTER SUPPORT ASSEMBLY
LOW & REVERSE CLUTCH ASSEMBLY
2-6 CLUTCH ASSEMBLY
26 CLUTCH
ACT FEED LIMIT VALVE
1234 CL BOOST VALVE
4-5-6 CLUTCH ASSEMBLY
CBR1/C456 CL REG VALVE
456 CL BOOST VALVE
EX BACKFILL PRESSURE RELIEF VALVE
3-5R CL BOOST VALVE
SHTL 1-2-3-4 CL REGULATOR VALVE
3-5 REVERSE CLUTCH
1-2-3-4 CLUTCH
CONTROL SOLENOID VALVE ASSEMBLY
PCS TCC

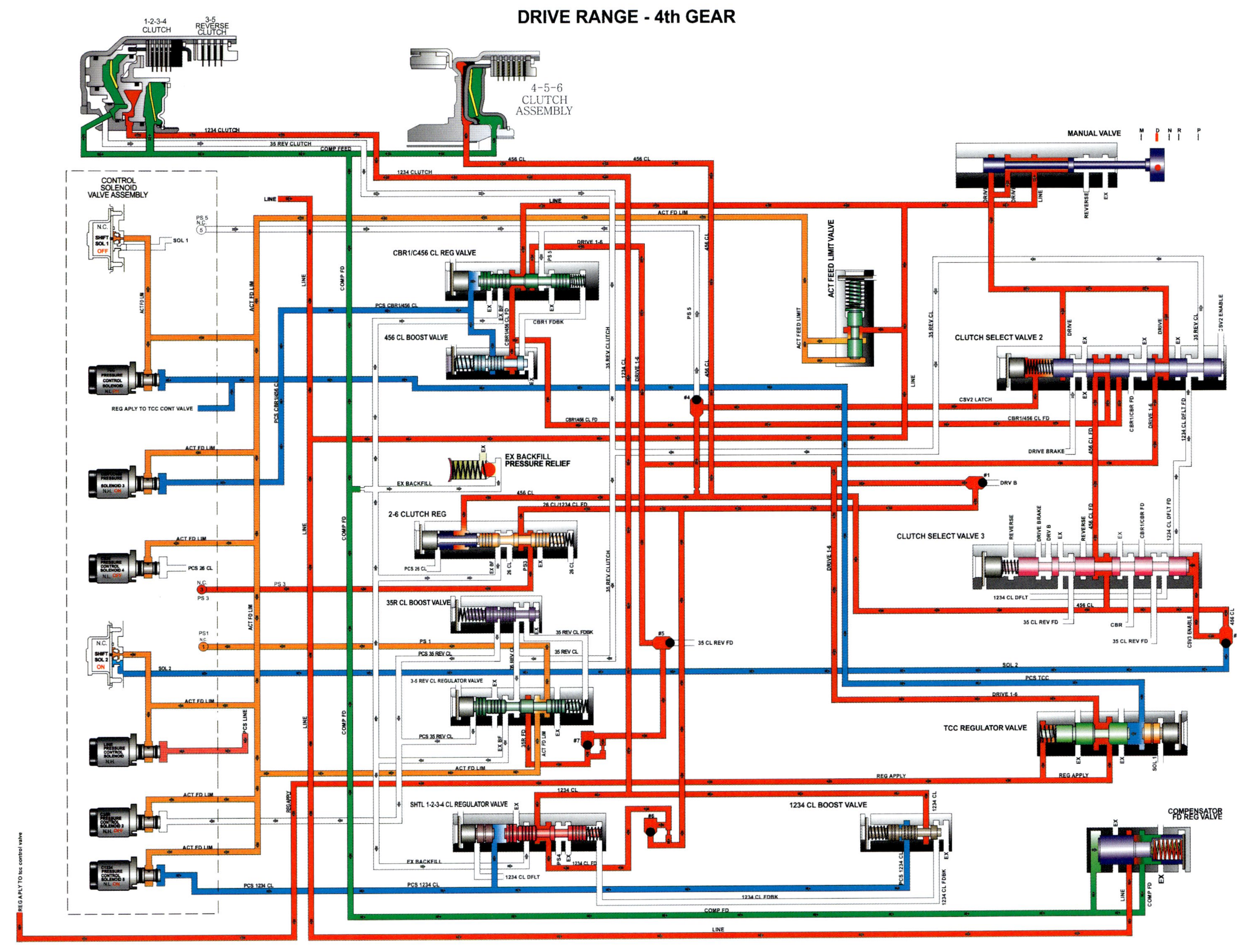
DRIVE RANGE - 4th GEAR
1-2-3-4 CLUTCH
3-5 REVERSE CLUTCH
4-5-6 CLUTCH ASSEMBLY
CONTROL SOLENOID VALVE ASSEMBLY
REG APLY TO TCC CONT VALVE
MANUAL VALVE
CBR1/C456 CL REG VALVE
456 CL BOOST VALVE
ACT FEED LIMIT VALVE
CLUTCH SELECT VALVE 2
EX BACKFILL PRESSURE RELIEF
2-6 CLUTCH REG
CLUTCH SELECT VALVE 3
35R CL BOOST VALVE
3-5 REV CL REGULATOR VALVE
TCC REGULATOR VALVE
SHTL 1-2-3-4 CL REGULATOR VALVE
1234 CL BOOST VALVE
COMPENSATOR FD REG VALVE
REG APLY TO tcc control valve

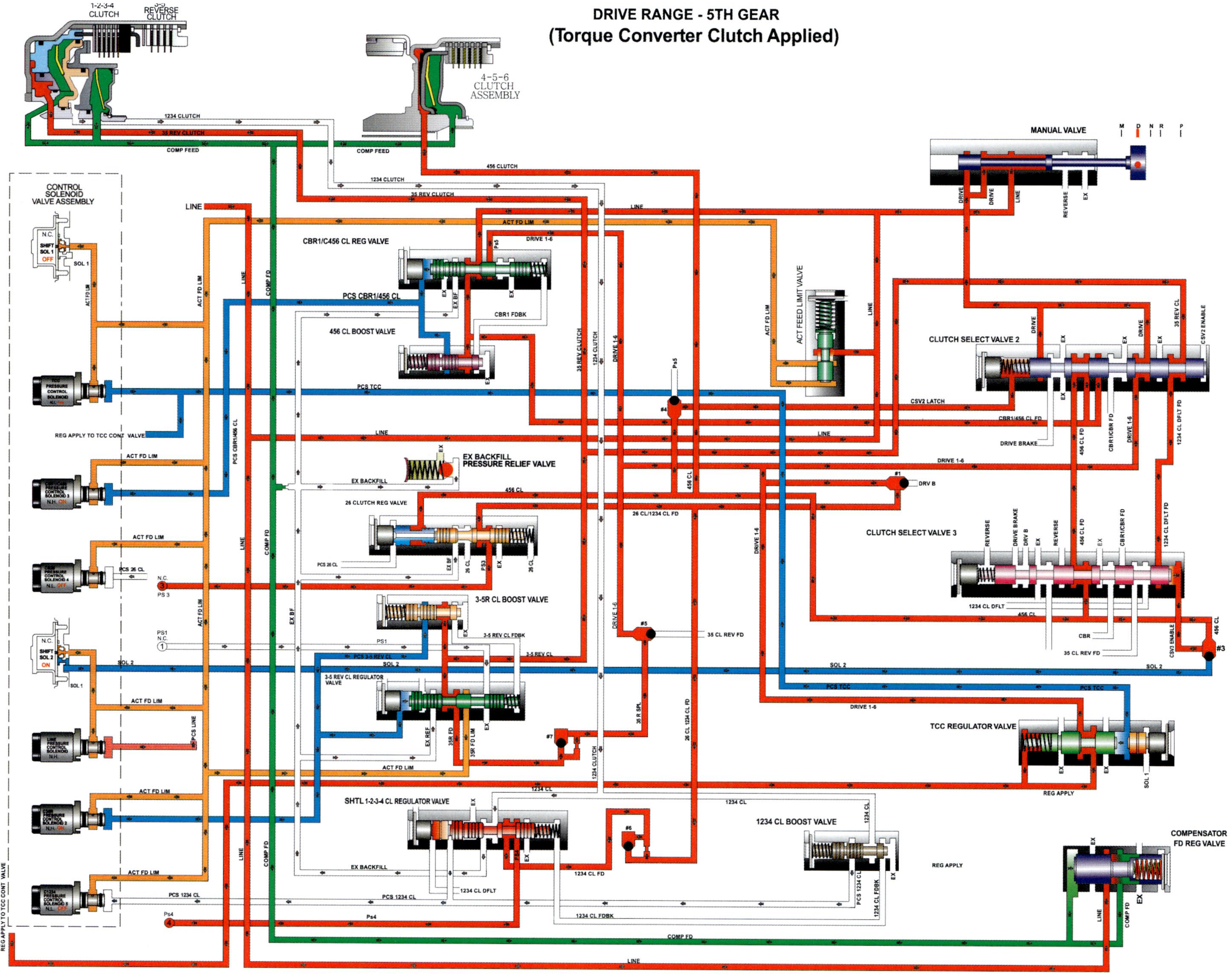
DRIVE RANGE - 5TH GEAR
(Torque Converter Clutch Applied)
1-2-3-4 CLUTCH
3-5 REVERSE CLUTCH
4-5-6 CLUTCH ASSEMBLY
MANUAL VALVE
CONTROL SOLENOID VALVE ASSEMBLY
CBR1/C456 CL REG VALVE
456 CL BOOST VALVE
ACT FEED LIMIT VALVE
CLUTCH SELECT VALVE 2
EX BACKFILL PRESSURE RELIEF VALVE
26 CLUTCH REG VALVE
CLUTCH SELECT VALVE 3
3-5R CL BOOST VALVE
3-5 REV CL REGULATOR VALVE
TCC REGULATOR VALVE
SHTL 1-2-3-4 CL REGULATOR VALVE
1234 CL BOOST VALVE
COMPENSATOR FD REG VALVE
REG APPLY TO TCC CONT VALVE

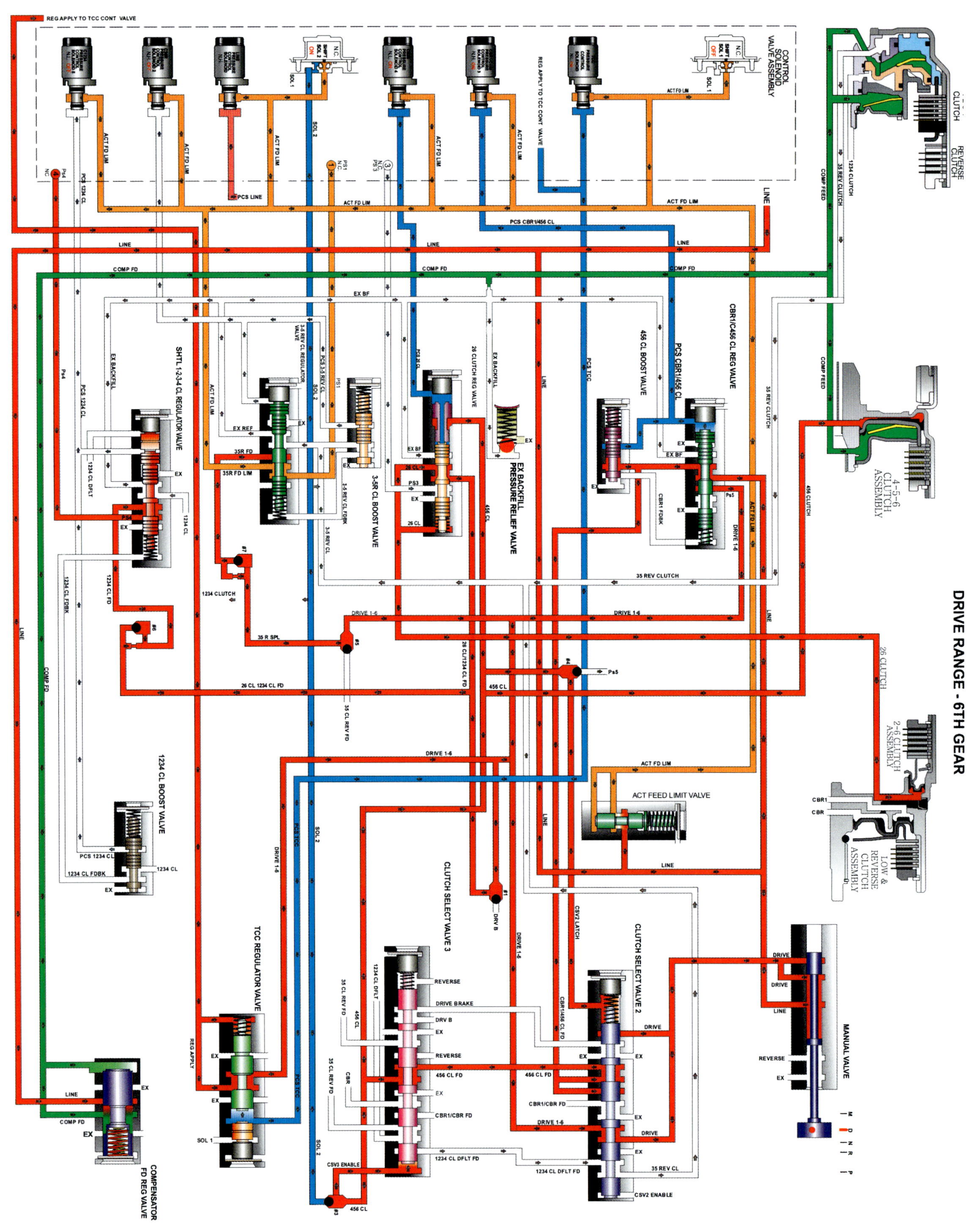
DRIVE RANGE - 6TH GEAR

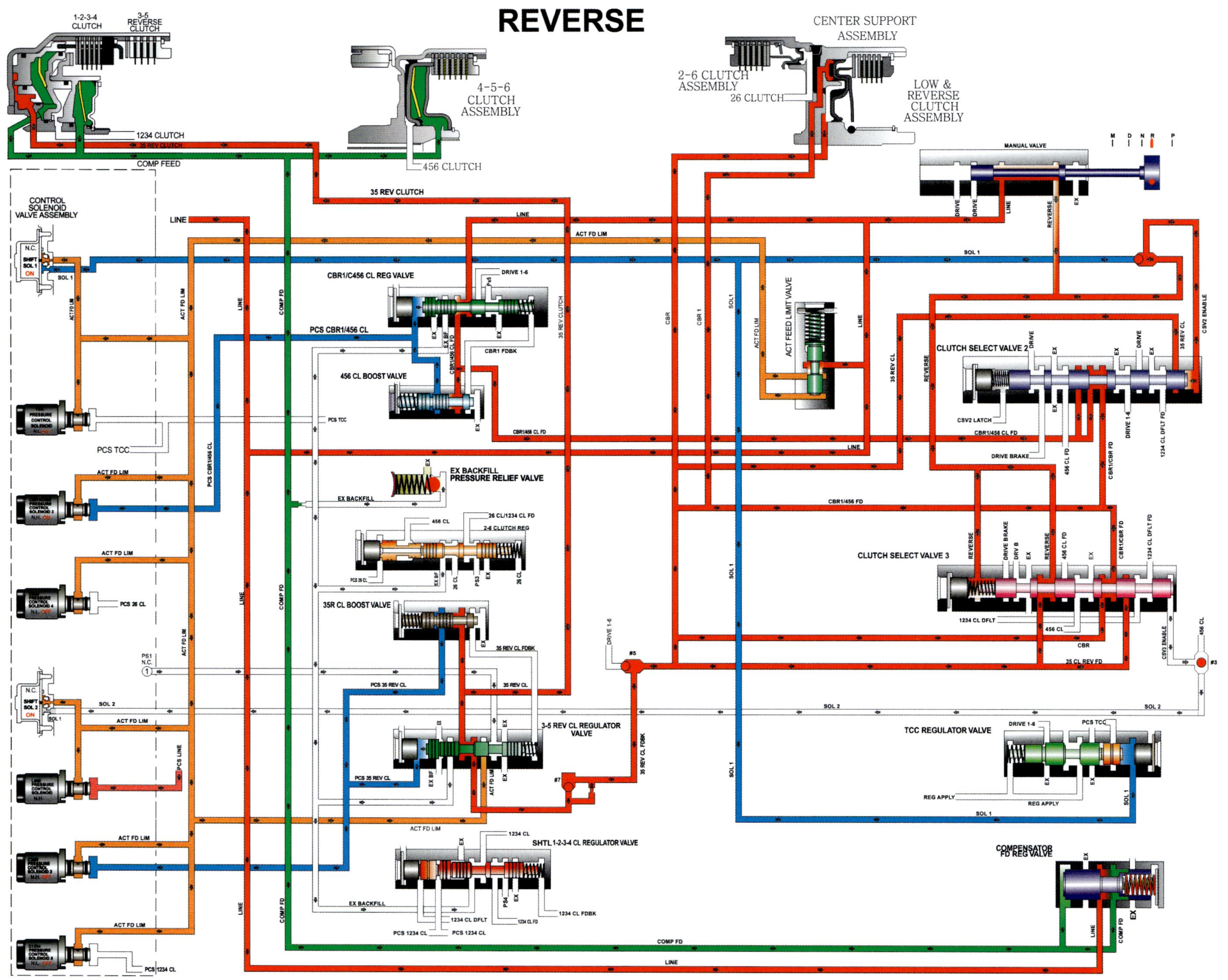
REVERSE
1-2-3-4 CLUTCH
3-5 REVERSE CLUTCH
1234 CLUTCH
35 REV CLUTCH
COMP FEED
4-5-6 CLUTCH ASSEMBLY
456 CLUTCH
CENTER SUPPORT ASSEMBLY
2-6 CLUTCH ASSEMBLY
26 CLUTCH
LOW & REVERSE CLUTCH ASSEMBLY
MANUAL VALVE
CONTROL SOLENOID VALVE ASSEMBLY
CBR1/C456 CL REG VALVE
456 CL BOOST VALVE
EX BACKFILL PRESSURE RELIEF VALVE
35R CL BOOST VALVE
3-5 REV CL REGULATOR VALVE
SHTL 1-2-3-4 CL REGULATOR VALVE
ACT FEED LIMIT VALVE
CLUTCH SELECT VALVE 2
CLUTCH SELECT VALVE 3
TCC REGULATOR VALVE
COMPENSATOR FD REG VALVE
PCS TCC
LINE
SOL 1
SOL 2
COMP FD
ACT FD LIM

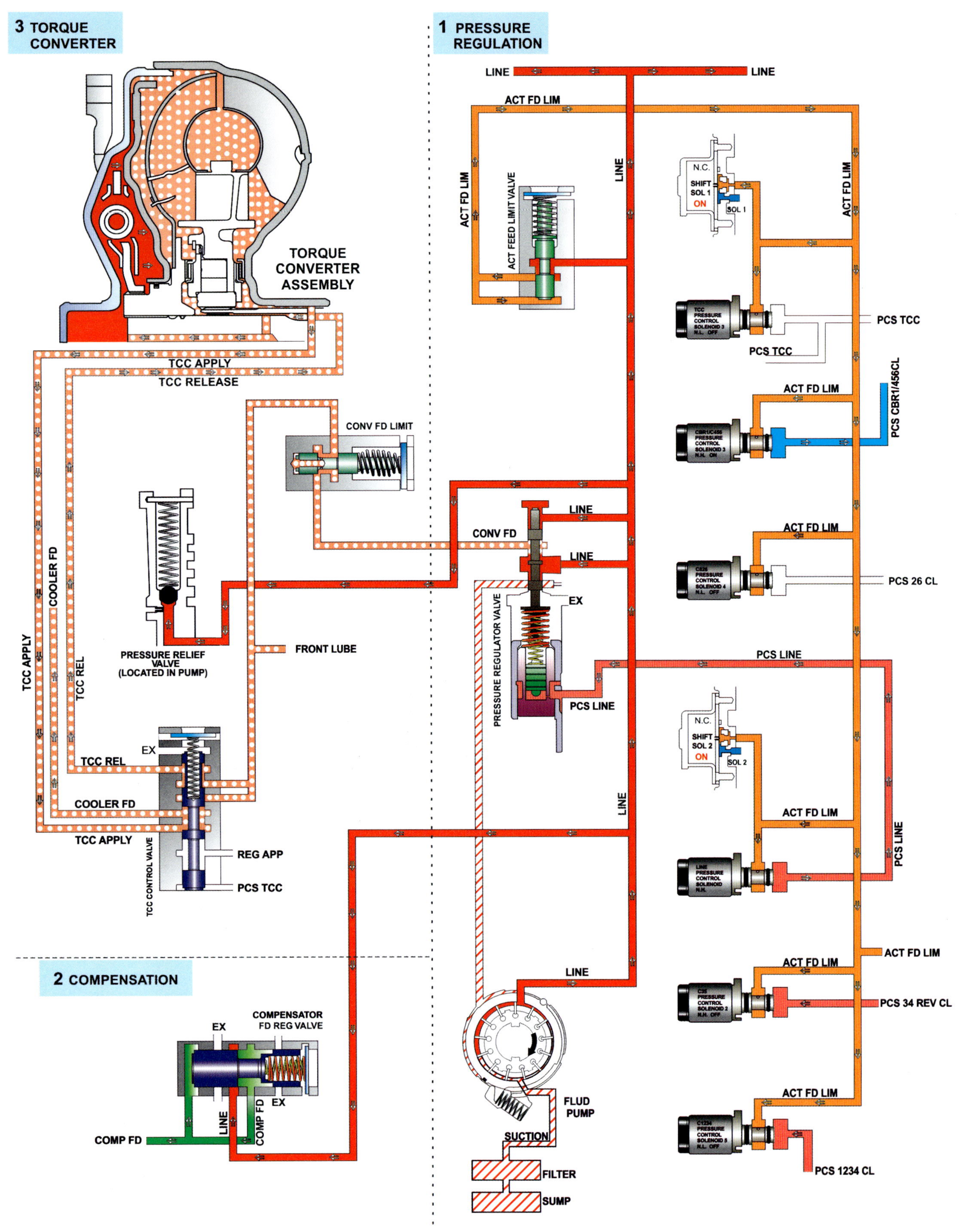

3 TORQUE CONVERTER
1 PRESSURE REGULATION
2 COMPENSATION
TORQUE CONVERTER ASSEMBLY
LINE
ACT FD LIM
ACT FEED LIMIT VALVE
N.C.
SHIFT SOL 1
ON
SOL 1
PCS TCC
TCC APPLY
TCC RELEASE
CONV FD LIMIT
PCS CBR1/456CL
CONV FD
EX
PCS 26 CL
PRESSURE RELIEF VALVE (LOCATED IN PUMP)
FRONT LUBE
PCS LINE
PRESSURE REGULATOR VALVE
COOLER FD
TCC REL
SHIFT SOL 2
SOL 2
REG APP
TCC CONTROL VALVE
PCS 34 REV CL
COMPENSATOR FD REG VALVE
COMP FD
FLUD PUMP
SUCTION
FILTER
SUMP
PCS 1234 CL